...Whereas We for divers good causes
and considerations Us thereunto moving are
graciously pleased to confer on the Town
of Perth in Perth and Kinross the status of a City.
Now Therefore Know Ye that We of Our
especial grace and favour and mere motion
do by these Presents ordain, declare and
direct that the Town of Perth shall henceforth
have the status of a City and shall have all
such rank, liberties, privileges and immunities
as are incident to a City...

Extract from the Commission in Favour of the Town
of Perth to be a City, dated 31 May 2012.

JEREMY DUNCAN is proud to consider himself a Perth man, despite his ancestral roots in Fife, Edinburgh and Aberdeenshire, not to mention south of the border. He was born in the city (when it still was a city) and educated at Perth Academy before moving on to St Andrews and Loughborough. His unspectacular career in librarianship began in Staffordshire before he returned first to Fife and then to Perth to work in the Sandeman Library. He enjoyed 16 years as local studies librarian before leaving to focus on a different aspect of the book business.

His previous books include *Perth and Kinross: the Big County* (1997), *Perth: a Century of Change* (2008), *Lost Perth* (2011) and *A Roof Over One's Head: A Short History of the Gannochy Trust* (2012).

He has been a proud father to two children and is now embarking on grandparenthood – and still trying to work out which end of a baby is which.

Perth: A City Again

A revised and extended edition of
Perth: A Century Of Change

JEREMY DUNCAN

Luath Press Limited
EDINBURGH
www.luath.co.uk

First published as *Perth: A Century of Change* by
The Breedon Books Publishing Company 2008
Revised and extended edition 2012

ISBN: 978-1-908373-56-4

The paper used in this book is recyclable. It is made from
low chlorine pulps produced in a low energy, low emission
manner from renewable forests.

Printed and bound by
Charlesworth Press, Wakefield

Typeset in 11 point Sabon
by 3btype.com

For Wendy,
a Fair Maid by adoption,
and for
Alexander McDonald,
born April 2012

Contents

Preface to the First Edition

I WOULD LIKE to thank a number of people for their kind assistance with this first account of Perth's progress through the 20th century. My former colleagues in the local studies section of the A.K. Bell Library, the ever welcoming and helpful Sara Ann Kelly, Yvonne Bell and Marjorie Donald, made many volumes of local newspapers available to me, as well as their photographic collections which have been plundered for this book. Archivist Steve Connelly and his assistants, Jan Merchant and Christine Wood, have been equally kind and efficient, as have Eddy Durkin and Jill Reid in the reference section. Paul Adair, photographic officer with the council's heritage service, gave many hours of his time to assist with the selection of photographs from the tens of thousands in his care and to him I am most grateful, as indeed I am to the heads of the library and heritage services, Liz Knowles, Caroline Beaton and Robin Rodger, for their cooperation in making this book possible.

Several others have supplied information or photographs, including Bill Anderson, Jane Anderson of Blair Castle archives, Mike Beale, Mike and Carolyn Bell, David Bowler and Derek Hall of SUAT, Bill Colburn, Alastair Cruickshank, Helen Dixon in Australia, Jim Ewing of Perth College, Archie Gilmour, Iain Gilmour, Ruth Ingham, senior registrar in Perth, Stan Keay, Eric Knott, Alison Lowson, editor of the *Perthshire Advertiser*, Elizabeth Nisbet, Ralph Tilston, Bill Wilkie, Ian Wilkie, members of the reminiscence group of the Perth and Kinross Society for the Blind, and my father, Andrew Duncan, who has worked and lived in the city since the 1930s and who provided several details about the people and places which feature in the book.

Warmest thanks go to the following who have read various chapters, corrected mistakes of commission, omission and emphasis, and made many useful suggestions: Steve Connelly, Perth and Kinross Council archivist, Denis Munro, former director of planning with Perth and Kinross Council, Susan Payne and Robin Rodger of Perth and Kinross Council's heritage service and Tommy Smyth, archivist at The Black Watch Museum. I owe special thanks to Harry Chalmers who allowed me access to his magnificent collection of photographs and postcards of Perth and who generously allowed me to use several, and to Rhoda Fothergill who kindly read virtually the whole manuscript and made many pertinent observations. I continue to be in awe of her immensely wide and detailed knowledge of Perth history though we have agreed to differ on matters such as commas and capitals. The responsibility for any remaining errors lies, of course, entirely with me, and should anyone be offended by my failure to capitalise, among others, the title of Perth's civic chief then I can only apologise – no offence was meant and Rhoda was right.

My main written sources have been the local newspapers, particularly the *Perthshire Advertiser*, the only one of Perth's several newspapers to last the entire century. I have also dipped into the standard histories of the city, including Bill Harding's excellent book on Perth during World War One, *On Flows the Tay*. Of equal value are two recent publications: John Gifford's meticulously researched *The Buildings of Scotland: Perth and Kinross* and Margaret Lye's colourful two-volume edition of *The Diary of the Very Rev. G.T.S. Farquhar*.

Photographs and other illustrations have come primarily from the collections of Perth Museum and Art Gallery, from the local studies and archive collections of the A.K. Bell Library, and from the private collection of Harry Chalmers of Perth. Photographs credited to Iain McDonald, to whom I am most grateful, and those by me which are uncredited, were taken in the summer of 2008. Care has been taken to seek permission to use copyright material but if copyright has unintentionally been infringed then I accept full responsibility and apologise to anyone concerned. Thanks are also due to the following for kindly granting me permission to enter their property and take photographs: the headmaster of Craigclowan Preparatory School, the rector of Perth High School, the provost of St Ninian's Cathedral, the staff of Friarton Prison, Mr Taylor (junior), the trustees of The Black Watch (Royal Highland Regiment), the receptionists and security folk at Norwich Union, St Johnstone FC, Tayside Police and the lady who welcomed me to her New Row balcony to snap the Korean War Memorial.

Finally I would like to thank my publishers for their patience. The book was first commissioned in 2002 shortly before the accidental death of my son, Adam, in New Zealand whereupon all thoughts of research and writing temporarily ceased. I pay tribute to my daughter, Genevieve, who despite her own grief brought sunshine into those dark days, and still does, and to my wife, Wendy, who with her gentle encouragement and advice, not to mention her gainful employment, has been a wonderful support throughout. It is dedicated to her, with much love.

Inevitably, since the above was written in 2008, a number of those mentioned have died and several have changed jobs. It felt important, though, to reprint the preface exactly as it originally appeared.

Preface to the Second Edition

Perth: a Century of Change was first published in 2008 and has been one of the fastest-selling books about the city in recent years, reaching as high as number three in the Waterstones Scottish history charts. It was sadly cut off in its prime when the publisher, Breedon Books, went into administration in 2009, so I am delighted that, thanks to a suggestion of Ross Maclachlan, manager of the Perth branch of Waterstones, Gavin MacDougall of Luath Press has agreed to publish a new edition. It has been revised and updated, and given a new title to mark the fact that Perth is indeed a city again. My principal thanks must therefore go to Ross and Gavin.

No less deserving of my appreciation are former provost of Perth and Kinross Council, Dr John Hulbert, who over a lengthy coffee gave me much background material regarding the bid for city status, and Perth and Kinross Council archivist, Steve Connelly, whose knowledge and understanding of Perth's historic status as a city is second to none. I am most grateful to them both for their assistance so willingly given. In addition it is my pleasure to acknowledge the help received from the following: Paul Adair of Perth Museum and Art Gallery; Barbara Briggs of D.C. Thomson and Co. Ltd, Dundee; the Rev. Scott Burton of St Matthew's Church, Perth; Iain Flett of Dundee City Archives; James Gerard of the Office of the Deputy Prime Minister, London; Michelle Glencorse of Perth and Kinross Council; Bruce Gorie of the Court of the Lord Lyon, Edinburgh; Lt David Gosling of the Salvation Army, Perth; Stewart Grant of Perth and Kinross Council; Leanne Jobling of the National Records of Scotland, Edinburgh; Dr Robin Mundill of Glenalmond College; Fiona Musk of Aberdeen City and Aberdeenshire Archives; Colin Proudfoot of the A.K. Bell Library's local studies section; Tommy Smyth of The Black Watch archives in Balhousie Castle, Perth; Jill Winn of South Lanarkshire Libraries; John Wright of Glenalmond College; and the staff of the archival collection of Perth Academy.

The photographic credits outlined in the preface to the first edition apply to the second as well, but with the following amendments. Harry Chalmers has since died and I regret that I have been unable to track down his family to request their permission to use his photos again. If they would care to get in touch, due acknowledgement will be made in the next edition. Sara Ann Kelly is now visitor and commercial services coordinator with Perth and Kinross Council and has kindly given permission for those photos from Perth Museum and Art Gallery and the local studies and archive sections of the A.K. Bell Library, which appeared in the first edition, to be used again. My grateful thanks go to her. Iain McDonald, astrophysicist extraordinaire, has since become my son-in-law and now lives near Manchester. Many thanks to those not mentioned above who kindly consented to their photos being used a second time. For permission to use images which are new to this edition I am grateful to D.C. Thomson and Co. Ltd, to the *Perthshire Advertiser* and to the Perthshire Picture Agency.

It is my great pleasure to dedicate once again this new edition to my beloved wife, Wendy, and, with grandfatherly pride, to the newest member of the family, Alexander.

CHAPTER ONE

A City Again

DR JOHN HULBERT, provost of Perth and Kinross Council, was an anxious man. The whole focus of his provostship since he took office in 2007 had been on the restitution of city status to Perth and now, in March 2012, with new elections only a few weeks away, he had heard nothing about the outcome of the council's participation in the Diamond Jubilee civic honours competition. The results had initially been anticipated at the start of the Jubilee year, and failing that in February on the anniversary of the Queen's accession, but when still no news was forthcoming the provost feared that the next likely date would be the Jubilee weekend in early June – after the council elections when he was due to retire. And then came word on the twelfth of March that an announcement would be made on the fourteenth.

Tuesday 13 March was a day of rumours. Perth MP Pete Wishart phoned the provost from London to say that there was mounting speculation that Perth and Reading had been successful. The provost spent that evening at home, preparing for the press interest that would follow the announcement, good or bad, the following day. Then at around 8.00 pm the phone rang again. David Mundell, Under-Secretary of State for Scotland, was on the line, asking to meet with the provost in his office in the morning at 9.15. He added that an order would be laid before Parliament at 9.30 am announcing the long-awaited result of the competition. Hulbert was beginning to sense that the rumours might be true and asked Mundell for confirmation. The latter, though, would not be drawn, fearing (jokingly) that by leaking information he might end up in the Tower of London, and said only that there were grounds for optimism. Later that evening *The Courier* phoned and asked if the rumours they had also heard were true. Hulbert could not say but mentioned the newly scheduled meeting with David Mundell. That was confirmation enough for the Dundee newspaper which set the presses rolling with 'It's Perth City' as the headline.

The following morning, as an expectant group gathered in the provost's office at the foot of the High Street, a civil servant almost 400 miles away in the Cabinet Office in London was about to add her name to the

The Courier correctly anticipates the formal announcement of Perth's success in the civic honours competition. Leader of the Council Ian Miller, Provost John Hulbert and chief executive Bernadette Malone, of Perth and Kinross Council, pose outside the council's High Street offices.
Courtesy and copyright of D.C. Thomson and Co. Ltd.

history books of Perth. Noelle O'Connor, deputy head of the constitutional policy team, had written the official letter, addressed to council chief executive Bernadette Malone, notifying her that Perth's application had been successful. The letter was attached to an email and at 9.30 am, at the same time Parliament was being informed, the email was sent on its way. It arrived in the provost's office at around 9.35 and once again, after an interval of almost 37 years, Perth was officially a city. After a small celebration the provost picked up one of the two press releases that had been prepared for either outcome, and went to meet the assembled media.

The decision to go for city status, taken after the council elections of 2007, was a bold one. The concomitant of applying to be regarded as a city was, after all, a tacit acceptance that Perth no longer enjoyed that civic rank, despite what the signs on the outskirts of Perth said, despite the presence of a City Hall, and despite what many residents felt, that Perth always had been a city. Had the campaign been unsuccessful any subsequent references to the city of Perth would have sounded hollow indeed.

The continuing SNP-Liberal Democrat coalition, under the leadership of Provost John Hulbert and with cross-party support, set to work on what they knew would be a lengthy campaign. There were significant milestones along the way, including Homecoming Scotland 2009 and the year-long Perth 800 celebrations in 2010, which it was felt would help to build up momentum towards the campaign's conclusion in the year of the Diamond Jubilee. With competitions for city status having previously been held to mark the millennium and the Golden Jubilee it was believed to be almost certain that another would be held in 2012. It was only in the autumn of 2009, though, when there had still been no word of a city competition, that the provost checked with the Ministry of Justice who replied that there were no plans at all for such a competition. The council quickly decided to incorporate the campaign with the Perth 800 celebrations, scheduled to start in January, even though that meant they had a significantly shorter period to make their case. The formal launch took place on 7 December 2009 at a high-profile dinner in the House of Commons dining room, hosted by Pete Wishart and the provost, which included a presentation to the guests aimed at publicising the campaign and increasing support for it. Also launched at the dinner was the official document presenting the claim for city status, an impressively argued and well-presented brochure notwithstanding the speed with which it had to be produced.

Within four weeks of the launch, however, the campaign had to change direction again when it was announced by Lord Mandelson that there would, after all, be a Diamond Jubilee competition. The disappointing addendum was that only one town in the United Kingdom would be elevated to a city. As the year progressed a number of strong candidates from south of the border put themselves forward, some several times the size of Perth and closer politically to the new Conservative-Liberal Democrat coalition government. Relatively small Perth with its SNP representatives was hardly likely to attract the attention of Whitehall amongst such a field. What was in Perth's favour, though, was the fact that no other Scottish town intended applying, and without any potential conflict of interest all of Scotland's politicians were able to get behind the Perth campaign. And this they did. Scottish Secretary Michael Moore and First Minister Alex Salmond lobbied the prime minister on a number of occasions and the provosts and lord provosts of Scotland's six existing cities also lent their weight to the campaign – as did leaders of industry, commerce and the public sector. Also supportive were Perth's twin towns, the people of Perth themselves and the many Perth exiles across the globe.

Even so, it was recognised that Perth's chances of success were extremely limited as long as only one award was to be made. In February 2011 Alex Salmond asked David Cameron to consider granting city status to one town from each constituent part of the United Kingdom. At the same time, the provost wrote to David Cameron pointing out that Perth was the only candidate seeking a restoration of city status and that the royal family's long and happy relationship with Scotland might be affected if only one English town was successful. This twin-pronged approach seemed to work as shortly afterwards it was announced that the competition might indeed have more than one winner.

Meanwhile, behind the scenes in Perth, the council's design team were hard at work on a second campaign document, the first having been so quickly rendered redundant, and in May produced something even more substantial and impressive than its predecessor. It was delivered that month to the Cabinet Office by the provost and Pete Wishart in person and was later described as one of the best, if not the best, of the documents submitted to the competition.

This, though, was not the end of the campaign. Continuing efforts were made to garner support from all over the world and when in October 2011 the Cabinet Office said they would accept any evidence in support of their entry up to the middle of November, the many messages of support received in Perth were collated and bound into a volume with the more significant ones highlighted. This too was submitted to the Cabinet Office. The provost was particularly grateful to Sir David Edward, a distinguished son of Perth, who wrote: 'I was brought up to be conscious of Perth's history and ancient civic status. Successive lord provosts were knighted, and were significant figures in Scottish public life. The loss of Perth's status as a city was, for me, an act of bureaucratic vandalism. So I most fervently support the campaign to restore Perth's ancient and honourable title.'

The submission in November of the messages of support marked the end of the campaign as such. The final recommendation – for submission to the Queen – was now in the hands of Nick Clegg, Deputy Prime Minister, and his team which comprised Mark Harper MP, minister for political and constitutional reform, and the officials in the constitution group of the Cabinet Office. All that was left in Perth was the waiting and, for those so tempted, a bet on the outcome. By February both Ladbrokes and William Hill had Reading as firm favourite, so much so that the former stopped taking bets on the front runner. But Perth was not far behind, some bookies putting it in second or third place. The waiting came to a sudden and joyful end on 14 March 2012 and it is hard to imagine that any betting business or anyone in Perth could have been disappointed to hear the news – unless of course they were from Reading on holiday. The official charter, or in proper terms Her Majesty's Commission in favour of the Town of Perth to be the City of Perth, appended by the impression of the Great Seal of Scotland in beeswax, was received in the summer.

A second reaction to the news, at least as observed by this author, was the statement: 'But, of course, we've always been a city, haven't we?' and the answer to that question is no. For all of its recorded history, up to 1975, Perth had been a royal burgh, the ancient and highest rank to which for many centuries any Scottish town could have aspired. In contrast, city status, north of the border at least, was a somewhat nebulous concept and one that lacked any clear defini-tion. A few large Scottish royal burghs such as Aberdeen and Edinburgh were described as cities in 16th-century documents, so Perth was by no means unique in being similarly

The Commission in favour of the town of Perth to be the city of Perth, with the Great Seal of Scotland at the bottom.
Courtesy of the National Records of Scotland, Edinburgh.

described in the Golden Charter of 1600. And while the magistrates of the time would have known exactly what was meant by a royal burgh and what rights and responsibilities such a status conferred upon them, they would have been hard pushed to explain what a city was and exactly how it differed from a royal burgh. The fact that in practical terms there was no difference at all – and certainly no additional privileges – leads one to the conclusion that the 'city' appellation was more of a nod, than anything else, to a royal burgh's size or importance within the kingdom. This might explain why, when the Golden Charter was translated from Latin into English in 1653, the Latin word 'urbis' – which anyone with schoolboy Latin will recognise as 'city' – was translated as 'burgh' rather than its more generally accepted definition today. For almost two centuries, then, Perth had a charter which in the original Latin described Perth as a city and which in its more widely known translation had Perth as a burgh.

The general lack of awareness of city status seems to have changed in the years following 1786 when the town council was advised by James Beveridge, its legal agent in Edinburgh, that it should have a modern and accurate translation made of its charter, one that should be printed and referred to whenever necessary. It was not made clear in the council minutes why a new translation was required but, reading between the lines, we can perhaps guess that Perth's ancient rights and privileges were once again being questioned by rival royal burghs. (By way of example, the town council minutes of 1801 refer to Glasgow in particular as having tried on several occasions to usurp the Perth commissioner's position in the Convention of Royal Burghs as second to only that of Edinburgh.) The translation was duly made and printed, and for the first time in an official document in the English language Perth was described as a city. Even then, though, the council was seemingly unaware of the significance of that little word, for the title page of the printed translation simply refers to the 'Charter by King James VI in favour of the town of Perth...' However, within a very few years, a distinct change is evident in the writings of the period with 'city' being used increasingly frequently in publications and official documents. As this author has mentioned in an earlier publication, an entry in the town council minutes of 1792 demonstrates the change very clearly when, with a deft stroke of the pen, 'town council' was amended to read 'council of the city of Perth'. It was a gradual change, as evidenced by the 50 pages of the *Old Statistical Account of Perth*, penned in 1796, in which the word 'city' is rarely, if ever, used. Ten years later, though, the city-ness of Perth is firmly emphasised in books and maps of the time, such as *Memorabilia of the City of Perth* of 1806 and Robert Reid's manuscript map of the 'city' of 1808. By the first decade of the 19th century Perth was proud to be known as a city and whenever its newly proclaimed status was queried, as it occasionally was, a copy of the translation of 1786 was sent in reply.

Despite the apparent evidence it seems inconceivable that no one in Perth between 1600 and 1786 was aware that Perth had been called a city in the Golden Charter. The magistrates and town clerks were generally not ill-educated men and some at least would have studied Latin at the Grammar School. The problem seems to have been that the definition of 'city' was too vague to be meaningful and that only in the 18th century, perhaps following the Union and the resulting closer links with England, did it begin to acquire connotations of a status beyond that conferred by size or significance. Even today, as the Deputy Prime Minister's private secretary was at pains to point out in a letter to the author, 'the award of city status is purely honorific and confers no additional powers, functions or funding.'

The growing confidence amongst the magistrates in emphasising Perth's historic position within the kingdom was seen not only in the assertion of city status. Magistrates started wearing gold chains in the 1790s to mirror their counterparts in other large towns and in around 1802 the provost of Perth started using the title lord provost instead. This was a particularly contentious issue and only resolved in 1836 when the Law Lords, sitting in the Court of Session, debated whether Perth had a right to that title and grudgingly, and with a certain amount of dissent, accepted that it did. One of the strongest arguments was that during the visit of George iv to Scotland in 1822 Perth's chief magistrate had been introduced to the king as lord provost. As one learned m'lud remarked, though, had the provost been announced as a duke would the king have been any the wiser and would his ennoblement have been allowed to stand?

Within a period of 50 years Perth had asserted its right to be called a city, had its claim to a lord provost accepted in the law courts, and thanks to the handsome developments alongside both Inches, as well as the new County Buildings and waterworks where Tay Street now is, had the architecture to match. But of course it was not destined to last. In that great shake-up of local government in 1975, the royal burghs were abolished and Perth lost both its lord provost and its status as a city. The latter has at last been restored and while royal burghs will never come back there is certainly a possibility that Perth will once again have a lord provost as civic head. It is understood that the granting of such a title is in the gift of Scottish ministers and it must surely be the hope of many in Perth that they would look favourably on any such petition from either this present council or one in the future.

As Provost John Hulbert stated in 2011, Perth was the only town in the civic honours competition applying to have an ancient honour restored.

Looking back at the start of the 20th century Perth was a city and royal burgh not only in name – it actually felt like a city. There was an enormous sense of pride about the place, as evidenced by the coat of arms which adorned everything from the city's fever hospital to electrical installations and lamp posts in the street, and Perth folk were proud of its history, its appearance, its world-class businesses, its fine public buildings and even its trams. Perth took a number of knocks in the course of the century, not least of them from war, unemployment and emigration, and when in the later 1960s and early 1970s those charged with drawing up plans for local government reform looked at Perth dispassionately, they saw not a city but a medium-sized town struggling with the same problems affecting many others across Scotland. The loss of city status in 1975 was a major dent to civic confidence but one that merely reflected reality. But Perth has been fighting back hard in recent years and once again a real sense of cityhood pervades the air. Of the many themes in this book about 20th- and early 21st-century Perth perhaps the overarching one is that long journey from city to town and back to city again. And this is how, in 1900, that journey began...

CHAPTER TWO

Setting the Scene: Perth in 1900

JAMES AMES DID not have the easiest start in life. While his father, William, was respectably employed as a baker in the city, James had to cope with not only the death of his mother and a brother at an early age but also his father's choice of a new wife. We can speculate that James's relationship with his step-mother was difficult as aged only about 13 he was living and working as a servant across the river in Barnhill. He turned into a handsome young man, well-dressed in photographs, and could perhaps have led a comfortable life in Perth, either working as a clerk or perhaps behind the counter of a local tailor's shop. But a spirit of adventure led him, early in 1899 and at the age of 20, to enlist in The Black Watch and sometime later that year he set sail for the war in South Africa. As he leant over the side of the boat under a warm tropical sun, he might have reflected on how good life was and, as a soldier of the Queen, in the service of the British Empire, mused on what excitements lay ahead. We shall never know. In the early hours of 11 December, in the last few days of the 1800s, he and his fellow soldiers of the 2nd Battalion The Black Watch, now forming part of the Highland Brigade, found themselves trudging silently through a wet night on a surprise attack on the Boer positions at Magersfontein. But the enemy was waiting and it all went terribly and bloodily wrong...

A young James Ames with his sister, dressed up for a session with local photographer William Aimer.
Courtesy of Helen Dixon, Australia.

Survivors told of a pre-dawn ambush, of unexpected barbed wire fences and of compatriots, at the

23

end of battle, grotesquely impaled on that same barbed wire under a hot African sun, their bodies riddled with bullets. The rout of the Highland Brigade by the Boers at Magersfontein, and the death of their commanding officer, General Andrew Wauchope, was reported in the *Perthshire Courier* as early as 14 December. Two days later the first long lists of the dead, wounded and missing were received in the city and with The Black Watch battalion at the spearhead of action men of Perth and Perthshire bore the brunt of the casualties. In total 335 men of The Black Watch were on those lists, of whom 42 were reported killed, 182 wounded and 111 missing. As the *Perthshire Advertiser* said, 'many of the men are well-known in the city and it is pretty safe to say that there is scarcely a single family who have not some relative, or friend, or acquaintance in the lists.' The wounded included Lance Corporal Hugh Ramsay of Burrelton who survived eight bullets and Private James Williamson of Kinfauns who, badly wounded, lay on the battlefield for two days and a night before being brought to safety. Private James Ames was one of those who did not return home.

In those last two weeks of 1899 an 'air of subdued sorrow... overhung the city like a pall' and when the bells of St John's rang in the 1900s there were several families who heard them tolling for beloved sons and fathers and, for themselves, the end of an old life. But war and alcohol intensify the emotions, as does the arrival of a new year, so for the young and those unscathed by tragedy the bells signalled a release from the December gloom. According to the *Perthshire Courier*, 'the High Street on Sunday night shortly before twelve o'clock, and early on Monday morning, was a perfect pandemonium. The cursing and yelling, the shouting of drunken lads and lasses, were a disgrace to any civilised, not to say a Christian community. The air was polluted by foul-mouthed oaths and ribald songs.' The High Street, like Magersfontein three weeks earlier, 'was like a hell let loose.'

News of the war dominated the year and it is likely that some of the young men so criticised in the press for their Hogmanay boisterousness were later fêted in the same newspaper for volunteering for service in South Africa. Those who were selected were festooned with honours before marching away, some with gold watches from proud employers, keen to give General Cronje a bloody nose, and others with ceremonial dinners, complete with cigars and speeches. As the year progressed the news from South Africa improved. There was rejoicing in early March at the relief of Ladysmith – so much so that 'Ladysmith toffy' was on sale at one confectioner's – and even more so in May at the news of the relief of Mafeking which, under siege for seven months, had been successfully defended by Colonel Baden-Powell. Perth was extravagantly decorated with Union Jacks, streamers and bunting, bonfires blazed, the bells of St John's pealed in celebration, and impromptu choirs bellowed patriotic songs in the city streets. The corporation band squeezed onto a tram car and with trumpets sounding was drawn by horse through the city centre. Lord Provost David MacGregor gave a speech praising Baden-Powell, describing B-P, as he was known, as Britain's Pride.

Perth was also pretty good at celebrating home-grown success and the main cause for celebration in 1900 was the opening of the Victoria Bridge, which was first proposed in 1887 and begun 10 years later. The Pullar family, the city's great industrialists and philanthropists at the time, contributed much of the anticipated cost but what had not been foreseen was the lengthy legal dispute over the acquisition of land on the Kinnoull side of the river. The plans showed the bridge extending directly across the river from South Street, which probably seemed eminently

Rodney Lodge in c.1880. Mr Rollo's attractive riverside dwelling was almost entirely demolished to make way for the Victoria Bridge. Kinnoull Church can be seen on the left.
Courtesy of Perth Museum and Art Gallery, Perth and Kinross Council.

sensible to everyone except the unfortunate Mr Rollo whose property of Rodney Lodge, which enjoyed a fine view across the Tay and up South Street, lay exactly in the way. After expensive litigation the town council were given permission to use as much of Mr Rollo's property as was absolutely necessary – which amounted to the entire house apart from two walls – with the result that the eastern approach to the bridge was flanked by the surviving gable ends of Rodney Lodge for the next 30-odd years. At a cost of around £35,000 the bridge cost five times the anticipated maximum, a significant proportion of which went to lawyers rather than engineers.

Despite the expense and its regal name the bridge was far from an attractive or elegant structure. Even at the opening ceremony it was praised for its strength rather than its beauty. Some described it as a coal chute, presumably on account of the downward slope towards the town, and others as a roofless tunnel, with its high sides blocking the view of the river. Such aesthetic deficiencies were generally overlooked on 13 October 1900 when a crowd of 10,000 gathered to watch the opening processions and hear the speeches. The corporation band led the way followed by the lord provost, magistrates and councillors, the Society of High Constables, members of the school board and the other great and good of the city. Sir Robert Pullar performed the actual ceremony. As a

The Victoria Bridge in mid-winter, spanning a frozen River Tay...
Courtesy of the A.K. Bell Library Local Studies Department, Perth and Kinross Council.

... and the damage the bridge did to Rodney Lodge.
Courtesy of Perth Museum and Art Gallery, Perth and Kinross Council.

final flourish the name Victoria was lit up by electricity and a portrait of the Queen was illuminated by gas. It was not long, however, before Disgusted of Perth put Waverley pen to paper to complain to the local press: apparently large numbers of children from Watergate, Speygate and South Street, some of the poorer areas of the city, were playing on the bridge, attracted by the brightness of the lighting.

September saw the other big municipal event of the year, the opening of the brand new Perth Theatre and Opera House. This was widely, though not universally, welcomed, as theatres, along with Italian ice-cream shops, were still regarded by some, particularly churchmen, as dens of vice. Pantomime lovers would have been delighted, though, as *Dick Whittington and His Cat* had been performed the previous winter in the 'dismal, cold and cheerless' atmosphere of the old City Hall. The theatre was financed by a group of local gentlemen and leased by John Savile who, as owner and manager of Paisley Theatre, some 70 miles distant, nevertheless planned to run both theatres together. The long and narrow entrance to the theatre, as it still is today, was described as utilitarian but the auditorium was lavishly fitted out and the glittering opening night played host, to quote the *Perthshire Constitutional*, to 'one of the most crowded and distinguished audiences ever gathered together in the city at any form of entertainment.' Perhaps wary of Perth's reluctance to patronise the arts in financially viable numbers Savile urged the public to support their new theatre. The opening night's entertainment was provided by the English Opera Company.

A view of the interior of Perth Theatre in 1953.
Courtesy of Perth Museum and Art Gallery, Perth and Kinross Council.

Besides the bridge (the theatre was at this time independent of the local authority) the town council had plenty of other things on its mind, not least of them the urgent need to build a fever hospital, the electric lighting of the town, and whether or not to take over the tramway system. The fever hospital crisis arose in 1898 when the infirmary at York Place (the site now occupied by the A.K. Bell Library) announced it could no longer provide enough beds for scarlet fever cases and that the town and county authorities should make their own provision for the care of such patients. The county fever hospital opened at Hillend in March 1900 while the town, having decided against a joint hospital with the county, spent much of the year deliberating between sites at Cherrybank, Burghmuir, Hillend and Friarton. The last-mentioned was ultimately favoured and the city's fever hospital opened there in 1906.

Gas had been powering the city's lighting since the 1820s but it was a dangerous substance and frequently the cause of accidental deaths, not to mention a peaceful way out for the old and lonely. In March 1900 the council was given permission to build an 'electric lighting station' at the Shore and by late summer cabling was being installed beneath the South Inch before branching off to serve the various districts of the city. Advertisements were placed in the local press asking householders who wished to have electric lighting in their homes to let the authorities know immediately. Gas, however, was still the fuel of choice for many and just before the electric power was switched on in June 1901 a brand new gas works at Friarton went on stream.

Since 1895 the Perth and District Tramways Company had been providing a horse-drawn tram service, running initially between Glasgow Road and Scone and later extending to Craigie, Cherrybank and Dunkeld Road, and according to the annual report it was doing well, with no particular problems and good reserves of cash. The *Perthshire Constitutional*, however, was urging the council to take over the trams

A horse-drawn tram just leaving the Scone terminus, heading for Cherrybank.
Courtesy of Perth Museum and Art Gallery, Perth and Kinross Council.

and electrify the system along the lines of those running in Glasgow and Liverpool, pointing out that if Perth's proposed electricity generating plant was only to provide lighting, mainly required during the hours of darkness, then it could equally well be made to power the trams during the daylight hours. Towards the end of the year the council made an offer of £20,000 for the tramway company which was rejected as too little even though the tramway directors were in favour of the take-over in principle. The acquisition was eventually made but the tramway almost immediately became a financial liability.

There were several other important council matters under consideration, one being local government reform, whereby the duties of town councillors and those of the commissioners responsible for police, gas and water, were, from January 1901, all to be performed in the name of Perth Town Council. Other issues included the continuing improvement of Perth streets which were now being tarmacadamed and paved, the covering over of the lade at the North and South Inches, the provision of better housing such as the 'working men's' block in the Old High Street, the extension to the waterworks together with the opening of a new reservoir at Muirhall, and the honouring of Lord Provost John Dewar. This late civic head and soon-to-be MP, in acknowledgement of his tireless involvement with the new Sandeman Public Library, the new streets and bridge, new housing and drainage, was presented with his portrait and a huge silver bowl at a well-attended ceremony in the City Hall.

The council was also busy with the everyday mundane issues: whether to buy boxing gloves for the gymnasium (certainly not, said one newspaper, decrying a 'so-called sport that is debasing the youth of our country'); the naming of streets, such as Inchaffray Street which was the third and ultimately successful suggestion of the Earl of Kinnoull (Inchaffray Abbey formed part of the Kinnoull estates); and whether to erect plaques to commemorate the recently deceased John Ruskin (yes, they decided, and one surviving example can still be seen in Rose Terrace). The increasing level of council work was reflected in two ways; firstly the town clerk successfully petitioned his employers for a typewriter and was also given permission to employ a lady typist at 30 shillings (£1.50) per month, and secondly there was a rise in the rates of fivepence (just over £0.02) in the pound which shocked city ratepayers and which prompted the press to complain about the council spending too much on civic improvements. By way of relief from the brickbats the councillors undertook their annual

A plaque in Rose Terrace commemorating John Ruskin's early association with the city and this particular house. His autobiography, Praeterita, describes idyllic holidays spent in Perth.

summer river trip from Perth to Broughty Ferry and back, enjoying food and speeches on the way.

Almost as influential in the affairs of the town was the school board. Elections were held in April 1900 and many column inches in the local newspapers were given over to the campaigns and speeches of the candidates. Francis Norie-Miller, the boss of the relatively young General Accident, topped the poll and served with such distinction over the ensuing years that he was awarded an honorary fellowship of the Educational Institute of Scotland. Eight others were elected, all to serve for three years, and all to grapple unsuccessfully – as would many others over the next quarter-century – with the accommodation crisis at Perth Academy. Was a new school the answer for its 400-plus pupils or should they rebuild on the existing Rose Terrace site? Not until 1925 was a firm decision made.

The medical officer of health, Dr Charles Parker Stewart (not to be confused with Charles Stuart Parker, the former MP for Perth), had wide-ranging powers over local health matters and in a pre-penicillin era when nasties such as diphtheria, smallpox and consumption were rife, and when the older generation could recall, with a degree of alarm, the terrifying cholera outbreak of the 1830s, his annual report was read with interest.

In 1900 he commented on the springing up of new tenement blocks which were improving the city's working class housing, though he lamented the lot of the very poor who drank too much and for whom 'cleanliness is an unknown and undesirable quality.' He also drew attention to the problem of smoking among children, claiming that some, 'scarcely able to strike a match', were becoming addicts. If cigarettes were sold in packets, he suggested, instead of individually, then the increased price might put them beyond their reach.

The *Perth Directory* of the time lists the names of 21 medical practitioners in Perth who treated the everyday ailments of the inhabitants. The more serious cases ended up in Perth Royal Infirmary where, taking a random week in August, the staff tended around 60 in-patients of which nine were Perth residents. Consumptives (those suffering from tuberculosis) and the other long-term chronically ill, if they could not be successfully isolated and treated at home, were housed in Hillside Home on the Dundee Road, though additional accommodation was being built at Barnhill, funded principally by Sir Robert and Lady Pullar. The mentally

Championed by Dr Charles Parker Stewart this building, originally the city's fever hospital, later formed the nucleus of the former Friarton Prison. The royal burgh's coat of arms can be seen in the pediment.

ill were cared for in the pleasant buildings and open spaces of Murray's Royal Asylum for Lunatics, a hospital which predated the Perth Infirmary by about ten years. Forty-eight patients were admitted in the year 1899–1900 of which six were from Perth and twelve from the county.

The poor and needy of Perth were looked after by a number of charitable organisations such as the Model Lodging House in the Skinnergate, the Indigent Old Men's Society, and the Ladies' House of Refuge for Destitute Girls. The poorest boys attended the Fechney Industrial School and girls the Perth Girls' School of Industry at Wellshill where they were assailed by regular exhortations from distinguished visitors to be good and to develop strength of character.

The 40 officers of Perth City Police were not kept unduly busy by the citizens of Perth. A total of 1262 crimes and offences were made known to the police in 1900 which works out at between three and four per day. Of the annual figures 39 were crimes against the person, 142 were against property, 13 were simple vandalism, and the rest, the over-

The once dingy appearance of Skinnergate House, formerly the Model Lodging House, has been greatly improved in recent years.
Courtesy of Iain McDonald, Glossop, Derbyshire.

whelming majority, were described as miscellaneous and presumably, therefore, fairly petty. Over two-thirds of offenders were male. Jail was the prescribed destination for 76 while several hundred more chose jail rather than pay the alternative of a fine. The chief constable noted in his report that crime figures were a little down on the previous year and that there was 'an entire absence of serious crime.'

There was little complacency about one particular statistic, the fact that around half of those apprehended by the police were drunk at the time of the offence. The abuse of alcohol was widely discussed across the country at that time – as indeed it still was over a century later – and was a significant issue in the general election of October 1900. The two-way contest between the sitting Liberal MP, Robert Wallace, and his Tory challenger, William Whitelaw (the grandfather of Margaret Thatcher's deputy), resulted in a victory for Wallace by a majority of 344 votes. Considering the total number of votes cast was 3998 and that no women and less than half the male population could vote, this was not as close as it sounds. The candidates were quizzed on the hustings about their attitude to temperance and Wallace, with his support for 'universal Sunday closing' and all other temperance legislation, turned out to be rather more anti-alcohol than Whitelaw who would only go so far as to support a bill prohibiting the sale of intoxicating liquor to children. Electioneering could be an uncomfortable experience at times as Whitelaw found to his cost when visiting a schools' swimming gala at the Dunkeld Road baths. According to the *Perthshire Constitutional* 'the building was packed by school children, and the moment the Unionist candidate showed his face there arose such an uproar as fairly astonished him and Mr Norie-Miller, the chairman of the meeting. The children hooted and yelled, and one or two attempted a faint cheer which only led to more booing. The din continued for some time and when quietness was at last restored Mr Miller had to inform the boys and girls that Mr Whitelaw had come "not as a politician but simply as a lover of sport". This assurance so far satisfied the youngsters, but Mr Whitelaw appeared to be somewhat crestfallen at the unwonted demonstration.'

The Tories may have failed at the Perth polls (though they won nationally) but it was not for want of trying. As recently as May they – that is, the Fair City Habitation of the Primrose League – were jubilant at having won the UK Champion Banner for being the most systematic and hardest-working Tory organisation in the United Kingdom. The banner was presented in London by the Conservative prime minister, Lord Salisbury. The Perth Tories' time would come, but not yet.

Amid the excitement of elections, a new bridge and a new theatre, the normal life of the community proceeded apace. Local businesses were still doing reasonably well in spite of a dip caused by the war: the Perth branch of the Royal Bank of Scotland was looking forward to occupying its prestigious new premises on the corner of High Street and Kinnoull Street; John Shields and Co, linen manufacturers, added an extension to the Wallace Works in the Dunkeld Road, providing accommodation for an extra 250 looms to complement the existing 650; Dewars announced an increase in net profits to £55,000 at the same time that a rival firm were mourning the death of their founder, Arthur Bell, at his Scone home; Pratt and Keith in New Row were taking full advantage of the advent of electricity to advertise their 'electricity, light and power installations...Bell's telephones...heating apparatus and everything electrical'; and Fenwicks, the St John Street bakers, proud of their finest Danish butter shortbread, were still serving refreshments in their tearooms, each marble-topped table provided with a sugar bowl, a vase of flowers and a bell to summon the waitress. The three livestock marts of Macdonald Fraser, Hay and Co. and John Swan and Sons were enjoying if not a roaring trade then at least a healthily bleating one, selling between them in three days in October a grand total of over 66,000 sheep and over 4300 cattle.

A view of industrial Perth in 1905 in which at least eight factory chimneys can be seen. Courtesy of Perth Museum and Art Gallery, Perth and Kinross Council.

But there were also tensions in the local trades and Perth was inconvenienced by a four-month painters' strike which was at times close to becoming violent. So real was the threat that painters working on the new theatre had to have a police escort home at the end of the day. Local printers also went on strike in protest at female labour being used and again strike-breakers found themselves threatened with physical harm.

The arts were beginning to flourish but the problem of the Perth public failing to patronise musical events in sufficient numbers was as evident at the beginning of the century as it was towards the end. In January the Scottish Orchestra, a forerunner of the Royal Scottish National Orchestra, gave a concert in the City Hall to a sparse audience. The following month the Perth Orchestral Society gave their 13th annual concert in an almost deserted City Hall. The reason given was a blizzard blowing at the time though a review in the press suggests another: 'Of Schubert's *Unfinished Symphony* we will not say much. There was a laudable effort to get through it, but it was patent that the music was above the players' abilities...' Perhaps it was all too highbrow for the majority of Perth folk. Gilbert and Sullivan's *HMS Pinafore,* corporation band concerts on the North Inch, an appearance by Harry Lauder, the second visit of the National Mod to Perth, and events such as Burns Suppers, were probably all far more popular.

If members of the Scottish Orchestra were feeling disappointed in January 1900 they were not alone. At their annual general meeting the members of Perthshire Cricket Club were ruminating gloomily on a generally disappointing season, despite the presence of a professional in their ranks. They raised their spirits, however, with recollections of R. Macgregor Mitchell's bowling feat in which he took six wickets for one run in less than three overs, a record which stood for many years and perhaps still does. They were to have a better season ahead, despite a disastrous start against Brechin when the county side was bowled out for only 43 runs, almost half of them coming from two well-known local names, Joe Anderson and A.K. Bell. This was perhaps not a match the latter would have discussed with the world's most famous cricketer, Don Bradman, when he visited Bell at his Perth home many years later.

There were a number of amateur football teams in Perth at that time, the pre-eminent ones being St Johnstone, who played at the Recreation Ground by the South Inch, and Fair City Athletic whose home was at Muirton Bank. Both then played in regional leagues. As well as cricket

Cricketing legend Don Bradman and his wife admiring the view from the Kinnoull Hill stone table, flanked by Mr and Mrs A.K. Bell.
Courtesy of the A.K. Bell Library Local Studies Department, Perth and Kinross Council.

and football the residents of Perth had access to a variety of other sporting activities, including swimming at the Dunkeld Road baths, bowling at the corporation green immediately adjacent, racing on the North Inch, rugby, gymnastics, cycling and tennis.

In spite of the tragic start, 1900 had generally been a good year for Perth. A new bridge and theatre were the highlights, with various other improvements in progress. But for many individuals, particularly in the lower working classes, life was difficult. Working hours were long, housing squalid, and disease rife. Suicide was a way out for some, such as the man who jumped from the Perth Bridge in April and who miraculously survived the 60-foot drop. He managed to clamber onto a ledge inside one of the arches before throwing himself back into the fast-flowing water and drowning. For the less desperate there were the siren songs from Canada, those little advertisements in the press whispering promises of a better life overseas. Others moved elsewhere in Scotland or south of the border and it was in 1900 that the London Perthshire Association was first formed, somewhat later than a number of similar

Advertisements such as these appeared week after week in the local press, encouraging thoughts of emigration. Some, eventually, would buy one-way tickets to distant destinations. Courtesy of the A.K. Bell Library Local Studies Department, Perth and Kinross Council.

Scottish county organisations. On the other hand there was also a sense that others were in a worse position and when yet another devastating famine struck India a public meeting was held in Perth to raise money for the relief fund.

The year was drawing to a close and although most people accepted that the new century began in 1901 and not 1900, there had been the usual centennial debate in the press as to which year was correct. The 19th century's 'great toe' was one description of the year, the last of that century sticking out awkwardly into the 1900s. Together with a very elderly Queen on the throne, already well past her Diamond Jubilee, there was a sense of an old era ending and new beginnings ahead. Victoria had still been travelling regularly to Balmoral by train, usually stopping off for breakfast in the Station Hotel on her way north and for dinner on the way south. On these occasions part of the station was temporarily roped off, the hotel itself was always highly decorated for her visits, and important local families sent flowers. Her final visit to the Station Hotel was probably made in November 1900 and less than three months later the last of the Hanoverians, a royal house which had ruled Britain since 1714 and which had been the focus of so much discord in Scotland, was dead.

The celebrations for the new century's arrival began in earnest on Hogmanay 1900. Public buildings had already been closed for several days though shops were busy and, as the late afternoon darkness fell,

Queen Victoria was a regular visitor to the Station Hotel en route either to or from Balmoral. The hotel was designed by a member of the Heiton family, a dynasty of Perth architects, and built in the later 1880s.

the windows were 'ablaze with light.' Excited people thronged the streets and the station bustled with travellers arriving, and others leaving, to spend the holiday with family and friends. In the evening large numbers attended entertainments at the theatre and City Hall, the latter presided over by the lord provost, and many too chose to attend the watch-night services in the city's churches. By 11.00 pm, the entertainments having finished, a huge crowd began to congregate at the Cross where music was played, accompanied by loud singing, and fire crackers were tossed in the air, alarming some with loud bangs and showering others with sparks. Such was the noise that many at first did not hear the bells proclaim the arrival of a new century. But then there was an outbreak of hand-shaking, a 'pop-pop' chorus of bottles being opened, and a general sharing of their contents. After midnight the crowd began to disperse to go first-footing. It was a happy occasion, and perhaps rather too happy for some as the press bemoaned 'the number of very young boys who were seen to be intoxicated.' The celebrations continued the following day with the city's museums being open free of charge and entertainments again being held in the theatre and City Hall. The latter consisted of patriotic songs, for the nation was still at war, such as *Rule Britannia* being sung with great gusto to the accompaniment of the thundering City Hall organ. Treats were organised for the city's children and others for the city's elderly poor who were addressed by Sir Robert Pullar.

For some, though, it was not a good start to the year. The police court sat on Ne'er Day morning and the first accused of the new century was a regular offender, one Alexander Page. Charged with being drunk and incapable, 'he did not deny the charge but put on such a woe-begone look as might have touched the heart of a bandit,' said the press. The facial gymnastics worked and he was excused. The next offender, a woman who admitted stealing a currant cake from the Co-op shop in Scott Street while drunk, was less fortunate and despite her seemingly genuine remorse was given the option of 14 days in jail or a £1 fine.

And so, with a great sense of hope, some sadness, and the concerns, successes and failures of everyday folk, Perth set off on what blurb writers might describe as a roller-coaster ride of ups and downs, twists and jolts, through the 20th century. If Perth residents then could have seen what lay before them in the century ahead, of how their cosy, self-controlled and relatively stable Victorian world was to be shaken to its foundations by external influences, and of how in 2012 they would eventually reinvent themselves as a modern 21st century city, they would have been fearful and astonished. How we made it from 1900 to 2000 and beyond is the story of this book.

CHAPTER THREE

Westminster Confessions: Parliamentary Politics in Perth

THE BURGH OF PERTH, having previously shared a Member of Parliament with Dundee, Forfar, St Andrews and Cupar, first obtained the right to send a separate representative to Westminster in 1832 and from that year until 1918, when there was a major change in constituency boundaries, the seat was held, almost without a break, by the Liberals. The one interruption to Liberal hegemony occurred between 1892 and 1895 when a split in their vote gave an unexpected victory to the Conservative candidate, William Whitelaw, who had been recommended to the Perth Tories by no less a figure than Coningsby Disraeli, the former premier's nephew.

The Perth Liberal Club, adjacent to the museum in George Street and since demolished, was the focus of Liberal activity within the town. The leading light amongst local Liberals was also the city's chief employer, Sir Robert Pullar. When Robert Wallace, the MP who had represented Perth since 1895, stood down shortly after his victory in the 1906 general election, Sir Robert was elected unopposed at the by-election, the Tories choosing not to mount a challenge out of respect for a distinguished local businessman and benefactor. However, with his hesitant speech and autocratic disposition he was never a natural politician and retired from national politics at the 1910 election. In his place the Perth seat was held for the Liberals by A.F. Whyte who remained the MP for Perth until 1918.

The rise of the Conservative Party in Perth dates from the later years of the 19th century when the Liberal Party nationally was polarising into those who supported the Irish Home Rule policy and those who supported the union. The drift of the Liberal Unionists towards the union-supporting Conservatives resulted in the ultimate merger of those parties to form, in Scotland, the Unionist Party in 1912. The growth of the unionist cause manifested itself locally in the fortunes of the Working Men's Conservative Association which by 1880 was sufficiently supported by way of cash and members to buy premises at 50 George Street, next to Albert Close. Eight years later, and with Gladstone's Home Rule policy now the topic of heated national debate, such had been the upsurge in Tory support that more capacious clubrooms were found at 19 George Street. One of the speakers at the opening ceremony, recalling a not too distant past, said that 'he had often been told that if he was to ask how many Conservatives there were in the city of Perth he might count them on his fingers.' As the Conservatives continued to flourish the clubrooms were later extended by the purchase and subsequent demolition of one of Perth's most historic inns, the King's Arms (entry to which had been from a close at the foot of the High Street). However, in spite of prestigious premises, an increasing level of support, visiting speakers with resonant surnames such as Coningsby Disraeli and Lord Randolph Churchill, and a highly respected candidate in the form of Samuel Chapman, the Tories were still unsuccessful at the polls. The results of fiercely fought elections were announced to crowds numbering thousands outside County Buildings in Tay Street and those particular days, which began with such hope for Tory supporters, usually ended with them trudging disconsolately homewards, licking their wounds.

East Perthshire Conservatives outside their constituency offices in Tay Street during the parliamentary election of 1892.
Courtesy of Perth Museum and Art Gallery, Perth and Kinross Council.

The first avowedly socialist organisation in Perth was probably the Perth Trades Council which was formed in 1897. Its aims, as regularly stated in the minute books, were 'the moral and social elevation of the operative class and the consideration of all such questions as affect the social and political interests of Labour.' In those early days 15 unions were affiliated to the Perth Trades Council which, having supported a number of lengthy and occasionally violent strikes, was regarded by many with distrust. Even the City of Perth Co-operative Society, from which some empathy might have been expected, was somewhat suspicious. The trades council was equally suspicious of others, particularly would-be town councillors who came looking for their support and whose subsequent perfidy was recorded in the minutes: 'Unfortunately one or two of these gentlemen after being returned have forgotten all about the promises they made to the Trades Council.' Probably for this reason they started fielding their own candidates in town council elections in 1903. Despite its lack of success at the polls the trades council made known its views on local issues and the town council was at least forced to take note of them. One issue, in around 1901, was the building of working men's housing on what was presumably a noisy and noisome site adjacent to the slaughter house at the Shore. The town council agreed to meet a deputation from the trades council but then, according to the minutes, 'had not even the common courtesy to write us stating what decision they had come to.' Thus aroused they held a well-attended meeting in the City Hall, after which the town council agreed to defer a decision until a new council had been elected. The minute-taker recorded with some satisfaction that with the advent of the new council they hoped 'to hear of [the matter] being buried in the bog at the Shore.'

Nationalist sentiment had been growing in Scotland since the end of the 19th century but did not dominate the political agenda to the same extent as did Irish Home Rule. The main vehicle for nationalist ideas was the Young Scots Society, a Liberal organisation, the Perth branch of which was set up in 1907 with Sir Robert Pullar as one of the office-bearers. Despite the strength of their campaigning, however, the Home Rule movement suffered a serious setback with the advent of World War One and Perth would have a long wait for her first nationalist MP.

The other big issue of the time was women's suffrage which first came to the attention of the local press in 1908 when the Women's Freedom League organised a number of well-attended but peaceful

Sir Robert Pullar (1828–1912), a leading local businessman and philanthropist, though not, perhaps, someone to be trifled with. He was also a Liberal heavyweight – with his decided resemblance to Gladstone could he have been anything else? Courtesy of the A.K. Bell Library Local Studies Department, Perth and Kinross Council.

demonstrations in the city. By the time of the January 1910 election the movement was being taken sufficiently seriously for both candidates, Whyte and Chapman, to come out in favour of votes for women on the same basis as for men. In April 1913 the more militant suffragettes struck at the very heart of the archetypal Perth male by burning down the Perthshire Cricket Club pavilion on the North Inch which brought in its wake an angry crowd of cricket-loving males and police ready for action with batons drawn. In November of that year, at a Home Rule meeting in the City Hall, suffragettes disrupted the proceedings with shouts of 'votes for women' and found themselves quickly bounced from the building by stewards. Law-breaking suffragettes from across the country were jailed at Perth where prison doctors had previous experience of force-feeding hunger-strikers. When the King and Queen visited Perth in July 1914 to open the new infirmary they were met with a banner unfurled from a window in North St John's Place which read 'Forcible feeding and torturing of women in Your Majesty's prisons must cease.' In the East Church four suffragettes stood up and chanted a prayer for their 'imprisoned sisters.' An elder stood up to remove them but was restrained by a 'significant look' from the minister, the Rev. W. Lee. The suffragettes held open-air meetings in, and processions through, Perth which were frequently the target of children throwing stones. They picketed Perth Prison and with the aid of a megaphone shouted encouraging messages to their sisters inside. One of the last local protests, just before the outbreak of war after which the women's suffrage issue went into abeyance, occurred in St Ninian's Cathedral whose clergy had long been expecting a protest of some sort.

Several women stood up during matins and tried to pray for Emmeline Pankhurst and others 'being tortured.' The softly softly approach of the East Church's Mr Lee was not followed here for it was alleged that at least one woman was grabbed by the neck by stewards, had her mouth covered, and was forcibly ejected from the cathedral, after which the door was locked. The incident is recorded in the diary of the Rev. G.T.S. Farquhar, who preached in the cathedral on that occasion and who wrote as follows: 'The service was interrupted by Suffragettes who are swarming in the town owing to some of the Sisterhood being in the General Prison. When I rose to give out a hymn, I noticed a seat-full of Women rise. I knew well what it was. But they had not sung more than two or three words before our hymn drowned them. About a dozen men had them out in the street before we had finished the first verse. I am afraid Norie-Miller was needlessly rough. They are the most exasperating vixens that ever breathed but so outrageously so that it was a pity he descended to their level.' In return for the suspension of protests and for their considerable war service women were rewarded with the *Representation of the People Act* of 1918, which gave the vote to eight million of their number over the age of 30. They still did not have full equality with men but it was an improvement.

A postcard view of the charred remains of the Perthshire Cricket Club pavilion which had been targeted by suffragettes in April 1913. They knew exactly where to hit a Perth man hardest.
Courtesy of the A.K. Bell Library Local Studies Department, Perth and Kinross Council.

Apart from the newly widened franchise the 1918 general election in Perth was notable for two things: firstly, the constituency of Perth while retaining the same name was enlarged to include the eastern part of Perthshire, from Abernethy in the south to Blairgowrie, Coupar Angus and Alyth in the north; and secondly, the victory of local Liberals proved to be their swansong. Nationally the Liberal vote had been in decline in inverse proportion to the rise of that of Labour and in Perth the growing prominence of Labour politics was reflected in the opening of the Perth City and County Labour Club in South Methven Street in 1918. In the summer of that year, in the last months of war, the Labour movement showed its strength by marching, together with trade unionists, through the city streets. So soon after the Russian revolution and devastating industrial troubles at Pullars they were careful to emphasise that they were reasonable men who wanted to work in harmony with their employers. But the threat was there and some folk in Perth voiced their fears of an imminent Socialist revolution in the country. Eighteen months later, in January 1920, a major debate was held in the City Hall in which the motion 'A Soviet system of government is impossible as a system of democratic government' was upheld by 1,000 votes to 600, indicating that those who espoused far left politics, although defeated in debate, had been given a huge boost by the events in Russia of 1917.

The 1922 election marked the start of a new era of Tory dominance. A.N. Skelton won for the Tories and although little remembered today he was considered by some as a future party leader. The general election of the following year returned local cricketer and Liberal, R. Macgregor Mitchell, before Skelton was re-elected with a sizeable majority in the 1924 election. The Labour candidate again came last but with a greatly increased share of the vote. In the early 1920s all three main parties were working hard locally to attract voters and there was a sense that there was still everything to play for. The local Labour Party held a big rally on the North Inch in 1921, and that same year the Liberals demonstrated their faith in the future by opening new club premises in Canal Street. The Tories, too, held a bazaar in the City Hall in 1923, which raised the considerable sum of £5000, and a big 'demonstration' at Balhousie Castle in 1925 which was attended by around 5000 people. And where the Tories were rallied by a visit from Stanley Baldwin in 1924, the Liberals responded with a visit from Lloyd George in 1927.

Skelton stood down shortly after his victory over Liberal candidate

Francis Norie-Miller in the 1929 election, and was replaced as Tory candidate by Lord Scone, son of the Earl of Mansfield. In 1931, in a closely fought election with a high turn-out of voters, he too defeated the recently widowed Francis Norie-Miller who had been the front runner until only a few days before. Helen Gault, the Labour candidate who no longer enjoyed the support of her local party, was squeezed out of the running and lost her deposit. This galvanised the party into a publicity campaign throughout the constituency the following year though they were somewhat hampered by a lack of funds.

Lord Scone's ennoblement as the 7th Earl of Mansfield, on the death of his father in 1935, necessitated his departure from the House of Commons and a subsequent by-election in April of that year. This was Norie-Miller's moment. By now in his mid-seventies he was the grand old man of Perth: as boss of a large and flourishing company, celebrating its Jubilee that very year, with the new park at Rodney named after him, a new wife in tow and the very great honour of the freedom of Perth bestowed upon him in 1933, he was virtually unassailable. And when the Unionists and Liberals came together to support him as the National Government candidate, he had only a Labour candidate against him. His success, though, was short-lived and when the general election came in November of that year he decided to stand down on health grounds, without even having given his maiden speech. Thomas Hunter, who was then on the point of demitting office as lord provost, was quickly adopted as the National Conservative candidate and as the Liberals were un-prepared for Norie-Miller's departure they did not field a candidate. With a majority of almost 15,000 votes over his Labour opponent Hunter, doubtless as surprised at the turn of events as Norie-Miller would have been disappointed, took the train to Westminster and served as the MP for Perth for the next ten years, right through the war years. He was knighted in 1944.

The coalitions which came together to form the National Govern-ments of the 1930s masked, perhaps, the reality of the underlying polarisation of rank and file politics at that time. Fascism was growing throughout the world, particularly in Italy, Germany and Spain, but also in the United Kingdom where Oswald Mosley had emerged as the leader of the British Union of Fascists. But owing to their ready use of violence at public meetings and their open support for the Nazi regime in Germany their support was already waning by the time they held an

PERTH DIVISION ELECTION

16th APRIL, 1935

Poll Opens at 8 a.m. and Closes at 9 p.m.

You are respectfully invited to record your Vote for

Mr NORIE-MILLER

(THE NATIONAL GOVERNMENT CANDIDATE)

By marking a **X** against his name, thus :

1	McKINLAY (Adam Storey McKinlay, 149 Kestrel Road, Glasgow, W.3, Organiser)	
2	**NORIE–MILLER** (Francis Norie-Miller, of Cleeve, Perth, Insurance Director).	**X**

Do not sign your name, or put any other mark than the one **X** or your Vote will be lost.   [*Over*

A simple request to vote for Francis Norie-Miller in the 1935 by-election. Little by way of hard campaigning was required as, fighting against a Labour candidate and with the support of Conservatives and Liberals, the result was never really in doubt.

Courtesy of the A.K. Bell Library Local Studies Department, Perth and Kinross Council.

open-air meeting in Perth in August 1936. The first intimation of a gathering was published in the *Perthshire Advertiser* on 15 August: 'Blackshirt meeting at North Inch, Perth on Sunday 16th August 1936 at 3.30 pm. For further information apply British Union of Fascists (Scottish Headquarters), 8 Hope Street, Edinburgh.' Next to it was another announcement: 'Perth Trades Industrial Council. Great anti-fascist demonstration will be held in Museum Square on Sunday 16th August at 2.30 pm (if wet, Large Co-op Hall). Speakers – Councillor Mrs H Gault, Glasgow, Councillor Mr M Shinwell, Hamilton, Mr F Douglas, Edinburgh, and other local speakers. Rally to the cause of democracy. Down with fascism.' (For the avoidance of confusion, the above-mentioned Councillor Shinwell was in fact Maurice Shinwell, the famous Manny's younger brother.) In the same issue was a letter from the acting secretary of the trades council, urging the people of Perth to 'demonstrate to the rest of Scotland that Perth has no time for the advocates of a military dictatorship.' He further stated his belief that the 'working class population of this city...will conduct themselves with their customary restraint, while expressing their disapproval of the anti-semitic and anti-working-class doctrines of the Blackshirts.'

In the event the sun shone and the Large Co-operative Hall was not required. The fascists arrived in front of the Old Academy in a black van, its windows devoid of glass but well protected by wire, through which they could doubtless see and hear the large crowd (later estimated at up to 4,000-strong) waiting for them. The van then drove slowly onto the Inch and its 20 or so black-shirted occupants stepped out, one of whom climbed onto the roof. The principal speaker was Richard Plathen, the party's Scottish organiser, who was dressed not only in a black shirt but in black breeches and black riding boots as well, but despite his use of a loudspeaker he was rendered completely inaudible by the jeering and shouting of the crowd. Particularly effective, apparently, was the singing of the old music hall favourite, *Daisy Bell*. When objects started being thrown the police stepped in quickly to conclude the meeting. The fascists then unfurled a Union flag on top of their van, gave it a salute 'in true Hitler style', and departed the Inch and the city amid much booing.

The Communist Party benefited from fascism, almost inevitably, by way of a steadily rising membership. The two opposing ideologies clashed on a monumental scale in the Spanish Civil War when Franco and his fascists fought the Republicans for control of that country. Many idealistic Communists and far-left sympathisers from across Europe flocked to the Republican cause and, as local historian Paul Philippou has described on his Alternative Perth website, several Perth folk made that hazardous trip to Spain. One such was James Moir of Craigie, a young Communist party member who had clandestinely made the journey and signed up with one of the International Brigades by early June 1937. He was killed in action at Brunete, near Madrid, the following month, and although his body probably still lies buried on the battlefield his short life is commemorated by a gravestone in Wellshill cemetery.

With the defeat of fascism in 1945 politics in Perth might have returned to its pre-war normality, had a new party not entered the scene. The SNP first contested Perth at the 1945 election and, while Attlee triumphed nationally and Unionist Alan Gomme-Duncan won locally, their candidate barely scraped a four-figure vote. In 1950, in a constituency now renamed Perth and East Perthshire (though covering exactly the same area as before), the SNP again lost their deposit but things were beginning to change. In the general election of the following year the SNP candidate and party leader, Dr Robert McIntyre, saved his deposit with a poll of almost 6,500 votes. The humiliating days were over and the SNP were on their way.

At this time the town council uniquely honoured two consecutively serving prime ministers with the freedom of the burgh. The first was Churchill who was presented with his burgess ticket in the City Hall in

1948 in a ceremony which was broadcast by the BBC. Some time prior to the ceremony Lord Provost John Ure Primrose asked to see him to discuss the proceedings and was granted 10 minutes in his room at the House of Commons. Primrose later recalled that, having been kept waiting for 45 minutes, he was summoned in by the great man who quickly scanned through the suggested programme and scored out various items with comments like 'Won't do that', 'No', and 'Shan't do it.' He glanced up, noticed Primrose's expression of annoyance, and said 'You don't like it, eh?' Primrose replied, 'It is for your convenience, sir, but ye ken your ain kenning best.' Churchill replied with a smile, 'Put that into basic English, please, Lord Provost', after which they enjoyed a lengthy and convivial conversation. Churchill was apparently surprised by the warm reception given him by Perth folk and was particularly moved when the entire City Hall rose to its feet to sing *Will ye no come back again?* Sir Anthony Eden was similarly honoured in May 1956, describing the occasion as 'a day I shall never forget.'

Colonel Gomme-Duncan was knighted the same year and retired from politics at the 1959 general election. There were two front-runners to replace him, Captain Humphrey Evans, who had married into the Drummond of Megginch family, and Ian MacArthur, a senior advertising executive. A journalist who had been at the somewhat acrimonious adoption meeting described the events in a newspaper article several years later. Although his version was later disputed he described how Humphrey Evans had been the choice of the majority but that 'the all-powerful Earl of Mansfield' backed MacArthur 'and naturally the faithful listened to the voice of the prophet.' Although his memory may possibly have been at fault there is little reason to doubt the method of selection which applied equally to Conservative Party leaders at that time.

MacArthur won the 1959 election, increasing the Tory majority to around 14,500, and Dr Robert McIntyre, as he had done in 1955, came second. In the 1964 election, after '13 years of Tory misrule', Labour moved into second place, a position they retained in 1966. Ted Heath was by this time leader of the opposition and aware of both the growing threat from the SNP and the Tories' declining popularity in Scotland. In a jaw-dropping statement to the Scottish Conservative conference in 1968, known as the Declaration of Perth, he attempted to stave off both threats by announcing plans to set up a Scottish assembly, thus turning Tory policy of maintaining and supporting the union, consistent over the last hundred years, on its head. The policy was further approved by the 1970 Tory conference and did little harm to their electoral prospects as later that year Heath took up residence in Downing Street while MacArthur was successfully re-elected to Westminster.

This was a period of considerable tension both in domestic and foreign affairs. Middle-eastern terrorism was rearing its head but generally at a safe distance from Perth. Or so the people of Perth thought until they opened their *Perthshire Advertisers* one morning in 1969 to find a full page advertisement for Al Fatah, the Palestine National Liberation Movement: 'Remember Palestine...the Palestinians are fighting back.' Indeed they were: in that year Al Fatah carried out over 2,000 guerrilla attacks against Israel. The Northern Ireland troubles were also in the news and there was disquiet at Perth's first Orange march in June of that year which attracted 400 marchers and several thousand spectators. A much bigger one was held in 1973 in which 6,000 marchers, mainly from outside Perth, and around 30 bands paraded through the streets. All police leave in the city and county was cancelled but there were no major incidents apart from disruption to motorists and shoppers. The main topic of debate, though, particularly in business and agricultural circles, was whether or not to join the EEC. At one stage local farmers were evenly divided with the Perth branch of the Scottish National Farmers Union voting in favour and the neighbouring Perth area branch voting narrowly against.

Britain joined the EEC in January 1973 (in the referendum of 1975 Taysiders voted emphatically in favour of staying in), and it might reasonably be supposed, wrongly though, that this was the impetus behind Perth's town-twinning partnerships. The longest and most successful twinning arrangement has been with the attractive riverside town of Aschaffenburg which is situated near Frankfurt in Germany. The link goes back to 1956 and still flourishes with regular exchanges of schoolchildren, musical and sporting groups, civic heads and various others. Since that time other formal links have been established across the globe: with the Russian town of Pskov, first suggested by theatre director Joan Knight in 1989 and which, after the collapse of communism, received hundreds of boxes of food and clothing aid from the people of Perth; with Cognac in France in 1991; with Haikou on the Chinese island of Hainan in 1992; with Bydgoszcz in Poland in 1998; and with Perth, Ontario in 2000. Even older than the Aschaffenburg link, and one which is now almost completely forgotten, was the post-war friendship with the French town of St Lô which resulted in several exchanges of schoolchildren between 1946 and 1949 and perhaps longer. Strangely enough, until the Charter of Mutual Friendship was signed in 2006, there had never been a formal twinning link with Perth in Australia though there had been regular exchanges over many years of people and gifts. These included, in 1937, four black swans which were released onto the South Inch pond, at a safe distance from their potentially more aggressive white cousins on the Tay. One of the warmest statements of friendship between these two cities was received in 1946: 'We are particularly proud in this City of Perth [Australia] to have the inspiring tradition of a mother city in Scotland who, in common with the cities of Great Britain, set a standard of courage and fortitude during the war unsurpassed at any other period in British history…We sincerely hope…that the happy liaison which exists between our two cities of Perth will help to strengthen the bonds of kinship and of Empire…' This was cemented in a very practical way with several tons of food aid gifted by the daughter city in the immediate post-war years.

While Perth was developing its European links and the nation as a whole tentatively shaking hands with Johnny Foreigner across the Channel, the swirling undercurrent of separatist politics in Scotland was about to hit the surface and cause a tidal wave of alarm across the country. In the first election of 1974 the SNP, already with one seat at Westminster, added a further six to their tally and in the second they added four more, making a total of 11. Out went balding Tory Ian MacArthur and in came curly-haired nationalist Douglas Crawford who, in press photographs, always seemed to look mildly surprised at finding himself an elected member. Crawford had a run a good campaign, listing in full-page press advertisements a number of well-known supporters including the St Johnstone manager Willie Ormond, actors John Cairney and Andrew Cruickshank, and athletics hero Lachie Stewart. In the first election, unsuccessful though he was, he increased the SNP share of the vote from 12 per cent to 27 per cent, and in the second to 41 per cent, just scraping home with a majority of 793.

Crawford was a popular MP and in the election of 1979 won almost as many votes as he had in October 1974, this in spite of his political organiser having defected to the Tories. However, in Jim Callaghan's memorable phrase, there had been a sea change in British politics and the Tories under Margaret Thatcher were returned to power. Their new candidate, Bill Walker, who had survived an attempt to deselect him in 1978 on account of his perceived lack of local impact, proved his doubters wrong and sufficiently mobilised the Tory vote to recapture Perth and East Perthshire with a majority of over 3,000. Shortly after, with John Purvis winning Mid-Scotland and Fife for the Conservatives in the first direct elections to the European Parliament, and with the Tories firmly in control of the district and regional councils, it looked as if Perth was once again true blue. Then again, considering the howls of protest from baying crowds outside the City Hall and some of the biggest security operations ever mounted in Scotland when Mrs Thatcher made her annual visits to address the Scottish Conservatives, maybe not.

Constituency boundaries changed in time for the 1983 election. Bill Walker headed north to fight the new North Tayside seat while the

A surge in Conservative support in Perth in the late 19th century allowed them to buy and develop these large clubrooms in George Street. They were designed by the architect of the Station Hotel with a view, perhaps, to impressing the wavering voter and intimidating the opposition. The premises were vacated in the 1990s. The photo was probably taken around a hundred years earlier.
Courtesy of Perth Museum and Art Gallery, Perth and Kinross Council.

flamboyant and frequently controversial Nicholas Fairbairn, after a close contest with David Heathcote-Amory, was selected for the new Perth and Kinross constituency. He comfortably won the election beating Douglas Crawford into second place, the Liberal-SDP Alliance into third, while the Labour candidate, tied to an extreme left-wing manifesto described as the longest suicide note in history, sank virtually without trace.

After this things began to go badly wrong for the Tories. An expensive revaluation resulted in an unacceptably high rates bill for Scottish householders and in an attempt to ward off the resulting backlash ministers urged Thatcher to proceed with all speed to introduce an alternative to the rates. Thus the poll tax was unleashed in Scotland a year ahead of England and if it is premature to say that this most hated of taxes drove the final nails into the Scottish Tories' coffin, they were at least being measured up for it. At the same time, and in the wake of the disastrous 1979 referendum on Scottish devolution, there was again a crescendo of demand, led by the Scottish Constitutional Convention, for some measure of home rule. With Ted Heath as unpopular with the next generation of Tories as the poll tax was with the electorate, his pro-devolution policy was dropped almost as quickly as he himself had been. While the Tories lost half their remaining seats in Scotland in 1987 both Fairbairn and Walker held on to theirs, as indeed they did in 1992, but with ever-diminishing majorities and the SNP snapping closer and closer at their heels.

The 1992 victory was quite remarkable given the deep antipathy towards the Tories in general and the poll tax in particular – especially when the actual figures payable were announced in 1989 and found to be around 25 per cent higher than previously indicated by the government. The local press regularly featured strongly worded letters about the tax and stories of sheriff officers in action against non-payers who, in 1991, were reckoned to total about 20 per cent of the population liable for the tax. The Perth Campaign Against the Poll Tax was busy offering advice about poinding and warrant sales, all highly embarrassing to the Tories, and in the midst of their woes the Perth Conservatives, with financial figures as wobbly as their electoral ones, put their George Street premises up for sale.

The Tories finally relinquished their hold on Perth in 1995. Not only were they virtually wiped out in the first election for the new unitary authority of Perth and Kinross Council, winning only two of 32 seats, but in the by-election following the death in harness of Sir Nicholas Fairbairn they were beaten into third place, with less than 22 per cent of the vote, by the SNP's Roseanna Cunningham. Roseanna, as she liked to be known in her election leaflets, held the recently created Perth constituency at the 1997 election and was joined in Westminster by the SNP's John Swinney in North Tayside. In 1999 both were elected to the new Scottish Parliament, set up by Tony Blair's new Labour government following a referendum, upon which both then stated that they would not seek re-election to Westminster. The following year Swinney was elected leader of the SNP and Roseanna his deputy, and both committed themselves to working for independence by 2007.

The departure from Westminster of both Swinney and Cunningham allowed two well-known names to appear on the local political scene. Annabelle Ewing, daughter of SNP matriarch Winnie, kept the Perth

Conservatives campaigning in the 1995 by-election. Candidate John Godfrey was soundly beaten by the SNP's Roseanna Cunningham, despite the help of prominent Tory MPs.
Courtesy of the A.K. Bell Library Local Studies Department, Perth and Kinross Council.

constituency in SNP hands at the 2001 general election, beating Tory Liz Smith by the narrowest of margins, and Pete Wishart, the keyboard player with Celtic rock band Runrig, managed a more emphatic victory over Conservative candidate Murdo Fraser and entered the House of Commons as the new member for North Tayside. Following another review by the Boundary Commission for Scotland the parliamentary constituencies changed again in time for the 2005 general election and Pete Wishart, despite strong opposition from the Conservatives, found himself as MP for the new constituency of Perth and North Perthshire, further increasing his majority in 2010.

The story of 20th century parliamentary politics in Perth is therefore one of a declining Liberal vote, the dominance of the Tories, and the ascendancy of the SNP. The Labour presence was stronger in certain areas of Perth and thus made itself known at local government rather than constituency level. It is noteworthy, however, that in the past 25 years Labour has fielded two strong candidates who have both gone on to high office, Jack McConnell in 1987 and Douglas Alexander in 1995. Although McConnell came fourth he must have been buoyed by a letter from an SNP supporter to the *Perthshire Advertiser* which stated: 'Jack McConnell showed too much promise to be given a no-hope seat for Labour such as this.'

CHAPTER FOUR

The Council:
Local Government in Perth

THE ONE SINGLE organisation that had the greatest influence on the development of Perth in the 20th century was Perth Town Council. Its successor bodies, Perth and Kinross District Council and Perth and Kinross Council, deserve credit for significant successes but taken together had only one third of the time to make an impact. The following chapter looks at how local government was organised and how it developed during the century. Its many achievements, in the fields of housing, transport, education, recreation, culture and others, are outlined in subsequent chapters.

At the start of the century Perth was divided into four wards, each electing six or seven councillors. The town council comprised 25 councillors, of which one was lord provost, one was treasurer, and four were bailies, plus the unelected dean of guild who made a total of 26. (By mid-century the wards had been increased to eight and the councillors reduced by one, though plans in 1934 to create an extra ward by bringing Scone within the burgh boundary were rejected, not least on account of the views of Scone residents.) The council further sub-divided into 16 committees dealing with matters such as property, finance, burial grounds, the Inches, the library, the baths, the slaughter house, police, lighting, fire engines, cleansing, paving, gas, electricity and water. Since that time, and by way of contrast, the local authority has passed responsibility for the utilities and police and fire services to other bodies, has inherited building authority from the Dean of Guild Court and education from the Perthshire Education Authority, has been given responsibility for housing and social work by Act of Parliament and has absorbed various other functions as widely ranging as trading standards, the museum service and economic development. Considering too that Perth and Kinross Council now covers a much wider geographical area, has 41 councillors and manages one of the biggest staffing establishments in the area, then the enormity of the change over the course of a century becomes apparent.

Council elections for much of the century were generally fought on issues rather than party politics, such as whether to build a new hospital or reconstruct the old in the first decade, and in the 1920s where the water for the new city supply should come from, and whether trams should be replaced with buses. In 1902, though, and for the next 20 years or so, temperance was one of the main issues. The relatively unregulated supply of alcohol brought many social problems in its wake, notably poverty, crime, poor health and domestic violence and there was therefore a powerful movement in favour of restricting the supply, either by degree or outright prohibition. All temperance candidates were in fact defeated in the 1902 election but the issue continued to be debated for many years to come and, perhaps because a considerable number of jobs depended on the prosperity of the whisky industry, later candidates generally met with the same lack of success.

In January 1909 an elderly, militant prohibitionist, Carry A. Nation (yes, really), arrived in Perth from the United States to wage war on its publicans, though whether she was at this time still genuinely motivated by moral issues or, as some thought, merely cashing in on her fame is open to question. From the station she headed straight to the Stormont Arms at 43 South Street where Bailie Douglas Lawrie was the licensee. The press described the ensuing verbal sparring which attracted a large crowd in the bar.

> Nation: There is one thing I want to tell you, and that is if you continue in this damnable trade you will go to hell.
>
> Lawrie: My good woman, if that is so you will be meeting me at the gate.
>
> Nation: What is your name?
>
> Lawrie: It is always the custom for ladies to be introduced first...

And so it went on. She then moved on to the Co-operative Hall in Canal Street and addressed a large audience before selling copies of her book and her little trademark axes, symbols of the direct action she employed in her young days to destroy bars. A crowd several thousand strong waited for her outside the hall and accompanied her to her lodgings at the St Johns Temperance Hotel, shouting and hissing. Temperance certainly had its adherents (of the 26 hotels in the city at that time, over a third were temperance establishments) but it was not widely popular

The Balmoral Bar in Castlegable, photographed in 1930, was one of the many public houses in Perth which temperance organisations campaigned against.
Courtesy of Perth Museum and Art Gallery, Perth and Kinross Council.

with the man in the street. One notably 'dry' area was Craigie which was granted a licence for its first public house as late as 1971.

While certain issues, usually those involving considerable expenditure and a corresponding increase in the rates, could arouse the passions in Perth voters it seems that in general the public was happy to let the council run the town in peace. In 1929 an editorial complained about 'the unfortunate disinclination on the part of citizens suitable for town council work to come forward and serve the community.' Neither did voters turn up in huge numbers. The council elections of 1950 were marred by a poor turnout and a general lack of interest. One political meeting in Dovecotland had to be abandoned after only one member of the public turned up. In 1953 Archie Martin, who was then in the early stages of a long and distinguished local government career, commented that the turn-out at local elections in Perth was low even by Scottish standards.

One reason, perhaps, that the public were satisfied with town council performance was a series of highly effective civic heads, men who demonstrably had the wellbeing of the citizens of Perth at heart. In 1931 Lord Provost Thomas Dempster, described as 'one of the most able civic chiefs of modern times', mainly on account of his strong support for the Woody Island water scheme, was elected to that position for a record third term and was brilliantly supported by Robert Nimmo as council treasurer. Nimmo himself was unanimously elected lord provost in 1935 but only after six years of steadily reducing the rate burden, by over 25 per cent in that period, and yet still managing to improve local services. Thanks to Nimmo, Perth in the 1930s had a reputation for setting some of the lowest rates among Scotland's large burghs. His popularity as treasurer was maintained as lord provost, a position to which he was elected four times, serving throughout the war years. He was succeeded in 1945 by another immensely well-liked figure, John Ure Primrose, the jovial farmer at Gannochy, who was elected for three terms and who, like the more restrained Nimmo, was also subsequently knighted. Between them they ran Perth for almost quarter of a century.

One of the many highlights of Lord Provost John Ure Primrose's tenure of office was the welcoming of Princess Elizabeth to the city in 1951.
Courtesy of the A.K. Bell Library Local Studies Department, Perth and Kinross Council.

In 1954, after 20 years on the council, Sir John Ure Primrose stepped down as lord provost, had his portrait painted and went into retirement in Fife. He had latterly presided over a relatively high-spending administration, with much of the increase being spent on education and housing, as a result of which the rates by 1951 had escalated to almost double the pre-war level. As the council embarked on a string of improvements in the 1950s – the crematorium, the Queen's Bridge, the Pomarium flats, and a new shopping centre, to name a few – so the rates bill soared, a situation not helped by a reduction in government grants to local authorities. The press asked rhetorically if the town could afford such developments and gave the answer that as society had changed so much in the previous 20 years, with the public expecting and demanding a higher standard of living, the town had to afford it. But in 1962 some people began to disagree and after a particularly steep increase in the rates that year a mass protest meeting in the City Hall resulted in the re-formation of the Ratepayers' Association and the first appearance on centre stage of Jean Hamilton as its president. She was a redoubtable campaigner who earned her name in Perth history through her fight for a new wash-house. She eventually served on the council itself but was more effective as a campaigner against the council than sitting on it.

The penultimate lord provost was David K. Thomson who served two terms between 1966 and 1972. This particularly popular civic head, with a distinguished war record behind him, was given the freedom of Perth and Kinross District at a packed ceremony in the City Hall in 1982.

Former Lord Provost David K. Thomson receiving the freedom of Perth and Kinross District in 1982. Many well-known faces can be seen on the City Hall stage.
Courtesy of Perth Museum and Art Gallery, Perth and Kinross Council.

Party politics did not feature significantly in local elections until the 1960s. The trades council fielded its first candidate in 1903, Labour candidates stood around the time of World War One and communists in the 1930s but in general, while they had limited success, it was the Moderates, a grouping of centre-right councillors, who held sway for much of the period. The second-largest grouping were the Independents who at that time would have rejected any suggestion that they were in fact a group. In 1962, as Tory popularity dwindled amid national scandal and intrigue, the political mood began to change and Labour success took them to within two seats of the Moderates. Five years later the Moderates lost control of the council (one of their seats being captured by the Independent Jimmy Doig at the start of his long involvement with local politics) though they still remained the largest party. In 1968 the SNP won their first seats and by the following year had a total of four and a 30 per cent share of the vote. Aware of the growing challenge from the political parties and united by a common distaste for party politics in local government the Moderates and Independents joined forces in 1971 to form the Moderate-Independent Alliance, thus giving themselves a large majority over Labour and SNP councillors. Moderates were now being challenged by the press to come out as Tories, which is how most Perth people regarded them, but they refused to do so, claiming that they stood only for 'the application of common sense to local government.' Coupled with this, the *Perthshire Advertiser* became increasingly vociferous in its demand that Conservatives should fight for council seats: if Labour thought they were worth fighting for then so should the Tories, they argued. The main concern for the newspaper was that, in the elections for the new Tayside Regional Council, scheduled for 1974, Labour would present a united front in 'the struggle for the control of regional councils.' The Tories must do the same, they urged, and should therefore cut their teeth on the last town council elections of 1972 and 1973. As the paper put it: 'At the moment there is no sign that anything other than five independently-minded persons, committed to keeping party politics out of local government, will be travelling up to Dundee from Perth to face the well-drilled forces of Dundee's experienced Labour representatives.' In the end the Tories put up two candidates for the 1972 elections, who were soundly beaten after what was regarded as an amateurish campaign, and stated they would aim to fight every district and regional seat in 1974. Finally, in the last council elections of 1973 and having been trying for more than half a century, Labour gained three seats and became the largest party in the council. Frustratingly for them, the success was short-lived as local government reform effectively moved the goalposts at which they had been aiming for so long.

Westminster was forever getting the screwdriver out and tinkering with local government: a bit more tightening here and a little adjustment there, all designed to make the machine work more efficiently and better able to cope with the rougher terrain of the advancing century. Major overhauls in the 1900s totalled only three but they had wide implications for the city of Perth and the way in which it was governed. The first was the *Local Government (Scotland) Act* of 1929 which came into force in 1930 and established a system of local government which survived until the introduction of district and regional councils in 1975. A more effective structure than had hitherto existed was ushered in, consisting of joint county councils, district councils, and three different types of town council which, depending on the size of the town, exercised control over a varying range of functions. Perth was thus designated a 'large burgh' and as such retained control over most functions as before.

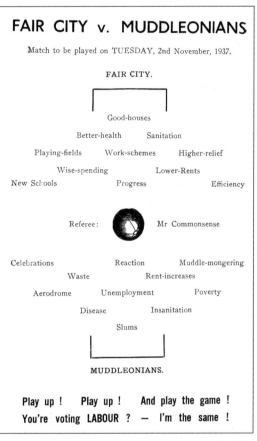

A clever Labour leaflet for the council elections of 1937, designed to appeal to the football-loving male and highlighting the contrasting policies of the local Labour Party and the council administration: good housing versus slums, playing fields versus the aerodrome and new schools versus celebrations. It was to no avail, though, as Labour failed to make any headway against the Moderates.
Courtesy of the A.K. Bell Library Local Studies Department, Perth and Kinross Council.

The 1929 Act also legislated for the abolition of parish councils which had been in existence since 1894. The duties of the Perth Parish Council, 'mourned by many', were thus transferred to the town council and included the responsibilities of running the Glasgow Road poorhouse, known as the Bertha Home, and providing relief to the city's aged, infirm and unemployed, duties which by common consent had been performed very well. The work of the parish council was supported by the poor rate, paid by local householders. In 1926 the staff and elected members of the parish council were described as 'quietly contributing their quota to the good government of the city.' Robert Stewart was the parish council's Inspector of Poor whose job it was to enquire after the poor and needy, their living conditions, and make provision for them. In that year, a year of relatively high unemployment, more short-time working and the General Strike, he dealt with almost 3,700 cases, a huge increase on the previous year when he had less than a third to deal with. Stewart acted in this role for the entire life of the parish council.

The next major reform of local government was first proposed in 1963 and, following the report of a Royal Commission (the Wheatley report) and a government white paper, resulted in the *Local Government (Scotland) Act* of 1973. This was not so much an overhaul of local

The former poorhouse on the Glasgow Road, having been converted to modern flats and townhouses, provides a much higher standard of housing than a century ago.

government as a completely new build. It could not have been a huge shock to the Perth councillors of the time, though, as the divisions between city and county, and even Perthshire and Angus, were not as clearly defined as before. As far back as the early 1950s a local plan emphasised the need for the town council to promote a balanced development in conjunction with the county council. In the mid-1960s the lord provost of Perth stated that the interests of city and county were closely interwoven and said 'we now travel together in many fields.' Even the title of the Tayside Development Plan of 1966 indicates the more inclusive and broader local government thinking of the time. The effect of the 1973 Act was thus to consign to the landfill site of history the centuries-old crumbling counties, rotten royal burghs and tarnished town councils, replacing them with shiny new regional, district and community councils. The new set-up, in which Perth at district level was lumped in with the rump of Perthshire and at regional level was required to rub shoulders with Dundee, was not popular. The demise of the ancient town council was bad enough but the prospect of playing second fiddle to the arch-rival along the Tay was even worse. The *Perthshire Advertiser* doubted that Perth would have much of a voice and proposed, as a counter-balance to the dominating influence of Dundee, that Perth should be the capital of Tayside, which stance received the support of most Perth councillors but which was nevertheless in vain. A further blow was dealt when Fife, instead of being divided between the Tayside and Lothian regional councils as had originally been proposed, was permitted to remain independent as a regional authority. Perth had regarded north-east Fife as an additional counterweight to Dundee but this was not to be so.

Thus came into being, as far as Perth was concerned, Tayside Regional Council, Perth and Kinross District Council (the old town council's preferred option of Perth District Council having been rejected) and, in time, a number of community councils. The regional council headquarters was established in Dundee and not, as Perth had argued, either in Perth or midway between the two. Perth's fears, however, about Dundee and Labour domination were allayed in a number of ways. In the regional elections the Tories won 22 of the 46 seats, an impressive total (given Tory disarray at national level) which was increased when an Independent crossed the floor and joined the party, thus ensuring that while still one short of an overall majority they at least could not be outvoted. When the 46 councillors came to vote for a chairman Perthshire's I.A. Duncan Millar and the ex-lord provost of Dundee each received 23 votes. Both drew aces when asked to cut a pack of cards and on the second cut Duncan Millar won with a second ace. Finally, when Perth's town clerk, Archie Martin, was appointed chief executive of Tayside, Perth folk perhaps began to breathe a little easier. The new regional and district councils shadowed the old councils for a year after which, on 16 May 1975, they assumed full authority. The last meeting of Perth Town Council, described as 'a sad occasion' by Lord Provost A.U. Cross, was held on 21 April 1975. One of the council's final acts was to commission a new window for St John's Kirk to mark the end of its long association with the church.

The old custom of providing provosts and bailies with civic lamps outside their homes disappeared with the local government reforms of the 1970s. Shown here is Lord Provost Ritchie's lamp outside his former home in Atholl Crescent.

After that it was a case of out with the old and in with the new. The district council was under Tory control (Labour being unable to capitalise on their success in the last town council elections) and one of their first decisions concerned the possible retention, unofficially, of the lord provost title which under the 1973 Act had become the preserve of Edinburgh, Glasgow, Aberdeen and Dundee. The kirk session of St John's were keen that the title should be retained in some way, as were many Perth folk, and a few councillors were in favour of it being adopted by the dean of guild. (The dean until 1975 had been an unelected member of the town council, with limited voting rights, and ranked second only to the lord provost himself in ceremonial and social occasions. The dean of guild title survived the reforms of 1975 but the office-holder thereafter had no further say in council affairs.) In the end, the council voted to give its new elected head the title of chairman and sent the lord provost's robes and chain of office to the museum, after which time Conservative values reasserted themselves and they successfully petitioned the Scottish Secretary to recognise the civic head as not chairman but provost of Perth and Kinross District Council. While attempts to preserve the lord provost title were thus in vain the council had more success with their new coat of arms. A request to the Court of the Lord Lyon that the royal burgh of Perth's double-headed eagle should be retained on the new arms was granted on the grounds of Perth's historic importance and it still survives on the arms of the unitary authority, Perth and Kinross Council.

Even the formation of community councils, the lowest level of Scottish local government, caused bitter debate in Perth where there was considerable opposition to the district council's proposal that seven community councils should be set up in the city, based on the electoral wards. Local Liberals were much against this notion arguing that as Perth as a whole was one community so it only required one community council. This, of course, after the demise of the town council, would have had the effect of conjuring up its ghost, a basically incorporeal and certainly toothless body, watching suspiciously over the new generation of decision-makers. Perhaps with such a spectre in mind the district council pressed ahead with dividing Perth into several community council areas. The first elections throughout the district were held in 1977, though by that time only one Perth community, Oakbank-Burghmuir, was sufficiently ready to have one, and even then the turn-out was less than

The royal burgh of Perth was proud of its coat of arms, particularly the double-headed eagle. This lamp, one of two outside the City Chambers, bears the eagle, the coat of arms and the royal burgh's motto, Pro Rege, Lege et Grege. It also has the date, 12 May 1937, which commemorates the coronation of George VI, a freeman of Perth. Courtesy of Perth Museum and Art Gallery, Perth and Kinross Council.

ten per cent. Despite an apparent lack of public support, though, there can be little doubt that they have an important role to play in local government, and by way of a recent example the Bridgend, Gannochy and Kinnoull Community Council has been a leading participant in the ongoing fight against a proposed incinerator and waste-to-energy plant in Shore Road.

When it came to public spending the old town council was generally recognised as prudent, so it would have come as a shock to rate-payers to see two rather more freely spending councils in charge of the purse strings. The mid-seventies was a period of rampant inflation which caused local government costs to rise annually by between 20 and 25 per cent, and indeed in the first year of the district council Perth house-holders found themselves paying almost 30 per cent more in rates than they had the previous year. Inflation was not entirely to blame as some top council officials, who had transferred from old town council jobs to equivalent district or regional posts, were paid almost 20 per cent more. New responsibilities assigned to the councils, new jobs, new equipment, and a computer for the district council, also led to higher costs. One of the district council's biggest purchases was its new headquarters, the former General Accident head office at the foot of the High Street. Such inexorably rising expenditure, mirrored at regional level as well, resulted in ratepayers' protests, a Westminster clampdown on local authority finances, and ever larger increases in the rates. This repeating cycle was one of the themes of Scottish local government in the late 1970s and 1980s and one which eventually led to the introduction of the poll tax. After one such tightening of the financial screws the Tory-controlled district council in early 1985 actually passed a vote of no confidence in its two Tory MPs, which Nicholas Fairbairn referred to as 'a cheap political trick.' Little love was lost between local and central government at that time.

Politically the Tories retained control of the district council for its first ten years and were helped to do so by councillors Jim Proudfoot and Norman Renfrew who in 1976 stated that there was no further room for Independents and joined the Conservative ranks. These nouveaux Tories, together with Councillor Hamish Young, all of them highly influential in local politics, were known as the Gang of Three. With its decidedly negative overtones, recalling Chinese communist dictators and British Labour Party rebels, this was an unfortunate sobriquet, as they were widely regarded as three of the most experienced councillors of the time. Indeed two of them, Young and Renfrew, served as provost in the early days of the district council. When they lost their seats at the 1984 elections they were described in a letter to the press as having far more knowledge than the rest of the council put together and were right almost 99 per cent of the time. Labour, meanwhile, was going through a turbulent period, both nationally and locally. Councillor Pat Reilly claimed that the Trotskyite Militant tendency had infiltrated his ward and later the highly-respected Labour regional councillor, John Stewart, found himself deselected by his party. There were, however, allegations of irregularities at the selection meeting and the decision was subsequently overturned by the constituency Labour Party. This growing influence of the far left gave rise in 1981 to the SDP which, in heady expectation, had candidates ready to fight the local elections by the following year.

In the mid-1980s, even though their local MPs did well in Westminster elections, the Tories lost control of both district and regional councils. Having refused to countenance any idea of power sharing on the district council they found themselves facing the massed pipes and drums of the other parties who had formed a coalition against them. By 1988 there were no Conservative councillors left in Perth at all. The end seemed nigh but in the 1992 district elections they bounced back to recapture control of the council, and elected former SNP member Mrs Jean McCormack as the district's first woman provost, and a deservedly popular one too. This was almost 60 years after Bailie Mrs John Wood had been elected Perth's first woman magistrate.

A degree of suspicion existed between the district and regional councils in the early days, but in time they developed a reasonably good working relationship. Tempers occasionally flared, however, such as when the district council's shopping policy was overruled by the region in somewhat heavy-handed fashion. There were also accusations of centralisation in Dundee and claims that the regional council was too remote from voters and the two-tier system too cumbersome. Inevitable were the demands across the great divide for one or other of the councils to be scrapped. When in 1988 there was a call for the regions to be abolished, not by a district councillor but by one of their own number, then perhaps the writing was on the wall. By the following year COSLA was canvassing views on the regions and in April 1996, as a result of the

Local Government etc (Scotland) Act of 1994, both Tayside Regional Council and Perth and Kinross District Council were replaced by the unitary authority of Perth and Kinross Council. By putting an end to the two-tier experiment, which had survived 21 years, this was the century's third and final overhaul of local government.

Elections to the shadow authority were held in 1995 and resulted in the SNP winning 18 of the 32 seats, and thus forming an administration. The Tories were routed, holding on to only two seats. It is, however, impossible to write off the Tories in Perth and Kinross and by 1999 they were sharing power in an anti-SNP coalition with Mike O'Malley having been elected Perth and Kinross's first Labour provost. The SNP succeeded in turning the tables in 2003 when, once again as the largest party though without an overall majority, they entered into a coalition with the Liberal Democrats, thus paving the way for the election of the council's first Liberal Democrat provost, Bob Scott. The coalition survived the 2007 elections, the first in Scottish local government to be held under a system of proportional representation, after which the SNP's Dr John Hulbert became provost. Following the 2012 election and having established an unlikely 'working relationship' with the Conservatives, the SNP decided to form a minority administration with Liz Grant taking over as civic head.

Reform did not end with the introduction of the unitary authority. The first years of the new council seemed to consist of endless reorganisation as, under pressure of continuing budget cuts, consultants were brought in, departments merged, directors paid off, staff shed and services axed. Sometimes the cuts went by relatively unnoticed but on occasions, such as when free music tuition was ended, public lavatories closed, and a grounds maintenance contract awarded to a private company, the voices of protest were loud and clear. On the other hand, the council was perfectly capable of spending large sums as well. Having taken over the functions and some of the staff of the former regional council, there was an obvious need for more office space. Various sites were considered as a home for the new council headquarters, such as the former William Low store in Victoria Street and Rosslyn House on the Glasgow Road, but in the end it was decided to convert the former Pullars factory in Kinnoull Street, a job which was completed by the end of 2000 at a cost of about £20 million. A public-private partnership over funding, however, helped to reduce the impact on council tax payers.

Councillors too were eligible for responsibility allowances as well as money for travel and subsistence, and one wonders what their counterparts of 1900 would have made of the £852,000 shelled out in 2012. Such a figure, unimaginable to them, would have paid for the Victoria Bridge almost 25 times over. One wonders too what that all-male gathering would have made of the appointment of the council's first female chief executive, Bernadette Malone, in 2003. A woman as town clerk… never!

CHAPTER FIVE

Blackboard and Black Gown: Education and The Church

The schoolmaster and the minister have generally been well respected in Scotland and have consequently exerted a considerable influence over individuals and society. From the 1960s, however, both found themselves struggling not just against the values of a consumer society but also against a rising anti-authoritarianism, and despite the best efforts of strong headmasters and charismatic churchmen they no longer enjoy the same elevated position in local society that was once theirs by custom and dint of study.

Scotland has long been proud of its education system which has steadily been improved by a number of Education Acts over the years. One of the most significant was that of 1872 which provided for compulsory elementary education, the establishment of school boards, and the creation of the Scotch Education Department, all of which laid the groundwork for the rapid development of schooling in the 20th century. The Perth School Board, as we have seen in the second chapter, was an organisation of some considerable standing, whose elected members had the authority to borrow money and levy rates and whose responsibilities were greatly expanded over the years. The building of new schools was a prime function and in the early 20th century these included the Advanced Department of Caledonian Road School, Central District School, Northern District School, and a major extension to Southern District School.

The increasing powers of the school board gradually turned it into an embryo social work department. As well as providing technical classes in subjects relevant to local industries, evening classes and employment advice to school leavers, it also carried out medical inspections of schoolchildren and in the many instances where the medical officer's advice was ignored a new school nurse service followed up the doctor's recommendations. This service was further extended in 1913 when the board was made responsible for the actual medical treatment of schoolchildren,

Northern District School was built by Perth School Board on the northern edge of the city
and has since been renamed Balhousie Primary School.
Courtesy of Perth Museum and Art Gallery, Perth and Kinross Council.

incurring an additional expenditure of £100 that year on medicines and
spectacles, and yet again in 1914 when the board was given responsibility for children with learning difficulties. The board also had the authority to compel parents to provide adequate food and clothing for their
children, to the extent of providing such basic necessities themselves and
later recovering the debt from the parents. Even in the winter months
many children used to turn up for school barefoot. With the opening in
1914 of a dining centre in the West Church Hall in South Street the
board also offered a school dinner service, the poorer ones being fed free
of charge, the others paying a nominal sum. In one nine-month period
at the start of World War One the board provided around 20,000 school
dinners. By the time of the board's demise in 1919 there had been a
noticeable improvement in the health and nutrition of schoolchildren.

The elected Perthshire Education Authority assumed the school
boards' responsibilities and was supported by a number of school
management committees. For the first time, though, the people of Perth
no longer had direct control over their own schools. The authority did
not last long, however, and despite a feeling that it had generally worked
well and had earned its reputation as the best in Scotland, it was
nevertheless abolished, along with all other education authorities, in the
local government reforms of 1930. Responsibility for education across
the entire county now passed to the new education committee of the
county council, while the final decision on matters of expenditure lay

The staff of Southern District School in the time of the Perth School Board. One of them, perhaps, may have kindled a love of rhythm and words in a young William Soutar who, as a great Scottish poet, ranks as one of the school's most famous sons.
Courtesy of the A.K. Bell Library Local Studies Department, Perth and Kinross Council.

with the finance committee. Friction between the town council and two county council committees was thus almost inevitable and was not long in coming. The first significant conflict occurred in 1933 when the town saw an urgent need for new buildings at Cherrybank School, where the existing premises were in poor condition, and at St John's Roman Catholic School, where pupil numbers were increasing. The county would not provide the funding, nor would they spend money on upgrading the recently vacated Old Academy to allow Balhousie Boys School to move in. Instead the county library service took over the ground floor of that building. The following year, however, the county council recognised that the old St John's RC School, just off the High Street, was in a deplorable condition and agreed to fund a new Roman Catholic school at Stormont Street instead, on the site of the former St Joseph's Convent (the Sisters of Charity having moved to Melville Street, beside St John's Roman Catholic Church). Such sources of friction were finally smoothed over in 1975 when town and county councils were abolished and education became the sole responsibility of Tayside Regional Council.

School's out, not just for the day but – as you can tell from the smiles – for a week or two.
The girls of St John's RC Primary start their potato holidays in October 1949.
The Louis Flood Collection.
Courtesy of Perth Museum and Art Gallery, Perth and Kinross Council.

Until the advent of comprehensivisation Perth Academy was regarded as academically the senior Perth school and as such it occupied a prime position in the dealings of the various education authorities whose responsibility it was. This was particularly so in the first quarter of the 20th century when the school's accommodation problem was acute. The situation became more complex in 1910 when the Perth Educational Trust handed Sharp's Institution over to the Perth School Board, complete with buildings and endowments. After lengthy debate the decision was made to merge the school with Perth Academy and by 1915 both premises were run as one single school under the rectorship of Edward Smart. In 1911, the acquisition of Sharp's Institution having made no difference to the accommodation crisis, the board decided to build a new Academy on land at Bellwood, on the eastern side of the Tay, an unpopular decision

The restricted accommodation at the Old Academy in Rose Terrace gave the education authorities many years of anxious thought. The cannon to the left of the building was a relic from the Crimean War and not a threat to latecomers.
Courtesy of the A.K. Bell Library Local Studies Department, Perth and Kinross Council.

which resulted in a ratepayers' protest to the Scotch Education Department whose pronouncement on the matter was a firm no. A site at Muirton Bank was the next possibility but when this too was rejected the board again considered whether rebuilding the Academy on its Rose Terrace site and extending it as far as Atholl Street might be the best option. They went as far as purchasing the required properties in Rose Terrace, Atholl Street and Barossa Street and holding a competition for local architects to design a new building, before World War One halted the proceedings.

It was only in 1925 that the education authority decided to build a new school at Viewlands on the outskirts of the city, on land owned by Macdonald Fraser, the livestock auctioneers. After further opposition to the plans, and another architectural competition, and a debate on whether or not to include a tuck shop (yes, they decided) and a swimming pool (no to that), work finally began in 1930, a year which also saw the retiral of the highly-regarded Edward Smart and the appointment of William Smail, a professor of Latin at a colonial university in Africa, as his replacement. As the building progressed the plans were altered slightly

The wide façade of the new Academy at Viewlands has the seriousness, if not the grandeur, of its predecessor in Rose Terrace. This photo was taken in 1960 on the 200th anniversary of the town council's decision to found an 'Academy for Literature and the Sciences' in Perth. There had, however, been a school in Perth since the 12th century.
Courtesy of Perth Museum and Art Gallery, Perth and Kinross Council.

to permit the erection of a clocktower, to which ex-rector Smart contributed the generous sum of £1,000. The school was completed at a cost of £95,000 and finally opened by the Duchess of Atholl in 1932. With accommodation for 900 pupils, girls and boys in equal numbers, and extensive playing fields for rugby, hockey and cricket, it was described in the press as one of the finest secondary schools in the country. The junior department of the Academy, meanwhile, was housed in Sharp's Institution and it took another ten years to build a new junior school adjacent to the new Academy. It was opened in 1942 and renamed Viewlands Primary School in 1966.

Quietly-spoken John Kerr took over as rector in 1950 and oversaw a series of improvements and extensions, as well as a visit from Prince Philip and Sir John Hunt in 1965, before his retiral four years later. One of the reasons for Kerr's resignation was the need, he felt, for a stronger man to deal with a growing unruliness among pupils and increasing levels of vandalism, and it is perhaps no surprise that shortly before his resignation some Academy pupils had made local news by spray-painting a trail from the city centre to the school where they had daubed the roof with the slogan 'Welcome to Kerr's café.' That stronger man came in the shape of the formidable Neil McCorkindale who, as the last of the Academy's rectors in the traditional mould, oversaw the change from selective to comprehensive education while continuing to insist on rigorous teaching and firm discipline from his staff and the highest academic and personal standards from his pupils. He retired in 1986 and his successor, James Waite, the fifth rector of the 20th century, led the school into the 21st, finally stepping down in 2001 at the time of an inspection report which made for less than happy reading. Charles Kiddie stepped into the breach and headed the school until 2008. The present rector is Andrew Smith.

The city's largest secondary school in terms of pupil numbers is Perth High School which was opened in 1950 in a collection of prefabricated buildings at Muirton. The first pupils of the school were the secondary girls from Caledonian Road School and the boys from Balhousie Boys' School, these two institutions having hitherto catered for the secondary education of pupils who did not proceed to the Academy. At their new school they were able to benefit from not just a three-year secondary schooling but for the academically more able a full six-year education as well. The school also offered a pre-nursing course open to anyone in the county. It was not long before accommodation at the High School was branded as unsatisfactory and within 20 years of its opening plans had been announced for a brand new school on a greenfield site at Oakbank, close to the Academy. Notwithstanding the state of the buildings the pupils seem to have enjoyed their time at Muirton. The *Perthshire Advertiser* published a letter from recent school-leavers who wrote: 'We would like the public of Perth to know how much we have enjoyed our schooldays. We would like to thank the rector... and all the staff who have helped us to make our education so happy and so worthwhile.' On 24 August 1971 the new Perth High School was opened, the same day that the city's newest senior secondary, Perth Grammar School, also opened, not in brand new premises but in those just vacated by the High School.

It was thus inevitable that the underlying issue in the Grammar School's early years would be the poor quality of its buildings. In early 1974 the Secretary of State for Scotland approved the plan to rebuild the school in a number of phases, the first of which was opened in 1977. Meanwhile the remainder of the school caught the attention of the prospective Conservative parliamentary candidate, Bill Walker, who made the telling point that if the school had been a commercial undertaking it

Built high above the city between 1968 and 1971, the five-storey Perth High School looks over the playing fields and buildings of its neighbour, the Academy, to Kinnoull Hill beyond.

would have been closed down under the *Factories Act*. By 1983 rector Robert Heeps described the conditions in some classrooms as appalling, with low temperatures a particular problem in winter. It was only in 1991, six years after Heeps' retiral, that work began on the fourth and final phase of the school's improvement.

Lying between the Grammar School and the North Inch was Perth's first Roman Catholic secondary, St Columba's High School, which opened in 1967 and which took its first pupils from the secondary department of St John's in Stormont Street. It originally functioned as a four-year secondary from where boys wishing to take Highers would generally have gone on to Lawside Academy in Dundee and girls to Kilgraston. Parent power flexed its muscles in 1973 and within three years the school had become a full six-year secondary, albeit with the smallest roll among Perth's senior schools.

That date in August 1971 when the new Grammar School and High School opened was also the date when Perth schools officially went comprehensive. In 1966, in response to the initial push towards comprehensivisation by the Secretary of State for Scotland, the county council's education committee gave 'long and anxious thought' to the reorganisation of secondary education in the counties of Perth and Kinross before finally agreeing to the radical change. Implementation was handed over to Lachlan Young, the county's director of education, who in 1970 announced that selective secondary education would end the following year and that advancement from primary schools would henceforth depend on a pupil's address rather than academic ability. The most controversial part of the plan, however, was the decision to merge Perth Academy with Goodlyburn Secondary, an arrangement which necessitated not just pupils in the first two years attending the latter site before transferring to the Academy building in third year but staff being ferried by taxi between the two campuses at some considerable cost of time and money. Neil McCorkindale and 80 of his staff, together with many parents, were much against the plan, and even Young himself said, of his own scheme, that it was 'full of holes and riddled with weaknesses,' the only problem being that no one else had thought of a better one. It was only in 1990 with the opening of a major extension at the Academy, that its pupils were once again accommodated on one campus.

The other major problem faced by Young during his career was the chronic shortage of school places. Between 1946 and 1958 the total number of pupils in the Perth and Kinross education system increased by 25 per cent, secondary pupils by 70 per cent, and senior pupils in fourth, fifth and sixth year by 100 per cent. The problem continued into the sixties and seventies, to the extent that by 1975 all Perth secondary schools were described as full, and even the Academy had soared from an already overcrowded 1,000 in 1955 to around 1,600 20 years later. The reason for the accommodation crisis was the post-war population 'bulge', combined with the raising of the school-leaving age to 15 in 1947 and to 16 in 1972. The situation was compounded by the many pupils who now lived in the new suburbs of Perth and thus at some considerable distance from the old city centre schools. The solution was a long period of school building, extensions and improvements, the costs of which were magnified by the accompanying need for more teachers, support staff, school meals, furniture, books and even school buses. During his tenure of office Young pushed through new schools at Goodlyburn, Letham, Oakbank, Tulloch, and North Muirton, as well as the new and extended secondary schools mentioned above. Tayside Regional Council continued his work but not with the same intensity with which he had transformed education in Perth.

Other contentious issues he grappled with were the showing of sex education films to primary school children in 1970, drug awareness campaigns in 1971, and a spate of 'there's a bomb in the school' hoax telephone calls which, while frustrating for staff, generally resulted in free periods for pupils. It was also a time when music in schools was considerably developed and when television and computers were being regarded as educational tools.

The early 1980s was a period of retrenchment in education. The government's restrictions on local authority spending forced the regional council to take unwelcome measures, including low wage increases for teachers and even some redundancies. This resulted in a teachers' strike and in the formation of the Perth and Kinross Parents' Association to combat the cuts. A lengthy and more damaging teachers' strike occurred in the mid-1980s during which Academy rector Neil McCorkindale tried to arrange out-of-hours tuition for his O-grade pupils, a brave if controversial move which earned him the support of parents and the condemnation of the Educational Institute of Scotland which proceeded to escalate strike action at the school. The withdrawal of extra-curricular activities during this long period had a particularly deleterious effect on Scottish sport for a number of years.

The practice of corporal punishment was finally abolished in the mid-1980s despite the great majority of parents in at least some local schools being in favour of its retention. It is interesting to note that steps were taken by the Perth School Board as early as 1904 to curtail its use, prompting much disquiet among teachers who feared that classroom discipline would be destroyed by such a move. It is indeed tempting to assume that school discipline has deteriorated since its abolition but there is strong evidence to the contrary. There have been many instances throughout the century of perhaps too highly spirited children giving their teachers a hard time, and even in 1902 the press reported that a class of girls was in open rebellion against their English teacher. Perth poet Willie Soutar recounted in his diary how he led a pupils' strike at Southern District School and how it ended with the ominous words that the strikers were now to be struck. There is also the testimony of William Nairne, the retired headmaster of that same school (who was always proud of the fact that his doctor father had delivered John Buchan), who wrote in 1937: 'Nowadays it is common to hear much of the lack of parental control and the consequent unruliness of children... but certain am I that the pupils in the schools today are much more amenable to discipline and more easily managed than those I knew in the earlier years of my teaching career.' It was not unknown, he said, for teachers to be faced with several rebellious and defiant pupils, if they even bothered to turn up at school in the first place, and cited an early personal experience when he with three other teachers faced a class of 200 shouting pupils. This is not to say that more recent teachers have had an easy time of it. The local press recounted the story of one Perth High School pupil who in 1977 picked up his physics teacher, put her out of the classroom and then proceeded to swear at the rector, which, considering the lack of respect for authority, was perhaps not the most auspicious start for a future army officer and Member of Parliament. On the other hand one should pay tribute to the many schoolchildren who work hard at their studies, get involved with charities, make wonderful music or perform on stage, and achieve notable results on the sports field and athletics track. Neither should we forget those pupils of the Grammar School who launched the talking newspaper for the blind service, which was supported financially by the Queen's Silver Jubilee Trust Fund in 1978, and other pupils of that school and also the Academy who on several occasions won prestigious school magazine competitions run by the *Sunday Times* and *The Scotsman*.

Education in Perth has taken a big leap forward in the first years of the 21st century, thanks to a bold and forward-looking investment in new schools. Under the umbrella of the multi-million pound Investment in Learning Programme the council has built six new community schools in the Perth and Kinross Council area, including two in Perth city. After years at the planning stage construction began in 2007 and two years later the Glenearn Community Campus opened, replacing the now redundant Caledonian Road Primary School and Friarton Nursery. Similarly, when the North Inch Community Campus opened in late 2011 as home to the new St John's Academy, the old St John's Primary and St Columba's High School both closed. The new campuses with their state of the art facilities have been highly successful, with figures released in the summer of 2012 showing that exam grades had improved, school libraries were being better used and more pupils were taking advantage of school meals.

Perth has been home to two independent schools in the 20th century. The first was the Bernard Holt School, a mainly boarding establishment which first opened near the South Inch in 1927. After 20 years or so the

Another school with superb views over the town is Craigclowan, the former home
of William Lovat Fraser and now an independent preparatory school.

school and its red-blazered boys relocated to Lockerbie leaving the field
clear for the blue-blazered pupils of Craigclowan. This coeducational preparatory school, which primarily feeds the neighbouring senior schools
of Glenalmond, Strathallan and Kilgraston, was founded in 1952 and
still occupies the former home – with its magnificent views over city and
river – of William Lovat Fraser, son of the founder of Macdonald Fraser.
It was saved from imminent closure in 1979 by the appointment of a
young and energetic headmaster, Mike Beale, under whose leadership
pupil numbers quickly grew. This in turn led to the building of new
classroom blocks and the development of sporting and musical facilities.
Beale retired in 2007 to take over the presidency of the Perthshire
Chamber of Commerce and was replaced by Andy Rathborne. In the
summer of 2012 Richard Evans from Bromsgrove Preparatory School
near Birmingham took over as Craigclowan's fifth headmaster.

Outside the classroom there has always been plenty for the children
of Perth to do. The Boys' Brigade was the main youth organisation for
boys at the turn of the century, the first company being founded at St

In the pre-digital world people enjoyed themselves in rather different ways. A group of school-children crossing South William Street in 1925 discover another use for yesterday's news. Courtesy of Perth Museum and Art Gallery, Perth and Kinross Council.

Stephen's (Free Church) in 1887. The organisation spread mainly through churches and in 1893, with seven such companies in existence, the Perth Battalion was formed, headed by Henry Coates. By the turn of the century there were 16 companies. Camping and sport were the main outdoor pursuits, while time was given indoors to drill and scripture knowledge. The Boys' Brigade also took part in major civic events such as the coronation celebrations in 1911. To mark their 50th anniversary in Perth over 400 boys staged a highly successful show, *Sons of St Johnstoun*, which played for six nights to a packed theatre.

The scout movement was founded by Baden-Powell, hero of Mafeking, in 1907 and like the Boys' Brigade enjoyed a rapid expansion throughout the country. Pitlochry is reckoned to have had one of the first scout troops in Scotland and scouts were certainly active in Perth by 1909 when, at the laying of the new City Hall's foundation stone, they were described as presenting 'an exceedingly smart turn-out in their kharki [sic] blouses and B-P hats.' The following year B-P himself visited the city and was given an enthusiastic reception. At this time there were around 135 scouts in Perthshire, a figure which had increased to around 1,100 in 1926. By 1930 the wolf cubs and sea scouts had been founded in Perth, the latter with their own eight-berth boat on the Tay. A major rally of 5,000 Scottish scouts and cubs was held in the presence of B-P

A group of scouts, one kilted and one signalling in semaphore, and a slightly unlikely-looking
scout leader, pose patiently for a photograph near Ballinluig, Perthshire, in 1912.
Courtesy of Perth Museum and Art Gallery, Perth and Kinross Council.

on the North Inch in 1933. Despite the difficulties of attracting scout
leaders the movement enjoyed a renaissance in the 1970s when scout
numbers increased by 25 per cent between 1970 and 1975, a trend which
continued into the '80s. There are still a few scout groups in Perth city,
perhaps the most active being the 10th Perthshire, formerly the Perth
Academy group, which boasts a waiting list and which still meets in the
school grounds, though now in a modern and purpose-built hut.

Guiding in Perth dates back to 1910 when the Perth city guides, one
of the first companies in Perthshire, were founded by Mrs Grainger
Heiton, wife of the well-known Perth architect. Brownies and ranger
guides followed later and by 1925 there were almost as many guides in
Perthshire as there were scouts, including in Perth around 380 guides,
200 brownies and 50 rangers. Guides, like scouts, held their mass rallies
and around 3,000 girls celebrated the movement's Jubilee at Muirton Park
in 1960. They too enjoyed a steady increase in numbers in the 1970s.

Other youth organisations included the following: the local Air Training
Corps which began as No 38 (Perth) Squadron in 1938 and was later
renumbered 38F to distinguish it as one of the first 50 ATC squadrons to
be formed; 'Open Door' which was run by St John's Kirk over two
winters in the late 1940s and which attracted hundreds of young people
to the City Hall on Sunday evenings; Perth City Boys Club which was

formed in 1947 and finally closed in 1990 after a wave of vandalism at its Dunkeld Road clubrooms; and the Duke of Edinburgh Award scheme which has instilled a sense of self-reliance and service to the community in many young people. In addition there were the myriad sporting clubs – football, swimming and cricket to name but three – art and drama societies, church organisations and Sunday Schools, and choirs by the dozen.

School-leavers who did not go onto university or straight into employment had the choice of further education at either Perth Commercial School, Watson's Business Training College or, later, Perth College. The first-mentioned organisation was founded in around 1902 and later moved to well-known premises in St John's Place. For many years the school supplied the General Accident (though not exclusively) with a steady stream of young people ready for the world of business. It was doubtless for this reason that Sir Francis Norie-Miller was for long the school's patron. The last lord provost of Perth, A.U. Cross, was also the last principal and proprietor of the school which closed in 1971.

Perth College began as the Further Education Centre in the former Southern District School in 1961 and by 1971, as Perth Technical College, had moved into purpose-built college buildings at Brahan. It achieved a

A view of Southern District School which was known to generations simply as Shand's.
Between closure and demolition it became the first home of the Further Education Centre
and later an annexe to Perth College.
From the collection of the late Harry Chalmers, Perth.

measure of national fame in 1985 when the press made much of its pioneering course in rock music and even though it proved to be a successful development one can imagine the letters to the *Daily Telegraph* when the course became national knowledge. In 2001, together with other colleges in the northern half of the country, it became a constituent campus of the UHI Millennium Institute (formerly the University of the Highlands and Islands Project) which achieved full university status in 2011. Perth might have been hosting graduation ceremonies back in the 1960s had its bid to provide a home for Scotland's sixth university been successful. Members of the University Grants Committee visited the city in 1964 and inspected the proposed site which straddled the Perth – Scone road. Of the seven towns in the running the UGC finally opted for Stirling and the Earl of Mansfield thus kept his land and Scone its distance from Perth.

Apart from educational institutions the city boasts two learned societies. The earlier years of the Perthshire Society of Natural Science are covered elsewhere in this book but suffice to say that as it approaches its 150th anniversary it can still attract good audiences to its annual series of lectures and still regularly publishes scholarly articles on subjects of local interest. The Royal Scottish Geographical Society, having considered almost 50 other possible locations across central Scotland, recently transferred its headquarters from Glasgow to Lord John Murray's House in Perth's North Port. The society also occupies the adjacent Fair Maid's House which has been skilfully modernised and extended.

In marked contrast to the exponential rise in expenditure on schools and education during the 20th century, the story of church life in Perth is one of steady decline, that 'melancholy, long, withdrawing roar' to use Matthew Arnold's phrase. The fact that the century began with an unedifying spat between two men of the cloth, one the Rev. David Manuel, minister of St Andrew's Church in Atholl Street, and the other his assistant, the Rev. Robert Barclay, did not help matters at all. No minor quarrel this, but one which saw Manuel trying to sack Barclay who left and, taking many of the congregation with him, set up a rival congregation in the Co-operative Hall. Despite his many faults, ranging from debt to womanising, Barclay successfully sued Manuel for slander in the Court of Session and was awarded the very considerable sum of £500 in damages. Exactly what Manuel said, and just how bad it was, is buried in 120 pages of court proceedings deep within West Register House in Edinburgh. In time Barclay's breakaway congregation was recognised by the presbytery and he subsequently built and became minister of St Mark's Church in Feus Road. In 1916 he joined up as a private and, rising to lieutenant, was killed in action in 1918. St Mark's was demolished in 1985, the occasion being memorable for the presence of an elderly lady who remembered witnessing the laying of the foundation stone over 80 years earlier. One particular feature of the 1902 dispute was the way in which it caught the imagination of the Perth public: on one occasion a crowd several hundred strong gathered outside St Andrew's Church to jeer Manuel who had to be escorted home by police for his own safety.

St John's Kirk viewed from St Ann's Lane.
Courtesy of Perth Museum and Art Gallery,
Perth and Kinross Council.

The oldest church in Perth is St John's Kirk, one of the great burgh churches of Scotland, and one which has been closely associated with not just the history of the town but at times the nation as well. It enjoyed a close relationship with both the Perth Guildry, as seen in the handsomely carved oak pews, and the town council, which is most clearly seen today at the annual service for the Kirking of the Council. Until the 1930s the ringing of the St John's bell announced the meetings of both organisations. At the start of the century, and as it had been since 1771, the building comprised three separate churches, imaginatively named East, West and Middle, each with its own minister and each firmly behind its own walls. By the later 19th century there was a clear desire among the townsfolk to demolish the interior walls and reunite the three congregations and indeed plans for such works had been drawn up in the 1880s but mere plans they remained. The calls for reunification continued into the 20th century and at the end of World War One it was decided at a public meeting, chaired by the Duke of Atholl, that the work would proceed as a memorial to the war dead of Perth and Perthshire. Sir Robert Lorimer was appointed architect and the work was carried out between 1923 and 1926. An estimated £50,000 was required for the restoration and when a subscription scheme raised only £34,000, including £1,460 from the *Perthshire Advertiser*'s 'People's Million Penny Fund', Lord Forteviot and other members of the Dewar family made up a large part of the shortfall. As a former lord provost of the city it must have given him immense pride to see, on the first Sunday in November 1926, the new congregation of St John's worshipping together for the first time since the 16th century.

The old Session House, viewed here from the Market Square, stood opposite the west end of St John's Kirk, roughly where the Lesser City Hall is now situated.
Courtesy of Perth Museum and Art Gallery, Perth and Kinross Council.

The church was officially opened in November 1928 and seven years later, although not part of the restoration process, the famous St John's carillon was installed.

The history of St John's for the remainder of the century would have been unremarkable had the controversial decision to invite Archbishop (later Cardinal) Thomas Winning to preach in early 1990 not enlivened a predictable succession of popular ministers and less warmly welcomed fund-raising campaigns. The invitation had been issued by the Perth Council of Churches to mark the culmination of the Week of Prayer for Christian Unity. It was almost inevitable that extreme Protestants would take exception to a Roman Catholic preaching in a church so closely associated with the Scottish Reformation and Pastor Jack Glass together with over 100 of his supporters duly turned up to protest. There was a big police presence during the service during which three hecklers were removed from the church and Glass himself threw '30 pieces of silver' through the open doors which were subsequently locked and the coins added to the collection plate.

The minister at the time, the Rev. David Ogston, was not only a distinguished and well-loved churchman but a talented writer in the Doric of his native rural Aberdeenshire. He retired in 2007 after 27 years of service to St John's and died the following year. A pair of specially commissioned silver candlesticks was dedicated to his memory in the summer of 2012. In 2004, during his ministry, A Vision for the Future was launched which aimed at raising around £2.75 million for the purpose of refurbishing the church fit for the 21st century. Funds were duly raised, the works carried out and the church was reopened in 2011.

The views of the above-mentioned Jack Glass were at odds with the prevailing mood of the century which was one of rapprochement between the main denominations. There was doubtless great joy in 1900 when the Free Church and the United Presbyterian Church, which could be regarded as the main historic offshoots from the Church of Scotland, united to form the United Free Church and again in 1929 when the United Free Church merged with the Church of Scotland. With breakaway congregations returning to the fold, and bringing with them church buildings whose names reflected their origins, an adjustments committee of the presbytery had to agree a number of name changes. As St Leonard's continued in King Street, St Leonard's UF Church became St Leonard's-in-the-Fields, and, as St Paul's still presided over the High Street, St Paul's UF Church (in Newrow) became St Columba's. More problematic was what to do with the large number of redundant church buildings which resulted from these denominational unions. One solution was simply to demolish them and a number disappeared in this way, including the historic Wilson Church, now the 1960s shopping development in Scott Street, and Bridgend Church, now Bridgend Court. Others have been secularised and found other uses, such as the original Free Middle Church in Blackfriars which is now used by the council. Ecumenism has developed steadily in the later 20th century, fostered partly by the 4th Kirk Week of 1965 which saw around 1,000 people from all churches and all over Scotland gathering in Perth for fellowship, partly by organisations such as Perth Action of Churches Together and Action of Churches Together in Scotland, and partly by individual initiatives of local clergy and congregations.

The gradual coming together of churches in the 20th century was in contrast to the gradual separation of church and people. Non-attendance at church was already becoming such a problem by 1913 that the council decided to provide heating in the three churches which (until 1929) it owned, St John's, St Paul's and St Mark's, 'thus offering one excuse less for non- or irregular attendance at divine worship.' In 1919 the minister of Kinnoull preached against the secular-isation of Sundays, arguing that sport brought out the worst in people, and three years later the press was comm-enting that dark and gloomy churches did not attract people in the same way as did the bright lights of the city's amusement halls. The approval of Sunday golf on Moncreiffe Island in 1931 led to a comment that 'the day of the dull and gloomy Sunday is receding into the limbo of the past.' Perth clergymen of all denominations sought to rectify matters by taking the Gospel message out into the streets and preaching in the open air, a move

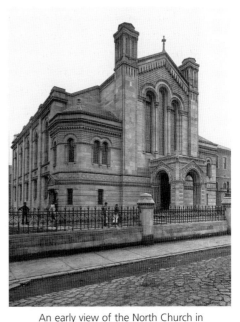

An early view of the North Church in Mill Street which is one of the few remaining in the city centre. Thanks to mergers over the years the church now represents several historic Perth congregations.
Courtesy of Perth Museum and Art Gallery, Perth and Kinross Council.

which was generally regarded as successful, though some came up against the scepticism of the Perth working man. The Rev. G.T.S. Farquhar, writing in his diary in 1921, recorded how the provost of St Ninian's Cathedral, having finished his oration, invited questions from the crowd. In reply to a query about baptism the provost offered to visit the questioner in his own home to discuss the matter and was rebuffed with 'I wouldn't allow you inside my house if you were to pay me.' The rehousing of large numbers of people in the new suburbs at some distance from the city churches, without a family car and with only a minimal Sunday bus service for transportation, would have led to a further decline in church membership in the immediate pre- and post-war period. There was a sudden concern in the 1970s about the steep drop in Sunday School numbers, both of teachers and children. In 1970 alone there was reckoned to be a falling away of about 1,000 children and over 100 teachers each month throughout Scotland, lured away by the attractions of weekend leisure and sport. The almost atheistic radical

The problem of declining church attendance was not helped by the advent of television
in the 1950s. A family relaxes together in their Hunter Crescent flat in 1959.
The Louis Flood Collection. Courtesy of Perth Museum and Art Gallery, Perth and Kinross Council.

theology of the 1960s, as well as popular television series such as the *Forsyte Saga*, may also have played its part. Neither were new people joining the church in great numbers: figures released in 1988 showed that of the 40-odd presbyteries in Scotland Perth occupied fifth bottom place in terms of new church members.

The Church's minimal presence in the new housing schemes called for serious thought from Perth Presbytery about the direction of its ministry in the city. As early as 1937 the presbytery had come to appreciate the need for a church at Muirton but when the Church of Scotland's Home Board refused permission for a new church the presbytery tried instead to persuade an existing congregation to move there. Both St Andrew's and St Paul's were asked to relocate and both declined to do so. By 1950, however, there were firm plans to build new churches in the housing schemes, the first of which was the Moncreiffe Hall-Church. This was followed by the move of St Stephen's to Muirton (during the ministry of the Rev. Joseph Shillinglaw who, on his retiral in 1965 at the age of 92,

The Riverside Church in North Muirton was opened in 2002, following the closure of the joint charge of St Andrew's and St Stephen's. It was described as 'the first of a new generation of Church of Scotland charges', with a new attitude to worship and, as evidenced by the lack of pulpit and organ, a new approach to church buildings.

was the oldest minister in the Church of Scotland), and by the opening of Letham Hall-Church in 1954. More recent has been the establishment of the new Riverside Church at North Muirton and a statement of intent to establish a church in the western edge housing estate.

The presence of new churches in the suburbs contributed to a further decline in numbers attending city centre churches. St Matthew's was created in 1965 in the former West Church in Tay Street, bringing together the dwindling congregations of the former West, Middle, Bridgend and Wilson churches. In 1971 Perth Presbytery approved plans to reduce the number of city churches to five, a decision which met with the approval of the Rev. William Smellie who, on the point of retiring as minister of St John's Kirk, said: 'I believe that 14 Church of Scotland churches in the city represents a completely unwarrantable extravagance in overhead expenditure.' St Paul's was physically in poor condition and was thus the first to be targeted by the presbytery, though it was saved from imminent closure by a large donation to help with repairs. It was thus the lot of Craigend Church to be the first to disappear, targeted not so much by the presbytery as the builders of the motorway interchange in whose path it lay. The congregation joined with that of Moncreiffe Church and by 1978 were worshipping together in a brand new church. Rationalisation was rapid in the 1980s and beyond: St Mark's merged with Letham Church (and in recent years have built new premises with a strikingly modern interior), Trinity Church with St Leonard's-in-the-Fields, St Leonard's with North Church, and St Andrew's, having turned down the option to build a new church at the western edge, with St Stephen's. St Paul's, the second-oldest surviving church in Perth, was finally closed in 1986, thus giving local planners the problem of what to do with a second high-profile empty church building, the Free Middle Church in Tay Street being the other. By the century's end there were only four Church of Scotland city centre churches in Perth: St John's Kirk, St Matthew's, St Leonard's-in-the-Fields and Trinity, and the North Church. Since then, the relentless pressure from falling rolls and stretched finances has forced the rationalisation process to continue. St Leonard's-in-the-Fields, having dropped the cumbersome Trinity suffix, has become a linked charge with St John's Kirk, and although they now share a minister the buildings, congregations and kirk sessions of both churches continue as before. Perth Presbytery has also agreed that all four congregations should work together as a parish grouping, whereby resources and activities – such as pastoral care and mission – are shared.

The old Congregational Church in Mill Street which, following a merger with the Evangelical Union congregation, moved to its present location in Kinnoull Street in 1899. The redundant Mill Street building was later taken over by Wordies.
Courtesy of Perth Museum and Art Gallery, Perth and Kinross Council.

In mid-19th century Perth the overwhelming majority of church-goers were Presbyterian, either members of the established church or one of the offshoots from it. There were also over 200 Roman Catholics, and a number of Episcopalians, Baptists, Methodists and Congregationalists. Since then the range of Christian organisations and churches in the city has widened to include the Salvation Army, the YMCA, Jehovah's Witnesses, spiritualists, evangelicals and others. The first Roman Catholic post-Reformation church in Perth was St John's in Melville Street which originated in 1832. Scotland's first post-Reformation monastery, St Mary's, was established by the Redemptorists on Kinnoull Hill in 1870 and though still owned and managed by them it functions today as an ecumenical spirituality centre, well-used by Perth's various denominations. The monastery building, however, on account of its size and outdated facilities, has been a considerable drain on the order's resources and in order to alleviate financial cramp they launched a fund-raising campaign in 2003. This was supplemented by a later attempt – which may yet prove successful – to sell some of its land for housing. By the 1960s the estimated Roman Catholic population of Perth had swelled to around 3,500 and two other churches have been built to cater to their needs. Episcopalians have two churches, St John's in Princes Street and St Ninian's Cathedral in North Methven Street, both built around 1850 although deriving from historically different, if not opposing, strands of Anglicanism. The arrival of English railway workers, in such numbers that an area of Craigie was known for a while as Little England, boosted numbers in their pews. The Congregational Church in Perth merged with the Evangelical Union church (familiarly known as the Morisonian Kirk and situated where Perth Theatre now stands) in 1896 and their present church, which provides a strong finish to the row of impressive and predominantly red stone buildings along the southern, and more recent, end of Kinnoull Street, was built three years later. The Baptist congregation in Perth had long worshipped in the old opera house in Tay Street and were dealt a severe blow in 1984 when the building was destroyed in a spectacular blaze. By 1990, though, the congregation had moved to a purpose-built church in Burghmuir, having raised the total cost of £345,000 entirely by themselves, without recourse to borrowing or a public appeal for funds. The Tay Street site was subsequently used for sheltered housing.

The Salvation Army has been in Perth since the later 19th century and their good works have been, and still are, warmly appreciated by clergymen and townspeople, so much so that much of the cost of building the South Street citadel, in around 1904, was borne by the people of the city. Its members have always excelled themselves in the care of the under-privileged and perhaps never more spectacularly than on Christmas Day 1919 when they organised eight Father Christmases, travelling in eight carriages, to distribute presents to 1,100 children in the city, though quite what the youngest believers would have made of multiple Santas is an interesting speculation. Despite the almost quaint Victorian name the Salvation Army in Perth continues to use modern methods to help the poor and disadvantaged, and when in around 2000 the citadel was improved and extended, care was taken to include kitchen- and computer-training suites, as well as offices, halfway flats for the

An interior view of St Ninian's Cathedral before the baldacchino was built over the altar in c.1911. A rood screen was erected in 1924 in memory of Claud Norie-Miller and has since been partially demolished. From the collection of the late Harry Chalmers, Perth.

formerly homeless returning to independent living, and (until recently) consulting rooms for dentists and doctors treating the homeless.

The Church of the Nazarene has had a presence in the city since at least the 1930s and is now situated in York Place following their purchase of the former Trinity Church in 1982. The church scored a notable success in 1972 when around 20 members of the Pack, a gang of youths with a string of charges for assault, mobbing and vandalism against them, turned up at Sunday evening fellowship meetings. 'A trifle boisterous and [they] don't behave too well' was the only judgment passed upon them. Most recently, and perhaps by way of a practical response from the churches to the regular city centre problems arising from alcohol abuse, has been the success of the non-denominational Street Pastor movement. The Perth project, the first in Scotland, started in 2008 and now has a sizeable core of active volunteers who patrol the streets on Thursday and Saturday nights, not preaching but offering assistance and a sympathetic ear as the situation demands.

The recent religious history of Perth is of course far more complex than the above would suggest. Paragraphs could have been devoted to the Glasite Church which survived in Perth until 1929, to the various mission organisations such as those of Thimblerow and Watergate, to the many distinguished churchmen of the city, and to the crusading evangelists Billy Graham and his son Franklin who preached to packed gatherings in 1955 and 1999 respectively. But their memory lives on, if not in this book then in commemorative plaques on walls around the town, in city churches and in lives touched by the selfless work of priests, ministers and other men of God.

CHAPTER SIX

Protecting the People:
Disease, Crime and Fire

IN PERTH IN 1900 over 13 per cent of all infants died before their first birthday, and 25 per cent of all deaths in the city were those of children under the age of five. Though appalling statistics by today's standards these figures were better than many other areas of Scotland. Diarrhoea was commonly cited as a cause of infant death and the prevalence of this easily treated condition was due in many cases to an organically and chemically polluted water supply. It was calculated around that time that the sewage of an estimated 45,000 people upstream of Perth went straight into the Tay and thus, despite the best efforts of Adam Anderson and the city waterworks, into Perth's drinking water. The *Perthshire Advertiser* of 1876 gave another example, describing how over 600 men of the Perthshire Militia were marched down to the Tay at 3.00 am one July morning and ordered to bathe. This, the first wash in a year for many, resulted in 'many fine salmon [fleeing] to the sea... while numbers of trout were picked up on the banks of the river in a fainting condition.' A clever pun made an equally serious point in the same paper in 1922: 'And drink ye not, my son, of the waters that flow past or thou shalt surely die, for verily, verily, I say unto you that many dyes do flow into this river, and he that drinketh of this water must have a stomach even alike unto Joseph's raiment.' Additional factors of poor sanitation and overcrowded housing allowed disease to develop and spread very quickly and, until the first medical use of penicillin in 1942, the only defence against bacterial infection was the patient's own body.

One of the most significant steps in the war against disease in Perth was the appointment of a medical officer of health. Dr Charles Parker Stewart was one of the first to hold this position and served Perth with distinction from around 1899 to 1937. The law stipulated that the medical officer had to be a qualified doctor and that his main duty was to keep himself informed of the sanitary condition of the city, with special reference to the origin and causes of disease, and to advise the

Staff accommodation, with the patients' block behind, at the former smallpox hospital at the Shore, well away from the inhabited areas of the city. The electricity generating station was later built next to it.

council on all matters affecting the public health. His extensive powers included the right to enter property in the interests of public health and examine anyone inside. He also had authority over food sold in shops, over poor housing and places of work, and had the final say on matters as wide-ranging as the treatment of smallpox to the removal of manure from the streets.

Parker Stewart had an enlightened approach to disease, believing firmly that patients with infectious diseases, instead of sharing the facilities of the York Place infirmary, should be segregated from other patients and from the community in a separate fever hospital. When a serious outbreak of scarlet fever occurred in 1901 he decided to make use of the temporarily empty smallpox hospital at the Shore (which continued until the mid-1930s), but almost as soon as it had been reopened a case of smallpox occurred and the scarlet fever patients were withdrawn and sent instead to the county's infectious diseases hospital at Burghmuir. A temporary fever hospital was erected at Friarton in 1902 and within two years the council had taken the decision to build a permanent fever

The Barnhill Sanatorium was built for the care of tuberculosis patients and funded mainly
by Sir Robert and Lady Pullar. After a brief half-century of existence it closed in 1958,
shortly after an immunisation programme against the disease was begun.
Courtesy of the A.K. Bell Library Local Studies Department, Perth and Kinross Council.

hospital at that site. It was opened in 1906. There was a further serious
outbreak of scarlet fever in the mid-1920s which affected over 1,000
people and resulted in 22 deaths, the cause being attributed not to the
water supply but to infected milk and ice cream.

Typhoid was another disease resulting from poor sanitation and
hygiene. The number of sufferers fluctuated from year to year with
around 40 or 50 cases reported in 1906 and only three in 1912. In 1919
62 cases were reported of which five were fatal, and householders were
advised to boil all water before use. This outbreak led to the full chlori-
nation of the city's water supply by 1928 after which there were no
further cases of this disease. Cholera was one of the most feared diseases
because of its rapidity of onset and in particularly severe cases a patient
could pass from good health to death within hours. When in 1909 it was
known to be prevalent in Russia foreign ships at the harbour were treated
with extreme caution: crews were inspected and all water on board was
sealed up. There was a major outbreak of diphtheria in October 1910,
one of the most severe in Perth for many years. War was waged on this
disease in 1941 when Dr Frank Main, Parker Stewart's successor as
medical officer of health, ran a highly successful campaign to immunise

almost all pre-school children in the city, using a mobile unit to visit the most populous areas. Diphtheria claimed its last victim in around 1945 and by 1947 it had virtually been eradicated. For those with the dreaded consumption, or tuberculosis as it is better known today, the only hope of recovery, in the pre-antibiotic era, lay in a long period of rest, fresh air and isolation either at home, in the Barnhill Sanatorium or, if they were recovering, in one of the cottages in the grounds of Hillside Hospital. By mid-century the steady decline in tuberculosis was attributed to the pasteurisation of milk (over 86 per cent of Perth milk was pasteurised by 1950), earlier diagnosis and better treatment. Immunisation against the disease began in Perth in 1955, the BCG vaccination being one of less pleasant memories of secondary education. By the later 1960s almost all children were regularly immunised against diphtheria and polio and many also against smallpox. At the end of the 20th century, with even more vaccinations available, only 0.5 per cent of babies died before reaching the age of one.

Dr Parker Stewart died in 1938 and was particularly remembered for his work among children through the Child Welfare Clinic which was opened in Princes Street in 1917. The initial monthly figures of 177 mother and children outpatients had increased to around 550 by 1933 and 1,000 by 1950. It quickly established itself as one of the best maternity and child welfare services in the country, its success being put down to its voluntary workers and a committee of particularly energetic ladies. A keen supporter of the clinic was Lady Georgina Home-Drummond who for many years held an annual garden party for mothers and children at her home at Hamilton House. In 1933, thanks to a large donation from William Watson of Scone, a new centre, named in his honour, was opened in a building between South Street and Canal Street. A branch of the clinic was opened in Muirton in 1941 and another in Letham in 1957.

The work of the medical officer of health, in tandem with sanitary improvements, better housing and the child welfare clinic, brought big improvements to the health of the city. Statistics show a steady decline in instances of major disease through the first half of the 20th century and as such figures declined so the life expectancy of Perth people increased by around 20 years in that same period. In 1950 half of all girls born could expect to live to the age of 75, and boys to 70. The huge strides forward in healthcare and the prevention of disease in the first half of the century become dramatically apparent when one considers that life expectancy for girls and boys born in Scotland in the early years of the 21st century has crept up by only around ten years since 1950.

Another major reason behind the steady improvement in health was the building of a new infirmary. The original County and City of Perth Infirmary at York Place, which was opened in 1838 with 68 beds, had outlived its usefulness (despite it having one of the first X-ray machines in the country by 1903) and by the early 20th century the council was debating whether to rebuild the old hospital or build on a completely new site. The decision was made in 1908 to accept the invitation from the Glover Incorporation to buy land at Tullylumb and after a period of planning and fund-raising, the new 120-bed County and City of Perth Royal Infirmary (Queen Victoria had approved the addition of Royal to the name in honour of the infirmary's Jubilee in 1888) was opened by George v and Queen Mary in July 1914, on a beautiful summer's day on the eve of war. Prior to the ceremony the King and Queen toured the streets of a gaily decorated Perth, the royal car being flanked by a military escort in case of trouble from suffragettes. The old infirmary was loaned, via the War Office, to the British Red Cross Society to be run as a VAD hospital during World War One and was eventually sold in 1920 to the Perthshire Education Authority. Over the ensuing years the new hospital was considerably expanded, with a maternity unit (donated by

One of the wards in the old County and City of Perth Royal Infirmary in York Place. A similar photograph shows a wall decorated with Biblical texts and a framed 'Rules for Patients.' Courtesy of Perth Museum and Art Gallery, Perth and Kinross Council.

Lord Forteviot), a nurses' home, further medical wards and operating theatres all gradually filling the Tullylumb site. Some of the funding came from the estate of Robert Douglas, the Scone benefactor, whose trustees decreed that in certain circumstances Scone patients should have priority.

Prior to July 1948 the hospital was funded primarily by patients' fees, regular subscriptions, voluntary donations and bequests, and its financial wellbeing was thus never on a particularly secure footing. The main funding came from the Ladies' Auxiliary Association, whose members trawled each street of the city and county, knocking on doors and asking for donations. As each donation, whether money or in the form of reading material, clothing or food, was listed in the infirmary's annual report there was a certain pressure, intentional or otherwise, on everyone to give. Charity events also helped and in 1921 Perth students at Scottish universities held a Perth and Perthshire Gala Week which raised £2,156 for hospital funds. In 1942 Sir Francis Norie-Miller, chairman of the hospital's board of management, ran an Infirmary Week in which a planned mile of pennies stretched to two and, together with flag days, yielded over £1,200 for hospital funds. But it was never quite enough and in the 1930s the local press carried advertisements outlining the increasing costs of running the hospital and the gradually widening deficit between income and expenditure. In 1933 the treatment of 3,000

The new County and City of Perth Royal Infirmary at Tullylumb photographed in May 1914, just before it was opened by George V and Queen Mary in July.
Courtesy of Perth Museum and Art Gallery, Perth and Kinross Council.

inpatients and 4,000 outpatients led to a deficit of £3,300. Six years later, in the first months of war, these figures had increased to almost 4,000 inpatients, 7,700 outpatients and a deficit of almost £10,000. In 1947, the last year before the hospital became part of the National Health Service, statistics show that 13,470 X-rays were carried out, 2,104 general anaesthetics given, and 758 babies born, all of which contributed to a deficit of £30,000. By the 1940s it was evident to at least some that this was not a way to run a modern health service. Apart from funding issues, comments in the press drew attention to the ridiculous situation whereby Perth still had two fever hospitals within its boundaries, one for city patients and one for county. Planning, they argued, should be done on a regional rather than local basis, though in 1943 they could not have envisaged how soon a radical Labour government would be in power and how quickly Beveridge and Bevan would change things.

The National Health Service came into being in July 1948 from which point responsibility for hospital funding and administration was transferred to the Secretary of State for Scotland, the Department of Health for Scotland and regional hospital boards. Perth Royal Infirmary continued to develop and expand under NHS management. A new outpatients' block, funded by a pre-war donation from a New Zealander, was finally opened in 1962, followed by a casualty department ten years later and a maternity block in the mid-1970s. Nurses were trained at Craigroyston House on the Glasgow Road, a nursing college (or Preliminary Training School as it was then called) which was opened in 1951. In the later 1970s, under the new Tayside Health Board, plans were drawn up for a major rationalisation of hospital services in the Perth area. Work began in 1979 on the first stage which was the construction of new geriatric facilities to replace the old Burghmuir Hospital (the former county fever hospital, having become virtually redundant following the development of antibiotics, had become a geriatric unit instead). The main work, however, was to graft a new district hospital onto the back of the 1914 infirmary. This £30 million 190-bed complex, with five operating theatres and a new outpatients' department, was opened in 1993, whereupon the Nissen-hutted wartime hospital at Bridge of Earn was finally closed. The final years of the century were notable for the acute services review which was announced by Tayside Health Board in 1999. Rumours of the transfer of maternity services to Ninewells Hospital in Dundee, the latest in a steady loss of Perth-based services to that city, resulted in a high-profile campaign by local residents, politicians and medical staff to retain the maternity unit in Perth. As far as campaigns go, 'Hands Off PRI' was successful in terms of mobilisation of support: not many, after all, could almost fill the City Hall or motivate 150 marchers to demonstrate through the streets of Edinburgh or persuade film star Ewan McGregor to sport a 'Born in the PRI' tee-shirt. Despite the best efforts of all concerned the review, when published in 2003, confirmed their fears: consultant-led maternity services were to be centralised in Dundee while PRI would have a community midwife unit instead. Even so, perhaps the strength of feeling in Perth had positive results as the health board gave assurances that PRI's future as an acute general hospital was secure and promised to invest in it a further £28 million. Cancer patients were some of the beneficiaries when the long redundant and decaying Cornhill House in the hospital grounds was demolished to make way for the Cornhill Macmillan Centre, the first specialist palliative care centre in Perth and Kinross, which opened in 2009.

Perth's other hospital, known today as Murray Royal, began in 1828 as James Murray's Royal Asylum for Lunatics and as such predated the old infirmary by ten years. This too underwent a series of expansions in the 20th century, including the Gilgal building which dates from the 1930s, new pavilion wards from the 1960s, and psychogeriatric wards and an industrial therapy unit from the 1980s. This last-mentioned work was part of the rationalisation which led to the closure of Murthly Hospital. In 2000, the future role of Murray Royal once again came under active consideration by Tayside Health Board and in 2006 NHS Tayside, its successor body, announced a massive redevelopment within the grounds. The plans comprised a brand new mental hospital, which included a medium secure unit for patients transferring from Carstairs, and around 200 new houses. There was the expected outcry, particularly from local residents concerned about the effect of such a large number of houses, not to mention the increased staffing levels at the new hospital, on the notorious traffic congestion problem at Bridgend, and Bridgend, Gannochy and Kinnoull Community Council, while generally supportive of the proposed new hospital facilities, argued the residents' case well. The contractors handed the new hospital over to NHS Tayside in the summer of 2012 and the demolition of at least some of the redundant buildings is imminent.

In 1948, although there was no compulsion on family doctors to provide services through the NHS, all 19 in Perth agreed to do so. The services of a family doctor and hospital treatment when required were now provided free of charge to all, though many workers were already entitled to free treatment under the terms of the *National Insurance Act* of 1911. Most doctors operated out of private houses, either their own or those converted into surgeries for a practice of two or more, and some premises at least were dark, shabby and under-equipped. In 1972 plans were announced for a single health centre in the city from which all doctors would operate. However, the initial support of only 17 out of 31 doctors soon dropped to a mere six and the plans were shelved until 1979 when, with renewed support from the city's medical fraternity, work began on the Drumhar Health Centre behind North Methven Street.

The gradual growth of preventative medicine and a move towards the earlier diagnosis of disease was noticeable from the 1940s onwards. Immunisation against common diseases such as diphtheria and polio was highly effective and a mass X-ray campaign in 1957, during which Lord Provost James Smart was the first to have his chest so examined,

Drumhar Health Centre, built as part of the major redevelopment of this area of Perth, was the first of the city's modern joint medical practices, since when several others have been completed.

aimed to detect tuberculosis in its earliest stages. A few years later the city's medical officer of health, Dr J.M. Aitken, ran Britain's biggest-ever diabetic detection campaign in which 75 per cent of the Perth population took part, resulting in 141 new cases being discovered. For medical and moral reasons the town council also urged Dr Aitken to organise a drive against an increasing number of illegitimate births, the Perth rate having been well above the Scottish average since 1955 and more than doubling in the ten years between 1958 and 1968. The town council declined to provide the Pill free of charge though free contraceptive advice was provided by the Family Planning Association at their clinic in South Street. There was also considerable concern over venereal disease which was reaching 'epidemic proportions' in Perth. Tayside Health Board later initiated campaigns for healthy living, fitness and immunisation.

One of the most controversial preventative campaigns was the proposed fluoridisation of the local water supply to improve dental health. The town council first debated the issue in 1963 but were reluctant to make a decision until the full implications of such a measure were properly understood. However, when the Secretary of State for Scotland offered to indemnify local authorities against any legal consequences the council decided to proceed, thus incurring the wrath of the Ratepayers' Association and reams of petitions of protest. The debate rumbled on until 1970 when, on the casting vote of Lord Provost David Thomson, the council decided against fluoridisation. In 1976 the matter was again discussed, this time by the regional and district councils, and by Tayside Health Board and Perth and Kinross Local Health Council. The upshot was that the health board overruled the objections of the district council and local health council and recommended that the regional council should proceed with fluoridisation, which, to the relief of many, they declined to do.

If Dr Charles Parker Stewart, the medical officer of health, led the war against disease at the turn of the century then his counterpart in the fight against crime was James Garrow, chief constable of the Perth City Police. Based at his headquarters in Tay Street he had a full staff of 39 under him, including two detectives, four sergeants and 31 constables. And with an average height in 1910 of almost six feet the men of the force must have been a formidable sight. Even so, this was not always a deterrent to the street urchins of the time. A Perth man, reminiscing about his childhood in the 1890s, recalled how the night-shift constables, each carrying a paraffin lamp, were marched out of the police station by a sergeant and as they were unable to break ranks the street children took every opportunity to yell insults without fear of reprisal.

William Izatt of Perth City Police.
Courtesy of the A.K. Bell Library Local Studies Department, Perth and Kinross Council.

The city police force achieved some distinctions in its long history, not least of them being its foundation in 1811 which made it the oldest component part of today's Tayside Police. It was also one of the first forces in the country to install radio communications in patrol cars, 'wirelessed cars' being the phrase used in 1949. In 1964 Perth City Police amalgamated with the Perthshire and Kinross-shire Constabulary which had been occupying Ardchoille, in Bridgend, since 1954. Since 1977 the Perth police station has been based in Dunkeld Road, in a modern cuboid building which also serves as the headquarters of the western division of Tayside Police.

A policeman's lot in the second half of the 20th century, if not always happy, was at least interesting. The police sergeant manning the public desk in Perth could well have had several years' experience as a village bobby in remoter parts of Perthshire, patrolling on foot or on bike and administering a friendly warning or a clip round the ear where required. There were few concerns in those days about being sued for assault or infringing human rights. Things began to change, though, in the 1960s and 1970s. Levels of paperwork increased and more use was made of panda cars, both of which meant less time on the beat and resulted in a more distant relationship between police and public. And of course they were kept busy by a steady rise in the crime figures. Statistics show that the number of crimes and offences in Perth city increased from 1,262 in 1900 to 1,526 in 1940, and to

Perth's present-day police station, which also serves as the headquarters of the western division of Tayside Police, was completed in 1977.

around 2,500 in the mid-1960s which very roughly represents a 100 per cent increase in crime in around 65 years while the population grew by only around 25 per cent. In the mid-1990s, though, figures for the whole of the Tayside Police area began to show a fall in the crime rate. Crime figures for the Perth and Kinross area in 2012 again show a small decrease from the previous year, the most common offence being theft, followed by vandalism and possession of drugs. Crimes of violence and indecency were relatively rare.

While there was certainly an ingrained lack of respect for authority among some children and some social classes, serious crime was not, nor has been since, a problem in the city. As we saw in 1900 almost half of all offences were alcohol-induced and therefore generally petty, though wives and children on the receiving end of physical and verbal abuse from drunken husbands and fathers may not have thought so. In some ways, too, it was almost inevitable. There was little desire among labouring men, living with a large family in one or two rooms in the slums of Perth, to stay indoors at the end of the working day. Cheap drink and companionship were easily found in the many public houses all around the city, and led night after night to arrests for drunkenness, theft, and assault.

There were the occasional more serious crimes such as embezzlement which was usually carried out by the town's apparently more trustworthy citizens. St Ninian's Cathedral fell victim to such a crime by one of its own congregation and even the town council itself was robbed of funds in 1904 by its treasurer, a local solicitor who paid for his misdeeds with three years in jail. The people of Perth also paid for them in significantly higher rates bills to cover the loss. In spite of such tales, and drunken and violent though the city's troublemakers may have been, Perth was at least a basically honest place. The police reported in 1910 that of the 1,425 articles reported lost during the course of the year a mere 24 were never returned to their owners. The figures for 1940 were even more impressive with 1,607 items reported lost and 2,393 [sic] found.

A spate of attacks on women in 1908 prompted the council to install street lighting in King Street, while ten years later young children were a target for one of Perth's most prominent and respected figures, a man who was even seen as a future Liberal candidate for Westminster. While serving as curator of the Perthshire Natural History Museum he committed 'various acts of indecent conduct towards young children' in the museum in May 1918. He suddenly resigned in early June and presumably fled the city as he was arrested by police in Nottingham just a few days later. He pleaded not guilty at his trial though the large number of witnesses suggests that his chances of acquittal were never very high. He was found guilty, recommended to leniency because of his age, and sentenced to six months' imprisonment.

While house-breaking and burglaries were a staple diet for the police, major robberies were few, though one stands out if only for the ineptitude of the perpetrators, a gang of safe-breakers who targeted Cairds just before Christmas 1957. Breaking into the shop at night, they packed explosives around the safe and then, to muffle the sound, piled a large number of dresses around it. The plan worked perfectly up to a point as not a sound was heard and the safe lock was successfully blown off. Unfortunately, though, so was the door handle, and thus being unable to open the safe they had to flee empty-handed.

Terrorism is not a word usually associated with Perth, but such a trial took place in the Perth courtrooms in 1989 which resulted in five

Orangemen being jailed for a total of 64 years on a charge of conspiring to supply arms and ammunition to the Ulster Defence Association, an outlawed loyalist paramilitary organisation. The court heard details of the usually well-hidden sectarianism of the city, of how a local pub ostensibly collected money for its own fishing club before passing it on to the Ulster Defence Association, and of how on one occasion a paramilitary colour party entered the City Hall during a function and presented the UDA cell leader with that organisation's flag before firing a volley of blank shots and departing. Men from the opposite end of the Irish political spectrum, members of Sinn Fein, were jailed in large numbers in Perth Prison in the 1920s and created a situation described as 'one of the most stirring periods' in the prison's history. They defied prison warders, bored through thick stone walls to communicate with each other and were apparently so close to taking over the building that reinforcements from the city fire brigade were called in.

The fire brigade were also busy dealing with a spate of arson attacks on local nightclubs in the 1990s. Roxanne's, the former Odeon cinema, went up in flames in 1992, followed by two others in 1993, Shenanigans in 1994, and Electric Whispers in 1995.

The first murder trial of the century took place in 1905 when Irish-man James Murray was accused of killing his wife in their Guard Vennel flat, an attack apparently so vicious that blood dripped through the floor-boards and into the flat below. He was nevertheless found guilty of the lesser charge of culpable homicide and jailed for seven years. The first execu-tion of the century, in 1908, was that of Edward Johnstone, 'the Saline Murderer', who had cut the throat of the young woman with whom he had been living. It was the responsibility of the magistrates of Perth to carry out the execution, the first in Perth since

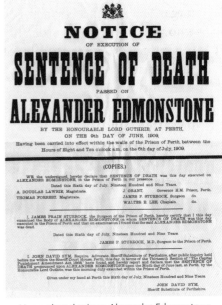

Unemployed miner, Alexander Edmonstone, robbed and murdered a young lad in a public lavatory in East Wemyss and fled the scene. He was apprehended in Manchester several weeks later, living under the name of Albert Edwards.
Courtesy of Perth and Kinross Council Archive.

1870, and they approached their counterparts at Glasgow to borrow a scaffold. This was duly erected in a shed in the prison yard, behind the wall facing the South Inch, by the well-known joinery firm of Soutar and McQueen (John Soutar was the father of the poet William Soutar) and the execution carried out by John Ellis. After almost 40 execution-free years in Perth there was another the following year when Alexander Edmonstone from Fife paid the penalty for the murder of a 16-year-old boy, despite the efforts of the Rev. Robert Barclay of St Mark's Church who had tried to organise a petition for a reprieve. Bailie Douglas Lawrie, who only months earlier had been assailed by prohibitionist Carry A. Nation, witnessed the execution and would doubtless have needed a strong drink afterwards. The scaffold was dusted down again in 1910, this time for Robert Ford Duff, a local glass-blower who was found guilty of cruelty to, and the murder of, his step-daughter in Craigie. Having had the dubious distinction of being handed down the first conviction for a murder committed within the city in 60 years he was given a reprieve and his sentence commuted to one of life imprisonment. The last execution at Perth was that of a Pole who was hanged in 1948 for the brutal murder of a woman in highland Perthshire.

Perhaps the most infamous murder, if only because no one was successfully prosecuted, took place at Cuddies Strip, near Buckie Braes, in 1935. The case, in which a young Perth man, David Kerrigan, was shot dead and his girlfriend indecently assaulted on a peaceful summer's evening, produced lurid headlines in the press at the time of the trial. John McGuigan stood in the dock and while found guilty of the lesser crime the capital charge was not proven.

Youth crime was a significant problem before World War Two and was another consequence of the lack of pleasure in home life. Friendship, fun and ultimately trouble were to be found on the street. Vandalism was relatively common though this could encompass anything from throwing stones through the windows of the new City Hall in 1911 to chalking – or even just striking a match – on public buildings. Even playing football in the street could result in a police caution. It seems, judging solely by press coverage, that vandalism and youth violence increased from the 1960s, as did car crime and drug abuse. Perhaps the earliest indication of this trend was the decision in 1960 to convert the Friarton fever hospital into Scotland's first junior detention centre. It was opened in 1964 and the boys of Perth seem to have wasted no time in trying to

The site of the Cuddies Strip murder in 1935. The dead man's girlfriend described how she had heard the distant bells of St John's chime through the quiet evening air. The noise of the adjacent bypass would make such an experience most unlikely nowadays.

An example of graffiti by members of the Pack in c.1980.
Courtesy of Perth Museum and Art Gallery, Perth and Kinross Council.

earn a place. Press reports of vandalism were depressingly regular and ranged from damaging trees, schools and public places, to spray-painting gang slogans, pushing over gravestones and, on one occasion, putting broken glass in a children's paddling pool. The council reported in 1972 that 50 per cent of all trees planted had to be replaced because of vandalism. One of the main culprits was the Pack, a tamer version of the Glasgow youth gangs, but one which nevertheless distressed and annoyed the generally peace-loving folk of Perth.

Violence on the streets manifested itself in gang fights, football hooliganism and muggings. In 1969, for example, the foyer of the City Hall played host to a fight between 30 knife-carrying youths, and two years later Scott Street turned into a scene from the Wild West when 200 football fans fought a 50-minute running battle after a Tayside derby at Muirton Park. Shoppers had to take shelter wherever they could and every available policeman in Perth was drafted in to help restore order. Of the 50 arrested most were aged between 13 and 17. When Rangers and other teams with (at that time) notorious supporters played in Perth a number of shopkeepers closed for the afternoon. Bailie David Keay wrote to the *Perthshire Advertiser* to say that 'gangs can be seen in Perth almost any night and many innocent people are molested and humiliated by their actions.' Judging by press reports, such behaviour reached its peak in the mid-1970s though it still carried on at a fairly high level throughout the 1980s and into the 1990s when at least one councillor was commenting on spray-painting, football violence, damaged trees and broken windows and describing the situation as 'out of control throughout the district.' And things, it would seem, are little better in the 21st century.

It is no surprise to find that underage drinking was increasing in line with vandalism and violence. In 1969 the Brewers' Association of Scotland ran an advertisement in the local press which read: 'Underage drinking. Warning. Too many people are openly attempting to defy the law. Underage drinking cannot and will not be tolerated.' Further attempts to halt the epidemic included an identity card scheme in the late 1980s and the launch of Pubwatch in 1994. Perth teenagers also experimented with soft drugs and glue-sniffing, and not even the death of a Perthshire schoolboy seemed to have any effect on the numbers adopting the latter habit. Not that anyone seemed to have any precise figures in 1971, as one source described solvent abuse as common in Perth schools and another as not a significant problem. By 1980, though, it was described as 'rampant' in the city and by the end of that decade Perth had been described in a Glasgow newspaper as a 'sniff city.' Drug use was also a growing problem, the number of offences across Tayside Region trebling between 1977 and 1978, and again doubling during the course of 1982. There was also a 'growing problem' for one less than thoughtful academic in Perth who grew cannabis on his window sill in full view of the police headquarters across the road. In the early 1990s local police said that drugs were now affecting all levels of society, a fact brought tragically home by the death from ecstasy in 1998 of the privately-educated daughter of a local businessman.

Looking back over the course of a century and beyond it is clear how malign an influence the misuse of alcohol has been on society. The temperance movement did much to deal with the root cause but ultimately failed. Others tried various ways of dealing with the effects. Youth organisations played a major part, as did some public-spirited individuals such as John Kelly who in 1968, in an attempt to curb vandalism and knife-carrying among local youths, set up well-attended boxing classes in Letham and Moncreiffe. The police and judiciary initially reacted strongly.

A late 19th-century trial, possibly posed, in the sombre surroundings of Perth Sheriff Court. Courtesy of Perth Museum and Art Gallery, Perth and Kinross Council.

Students on drug charges could find themselves remanded in custody as was a 15-year-old schoolgirl who in 1968 was found drunk in central Perth. Bailie Jimmy Doig took a tough line with a football hooligan in 1973, sentencing him to 30 days in a young offenders' institution. More recently the focus has been on media campaigns against alcohol and drug abuse, and police are more concerned with pushers and dealers on the streets rather than the frequently unfortunate end users. Whether city centre closed-circuit television cameras and suburban neighbourhood watch schemes have had a deterrent effect on drink- and drug-befuddled minds is open to question, though they have almost certainly contributed to the welcome drop in overall crime figures of recent years.

Those who fell seriously foul of the law might have ended up in the Edinburgh Road prison, one of the most forbidding buildings in Perth. Originally built to house several thousand French prisoners of war in the early 19th century, it was largely reconstructed in the middle of that century as the General Prison for Scotland which, as the name suggests, was designed to take offenders, serving terms of nine months or longer, from all over the country. As the building aged over the course of more than a century its accommodation steadily slipped below acceptable modern standards. Partly as a result of this the later 20th century history of the prison was characterised by a series of high-profile escapes, rooftop protests, suicides, a hostage crisis, and reports of extensive drug-taking. This was followed firstly by highly critical reports from the prisons inspectorate and subsequently, in the late 1990s, by a major multi-million pound refurbishment and upgrading of prisoner accommodation. This in turn was recognised by the inspectorate who praised the 'near unprecedented' turn-around and described it now as a model establishment. A major step forward in more recent years has been the demolition and replacement of C Wing where conditions were described by the inspectorate in 2005 as 'dreadful'. Friarton Prison merged with Perth Prison in 1999 and ten years later it too fell foul of the inspectorate. It was subsequently declared unfit for purpose and closed in 2010.

Perth's other prison, the former city and county jail, was built as a part of County Buildings in 1818, replacing the inadequate cells in the tolbooth at the foot of the High Street. It was almost entirely demolished in 1965 though the remaining thick, rough stone walls can still be seen at the Speygate car park which now occupies the site.

The city fire brigade at the turn of the century was situated adjacent

The city and county jail in Speygate which was demolished in 1965.
The site has been used as car park ever since.
Courtesy of the A.K. Bell Library Local Studies Department, Perth and Kinross Council.

to the police station in Tay Street and was presided over by firemaster Captain Robert McDonald who had 14 firemen at his command. In 1921, and now acting for the county as well as the city, the fire brigade moved into new premises in King Edward Street and became a fully professional service. No longer would insurance companies bemoan its speed of response nor the local press mock it, as did Onlooker in the *Perthshire Advertiser* in 1919, describing how 'the fire brigade arrived at the latest conflagration before it had burned itself out... despite the usual practice elsewhere this is an unusual occurrence for Perth.' The new county-wide service was also equipped with two new fire engines which had been donated by Miss Rachael Pennycuick who was subsequently given the freedom of Perth in recognition of her generosity. Supplementing the work of the municipal brigade during the most serious conflagrations was that of Pullars which, dating from around 1858, was the oldest fire brigade in the city. It had been formed to fight factory fires but, with the risk of such an event considerably reduced, the brigade disbanded in 1968. Three years later the Perth and Kinross Fire Brigade moved into new headquarters at Longcauseway where, now subsumed into Tayside Fire and Rescue, it still remains. It was announced in 2012 that the acting chief of Tayside Fire and Rescue will become the new head of the unified Scottish Fire and Rescue Service in 2013 which will have its temporary headquarters at the Perth Community Fire Station at Longcauseway.

There have been several major fires in Perth over the course of the century of which one of the earliest was the destruction of the King's Cinema in South Methven Street in July 1914, a mere five weeks after its opening. The city fire brigade arrived first but then suffered an equipment failure and by the time the Pullars brigade arrived, plus soldiers, it was too late to save the building. Two major industrial fires dominated the headlines in 1919, those at Campbell's Perth Dye Works which resulted in the shell-shocked directors selling the company to Pullars, and at the Bells bonded warehouse. The North British Glass Works brigade were first at the scene at the Campbells blaze, followed by the city and the Pullars brigades. Even the Dundee fire brigade was called in to assist. The four-storey building between the lade and Dunkeld Road was quickly engulfed in flames and such was the ferocity of the fire that there were fears not only for the neighbouring Balhousie Works and Wallace Works but for the barracks too, from where, as a precaution, ammunition was carefully removed. The Bells fire in Canal

The brightly-polished fire engines and equally well-polished firemen of Perth Fire Brigade, posing outside their King Edward Street headquarters.
Courtesy of Perth Museum and Art Gallery, Perth and Kinross Council.

Judging by posture and facial expressions this crowd might have been watching a football match rather than the major conflagration at Campbells dye works in 1919.
Courtesy of Perth Museum and Art Gallery, Perth and Kinross Council.

Street was described as 'perhaps the most spectacular ...in Perth's history' with gutters running with whisky and exploding whisky barrels creating a terrifying pyrotechnic display. Other major fires include those at Perth Theatre in 1924, the Friarton gas works in 1951, Woolworths in 1956, Bell's Sports Centre in 1968, Thomas Love and Sons in St John's Place in 1970, Balhousie Castle in 1977, the Baptist Church in Tay Street in 1984, the Isle of Skye Hotel in 1986 and the Wylie Recycling depot at Inveralmond in 2012. Occasionally the toll amounts to much more than buildings: Perth firefighter Roddy Nicolson lost his life trying to save two men from a Shore Road silo in 1995. This brave man is commemorated by a welcome wooden bench halfway up Murrayshall Hill, overlooking pastoral Strathmore and the mountains beyond.

After a century of battles against disease, crime and fire, this chapter ends on a peaceful note on the very last afternoon of 1999 when police were waiting for a telephone call they hoped would never come. Fearful of the effects of the so-called millennium bug on their computer systems they had an arrangement with police in Melbourne whereby, should the Australians experience any problems on the stroke of midnight, they would phone Perth and give them 10 hours' notice of impending computer doom.

CHAPTER SEVEN

The Traditional Industries of Perth

THE COMING OF the railway to Perth completely changed the face of the city, not just because of the long surgical scar of the track to the west and south of the central area, but because of the huge boost it gave to local industry. The best illustration of this is the 1901 Ordnance Survey map of Perth which clearly shows how the city's major industries chose to position themselves close to either the main line or a branch line. Between 1850 and 1900 the whole of the western side of Perth, the route taken by the railway for the north, was transformed into an industrial area where could be found dye works, glass works, textile factories and engineering workshops. The harbour was also linked to the rail network by a branch line and in this area too were brick works, dye works, a glass factory and the city's gas and electricity works. In that same half-century the railway itself spread out from the original station to fill the areas to the south and north with extensive marshalling yards and goods and engine sheds. And the station itself was huge by 1901: it equated in area to roughly the size of the city centre between Tay Street and Scott Street, and South Street and High Street.

That Perth developed into such a major hub on the railway network was due to its central location within Scotland. The Perth newspapers of the 1840s were full of advertisements offering shares in railway companies and of articles recounting their progress as lines began to criss-cross the Scottish lowlands. By 1848, without any overall plan in place, the lines of four railway companies had all converged at Perth. The original intention had been to build stations for them on the South Inch but following much local protest and then a public enquiry, it was decided to build a joint terminus at the edge of

An aerial view showing how the railway served the townspeople as well as nearby industrial premises such as Dewars and Macdonald Fraser. Animal pens can be seen at the bottom of the photo.
From the collection of the late Harry Chalmers, Perth.

the South Inch where the present-day station now stands. The original station was greatly extended in the 1880s at which time the Station Hotel was also built. The grandeur of the station architecture reflects the importance of the railway to Perth though, with the addition of the late 20th century entrance hall and large car park in front, this is not so easily appreciated today. Nevertheless it was regarded at the time as one of the finest station buildings in the country and thus eminently suitable for one of the premier junction stations in the British railway network.

In 1923 the many railway companies of the 19th century amalgamated into just four, two of which operated in Scotland: the London and North-Eastern Railway (LNER) and the London Midland Scottish Railway (LMS), the latter being the main employer at Perth Station. The 1920s were arguably the highpoint of the railway in Perth, a period when it provided comfortable and relatively inexpensive travel to wide areas of Perthshire and beyond. Descriptions of the station at that time suggest that its busiest time was the summer and autumn, beginning with the annual summer holiday exodus from Glasgow in July and followed, between August and October, by large numbers of early morning trains from the south rolling 'smoothly into Perth with their loads of sleeping-car passengers' destined for holidays and grouse shooting in the highlands. The future Edward VIII was a regular visitor to Glamis and not infrequently arrived at Perth by royal train. This most popular member of the royal family generally stopped for a chat with station staff before heading off to do some shopping at Frazers' High Street shop which thereafter proudly displayed the Prince of Wales feathers in their advertisements. Foreign visitors arrived, especially Americans – 'men with square-toed shoes, chewing gum, and women with horn-rimmed spectacles... who seemed to be quite well pleased with bonnie Scotland' but who, according to the porters, 'left as little behind them as an Aberdonian does.' Seasonal workers came and went, such as berry-pickers heading for the fields of north Perthshire and Angus and fish workers travelling to the ports of East Anglia, while for those at leisure weekend trains were laid on for football fans and excursionists. Throughout the year the main Perth employers depended on the railway for transporting goods and livestock.

Towards the end of the 1920s the railway's near monopoly on out of town travel began to be challenged. The advent of the motor bus, generally regarded as more convenient and which by 1927 was already

A busy scene at Perth Station in c.1900. The station was shared by all railway companies serving Perth and the booking offices of three of them – the Highland Railway, the Caledonian Railway and the North British Railway – are shown in the centre of the photo.
Courtesy of the A.K. Bell Library Local Studies Department, Perth and Kinross Council.

putting the very survival of Perth trams in doubt, was also enticing travellers away from the railway. In turn railway managers responded with cheaper fares and improved services and took care to point out that in August of that year, while there had been a number of fatalities on the roads, the railway had carried over four million passengers with no accidents at all. By 1929 the growing threat from buses was such that railway companies even considered branching out and offering bus services themselves. At the same time the private car was becoming more popular and affordable, and by 1937 scheduled domestic flights were being operated from Perth Aerodrome. Throughout the 1930s the railway had good and less good years. Football trains continued to bring in good revenue as did cheap Sunday fares and sleeping and dining cars, while evening excursions, 'holiday runabout' tickets, and one-off events such as the Scottish scout rally on the North Inch in 1933 all attracted extra passengers. On the other hand, the Empire Exhibition in Glasgow in 1938 drew much passenger traffic away from Perth and the station in that last year of peace was rather quiet.

The railway companies continued to emphasise the relative safety of rail travel though in the era before the *Health and Safety at Work Act* of 1974 the number of railway workers who were killed or injured in the course of their work, from being either struck by a train or crushed in the buffers, was remarkably high. There were suicides too, judging by the numbers of those falling in front of trains and by the decapitations on the track, and inevitably there were train crashes. The worst peacetime incident in British transport history occurred at Harrow in October 1952 and involved the Perth-London sleeper and two other trains. Over 100 people were killed and around 340 injured, though the lord provost of Perth, Sir John Ure Primrose, who had been in one of the sleeping cars, managed to walk away unhurt. One particular rail accident is remembered in a poignant brass plaque on the west wall of St Ninian's Cathedral. It commemorates the brief lives of Alasdair and

Adrian Kinloch, the 15-year-old twin sons of the honorary sheriff-substitute for Perth who were killed in an early morning collision in Yorkshire on 19 January 1905, while on their way back to boarding school after the Christmas holidays. The whole of Perth was shocked by the tragedy and thousands lined the streets as the cortege made its way to Wellshill cemetery.

As will be described in a later chapter, the railway played a major part in the domestic war effort and in the years immediately following 1945 struggled to return to pre-war normality. More attention was again paid to passenger comfort, dining cars were reintroduced, engines and carriages had their former colours restored and new rolling stock made an appearance.

A plaque on the west wall of St Ninian's Cathedral remembering the twin sons of Robert Kinloch who both died in the Cudworth railway accident of 1905.
Courtesy of Iain McDonald, Glossop, Derbyshire.

Women workers withdrew from their various wartime roles as men returned from overseas and resumed their former duties. Blackened roofs were removed from the station and replaced with clear glass, air raid shelters were dismantled and the station buildings given a coat of fresh paint. Then in 1948 came another upheaval when the railways were nationalised and placed under the direct control of the government. New experimental liveries were tried out and engines from various former companies, some from the south of England, were put through their paces on the Perth to Inverness line to determine which were best able to cope with the demands of the highland routes.

By the mid-1950s the nationalised railway service gave the impression of working well. Perth Station was looking fresh after its long post-war refurbishment and seemed to be as busy as it had been 20 years earlier, while sleeping car and new motorail services were proving popular. The £15 fare for the latter paid for a seat, a sleeper berth and the car itself, and an extra nine shillings and sixpence (£0.47) would buy a packed supper with a flask of coffee thrown in. Perth was also given its own direct daytime link with London when *The Fair Maid* was put into service, leaving Perth at 6.40 am and arriving in London at 3.20 pm. The reverse journey, with its arrival in Perth early enough for onward travel, allowed rail passengers for the first time to travel from London to the far north of Scotland in one day. When the British Transport Commission announced that it was going to spend £1.65 million on a new 20-acre marshalling yard at Tulloch (one of the most technologically advanced in Europe) and a power-operated signal box on the southern approach to Perth, replacing 13 older ones, it was hard not to believe that such developments boded well for the future of the railway at Perth. As the district traffic superintendent himself said, British Railways 'has demonstrated its faith in the future by capital expenditure in the city of Perth not equalled by any single organisation for many years.' But change was in the air and throughout the 1950s the press also featured stories about the reduction in a service here, the closure of a branch line there, and a bid to save a station somewhere else. Financial savings and faster journey times were achieved but at a cost to the communities outside Perth.

In 1961 the new marshalling yard was in operation and the *Perthshire Advertiser* chose to mark the occasion with a number of statistical illustrations of the work of the railway at Perth. Exported from the city in 1960–61 were: 100,000 tons of seed potatoes destined for England;

300,000 pounds of fresh fruit, sent by express passenger train to arrive in time for the first sales at Covent Garden; 110,000 sheep and 12,500 cattle; 30,000 tons of whisky; 45,000 dry cleaning containers from Pullars; as well as beef for Smithfield, flowers for the Midlands, and Tay salmon to all destinations. To cope with such a throughput the railway employed around 1,750 workers (about as many as it had at the beginning of the century), a figure which made it one of Perth's largest employers of labour. The railway was thus of vital importance to the trade and commerce of Perth and Perthshire, and to the economic and social well-being of the area.

It is ironic after such a proud fanfare of statistics that it all went wrong so soon afterwards. The Beeching report was published in 1963 but rumours of extensive job losses in the offing were so strong in 1962 that Perth railwaymen during a national one-day strike marched on the City Chambers to ask for the council's full support against the anticipated cuts. When the axe fell about 200 jobs went very quickly with the threat that another 500 would go over the next five years, thus reducing the Perth workforce to around 1,000. To most railwaymen this must have sounded like the death knell for the railway in Perth but in reality, though the job losses were tough, it was a brave attempt to trim down and reorganise the behemoth that British Railways had become. When it became clear that one third of the entire railway network carried only one per cent of the traffic and was losing out to a hungry and recently denationalised road haulage industry then something had to be done. But Perth was still an important junction in the Scottish network and while it remained so it could not be ignored altogether. So yes, Perth lost its district office but was then given an area manager instead, a new concourse was planned for the station with improved passenger facilities, and the future of the motorail service seemed assured when a terminal was created at Caledonian Road. Even so, by 1968 the local press was mourning the total loss of around 1,000 jobs, saying that the railway cuts were the heaviest of all economic blows suffered by the town and surrounding area in recent years. But more bad news was to come. The carriage and wagon workshops on the Edinburgh Road, which had served various railway companies since 1851, were closed in 1970 and at about the same time, following a public enquiry, the direct rail link with Edinburgh, via Kinross, was axed. Passengers thus had to detour via Stirling instead. With an inadequate road to Edinburgh, and now a downgrading of rail services, this was a particularly bitter blow to the council who were desperately trying to attract new industries and businesses to Perth.

There were still more cuts to come and indeed a gloomy NUR were predicting the end of all rail services in Perth and the loss of all 800 jobs by 1981. Motorail services were reduced in 1975 and axed completely in the early 1980s, at about the time the Perth area manager post was merged with that of Dundee. In 1984 the direct Perth-London sleeper service was ended, and henceforth sleeping cars from Perth were attached to the Inverness-London train. There were now under 700 railway jobs at Perth and they continued to trickle slowly away. But from the mid-1980s there was a sense that the precarious position of the railway in the city had finally stabilised. In 1988 Perth became the operations centre for the new Scotrail North area, for which 50 new jobs were created, and in the early 1990s the station façade and forecourt were given a facelift. In 1992, as if to underline the huge loss of railway jobs in 30 years, the Railway Athletic and Social Club closed its doors for the last time. And what of job numbers in recent years? A telephone call to Scotrail in 2008, attempting to elicit the number of employees at the station, resulted in no information at all because of 'security.' It was suggested, however, that simply going into the station and counting them would provide an approximate answer, a response which at least indicates that the numbers working there nowadays are relatively few.

It is no exaggeration to say that the railway network in 19th-century Britain was as important to business as the internet is today. So, as Perth quickly developed into a railway hub, the more enterprising local businesses began to exploit it to expand their trade. One such was the firm of Macdonald Fraser, live-stock auctioneers, which in 1875 moved from its Mill Street home to a site beside the railway at Caledonian Road. Together with fellow auctioneers Hay and Co. (which closed in 1992 after

The premises of Macdonald Fraser in 1980, an image which can still evoke memories of warm animal smells. From the collection of the late Harry Chalmers, Perth.

160 years) they were perhaps the two major Perth businesses which in the industrial age still depended on the Perthshire agricultural hinterland, and further afield, for their livelihood. Animals in their thousands would be sent to Perth each week, either by train or herded from nearby farms. In the early morning flocks of sheep would descend on the city from all directions and beware any householder who should forget to shut his garden gate on market day; fresh green grass or a particularly juicy chrysanthemum might well prove too tempting for a sheep which had just walked five miles. Perth Bridge was described as almost impassable on market day when sheep and cattle were vying for space with carriages and tramcars. That there were dangers too was demonstrated by James Duffy who, busy painting the County Inn one day in 1906, plummeted to his death when the fire escape he was standing on was hit by a passing animal. Stories of escaped animals abound, and include the occasions when a woman, on the top floor of a tenement opposite the mart, found a pig outside her front door, when a half-ton bull with a four-foot spread of horns smashed his way out of a pen and terrorised the Glasgow Road area, and when in 1982 a whole herd of cattle escaped into the city centre before being rounded up and returned to the mart.

Sheep and cattle were the mainstay of the Macdonald Fraser mart but turkeys, geese, horses and even deer passed through the auctioneers' hands. The old Perth Bull Sales were the firm's best known activity and for many years they had a reputation among leading cattle breeders, particularly of Aberdeen Angus, as the best place to buy stock. Indeed,

An early 20th-century view of sheep being herded along Tay Street with the Victoria Bridge in the background.
Courtesy of the A.K. Bell Library Local Studies Department, Perth and Kinross Council.

with visits by dealers from the United States and South America, tales of huge sums of money being exchanged, and appearances by film stars such as Greer Garson in 1950, all bringing touches of glamour to the city, it could well be said that the sales have had as distinguished a pedigree as the cattle themselves. The firm became part of the United Auctions group in 1962 and the following year the world record price for an Aberdeen Angus was realised when Lindertis Evulse, a 13-month-old bull from a farm at Kirriemuir, was sold to an American bidder for 60,000 guineas. The poor beast was later described as 'hard put to prove his virility' and when finally proven infertile was converted, as one Scottish journalist put it, 'into the dearest mince the world has ever seen.' By the 1970s, however, the export link to North America having dwindled and the February fortnight sales reduced to a week, the bull sales were no longer the world-famous events they had once been.

In the 1980s United Auctions decided to move away from their historic site next to the railway. Doubtless aware of the implications of the Beeching report, they had in the early 1960s switched from rail to

Farmers buying and selling cattle at the mart on Caledonian Road. The covered animal pens are situated just out of shot on the left.
Courtesy of Perth Museum and Art Gallery, Perth and Kinross Council.

road for livestock transportation with the result that large animal transporters, which brought hundreds of thousands of sheep and cattle into Perth each year, became a regular feature of the city streets. These added to the already high levels of traffic congestion and contributed to a feeling that the mart had outgrown the premises which had served it well for over a century. The last bull sale at the Caledonian Road site took place in October 1989 after which the company relocated to its new home, the £6 million Perth Agricultural Centre at East Huntingtower, and took with them five carved stone animal heads from the old site as a reminder of their origins. As in 1875 when proximity to the railway was critical to the company's success, so in 1989, with animals being brought in by road for auction, close proximity to the motorway network and the newly opened bypass was paramount. Animals, buyers, visitors, cars and lorries were now comfortably accommodated at the new mart, and although business suffered from the effects of the BSE crisis and in 2001 from the foot and mouth epidemic, few locals were prepared for the announcement in 2009 that the mart would shortly relocate to Stirling. The Perth Bull Sales, at Stirling, were still known as such until the summer of 2012 when United Auctions decided to drop the name in favour of the less confusing Stirling Bull Sales.

If the mart was a regular weekly reminder of the city's historic dependence on agriculture, then the Perth Show was the annual celebration of that link. In spite of the weakening of the agricultural ties between city and county during the course of the 20th century (the disappearance of the Little Dunning feeing market being a prime example), the Perth Show has gone from strength to strength. Its ever-growing popularity turned it into one of the biggest one-day events of its kind in Scotland in the 1970s and saw attendances booming from 16,000 at the centenary show of 1963 to 35,000 in 2000. Such was its success that it became a two-day event in 1980 and even attracted a display of the pope-mobile, minus His Holiness, after the papal visit to Scotland in 1982. But success also brought space problems and when in 1979 the council narrowly approved the application by the Perthshire Agricultural Society to hold the show on the main South Inch there followed such a howl of protest about the 'rape of the Inch' that the council had to back down. The Perth Trades Council was particularly outspoken, describing the council's original decision as 'a vote in favour of a privileged minority [which] ignored the legitimate interests and hereditary rights of Perth people who

A busy sweet stall on the corner of High Street and Meal Vennel during the Little Dunning Market of 1922. Milk caramels are being advertised at fourpence – presumably per pound or per bag. Courtesy of Perth Museum and Art Gallery, Perth and Kinross Council.

wish to make full and proper use of the South Inch' – which comment probably says as much about the perceived gentrification of the agricultural industry as it does about the old Labour politics of the time. The show, though, continues to flourish and, notwithstanding the centenary in 1963, celebrated the sesquicentenary in 2012.

The above-mentioned Little Dunning Market was another occasion when country met town. Held annually in October it was the main forum for farmers and farm workers to meet and discuss employment opportunities for the six months or year ahead. Filling the central streets, and of wider appeal, were the cake and sweet stalls and various entertainments such as boxing booths. Everyone, though, had to be wary of the 'cheap Jacks' who were experts at swindling the unwary out of their money. Ploughmen who had just received their arles, a payment which tied a labourer to a farmer for an agreed period, were prime targets and not infrequently fell for such tricks as paying half a crown for what appeared to be a paper bag containing three such coins, only to find the bag contained three pennies. Little Dunning survived as a feeing market until 1938, after which the advent of war put an end to an age-old autumn custom. The press in 1952 made mention of a few groups of ploughmen in the streets but observed that 'otherwise the Little Dunning Market was indistinguishable from any other Friday.'

Another firm which depended greatly on the railway network was Pullars of Perth, described by the *Perthshire Advertiser* in 1929 as 'the most famous firm in the city and the best known cleaning and dyeing works in the world.' From its small beginnings in 1824, engaged firstly in dyeing and later in dry cleaning as well, its rapid expansion was due largely to effective advertising, the use of the latest dry-cleaning technologies, and the establishment of a huge network of agencies, around 4,000 of them, the length and breadth of Britain. Such agents attracted custom locally and then sent cloth, garments, carpets and a whole variety of materials, even ostrich feathers, to Perth by rail for cleaning or dyeing. When Pullars was at the height of its success, in the earlier years of the 20th century, the name of Perth had probably never been better known throughout Britain.

By the turn of the century Pullars employed 2,600 staff and occupied extensive premises in the city centre, between Mill Street and Carpenter Street, and also at Tulloch on the then western edge of the city. The management was paternalistic in style and staff were generally looked after if they were regarded as good workers. If not, as in the case of an unfortunate employee who could not stay out of debt, the company went so far as to buy him and his family a ticket to

A Pullars van at Perth Station, either collecting packages from company agents across the country or sending out finished laundry. Courtesy of Perth Museum and Art Gallery, Perth and Kinross Council.

Australia and escorted them to the dock – presumably, one hopes, with their consent. The management were also wary of trade unionists and in an attempt to foster good relations provided the Tulloch Institute as a sports and social centre for its employees. However, with such a large workforce they were reluctant to increase wages and this resulted in a short strike of several hundred staff in 1912, the year which saw the

A semi-derelict section of the Pullars factory in Mill Street. It has since been replaced with the red-brick extension adjacent to Perth Concert Hall.
From the collection of the late Harry Chalmers, Perth.

deaths within ten days of each other of both Sir Robert Pullar and his brother, James. The strike resulted in a significant growth in the membership and power of the trade unions within Pullars which, combined with the general privations of war and the soaring costs of living, came to a head in violent industrial action in 1917. In September of that year, after weeks of tension, the infamous Battle of the Gates saw an angry mob of 2,000 strikers in Mill Street being charged down by mounted police. Worn down by such problems the Pullar family lost heart and within four months had sold the business to Eastman and Sons of London.

After the war there were outward signs that Pullars was again flourishing. The new management introduced works councils to improve management-employee relations and a little later allowed employees to buy shares in the firm. Business too was good as the high cost of living fostered a make-do-and-mend attitude among the public, and many customers, instead of buying new, sent older items of clothing to Pullars to be dyed and generally freshened up. In 1919 a rival to Pullars, Campbell's Perth Dye Works, where founding father John Pullar is believed to have learned his trade, was destroyed by fire. When the directors decided they no longer wished to carry on the business Pullars took over the firm, re-employed the staff and set about rebuilding the factory which became better known in recent years as Highland House. Another company, Eustace Brothers in Dublin, was taken over to get round punitive tariffs imposed by the Irish Free State in 1925. Meanwhile a string of new branch receiving offices was steadily being developed, opening at a rate of one a week. In an attempt to even out the industry's seasonal variations – dry-cleaning usually resulted from spring cleaning whereas dyeing was generally an autumn pursuit – the company offered reduced rates during the traditionally quieter periods. Some sales were a little too successful. In 1931, in the midst of the Depression, the firm held a Golden Summer Sale offering half-price dry-cleaning. Such was the rush of orders that the company had to take on more staff and operate a night shift for the first time in many years.

In spite of such valiant attempts the industry as a whole was in decline. The numbers employed in Perth's textiles and dyeing industries dropped significantly during the first half of the 20th century, due to increasing competition from rival firms in the bigger centres of popula-tion and by the difficult years of the 1930s. By mid-century Pullars

The ironing room at P. and P. Campbell's Perth Dye Works.
Courtesy of Perth Museum and Art Gallery, Perth and Kinross Council.

operations were once again concentrated in Kinnoull Street by which time dyeing had virtually died out in the city. In 1969, when the firm was taken over by the Johnson Group, the total number of employees in Perth had fallen to around 360. A further reorganisation in 1976 reduced the staff still further and freed up part of the Kinnoull Street premises into which the Presto supermarket moved in 1980. The Pullars chimney, one of the tallest but least attractive Perth landmarks, was dismantled brick by brick in that same year, a symbol of the gradual fading of the company from Perth consciousness. Finally in 1989 the company announced plans to vacate the city centre altogether and move to the Inveralmond Industrial Estate where it now operates as Johnsons Apparelmaster Ltd, that most famous of business names, Pullars of Perth, no longer surviving.

Pullars suffered from competition from England but also had rivals much nearer at hand. The Campbell works were, as we have seen, taken over after the fire of 1919, but that still left the firm of Thomsons who, as well as drycleaners and dyers, were also laundrymen. Referring to the laundry side of the business the firm wrote in 1931 that 'careful analysis shows that year by year more households are coming to depend on the commercial laundry services of washing and ironing. Washing at home

Pullars' staff concentrating on mending stockings. The notice at the back reads: 'As you pack each order ask yourself – is this a good sample of our work? – will it bring us a repeat order?'
Courtesy of Perth Museum and Art Gallery, Perth and Kinross Council.

is rapidly becoming as old-fashioned and out of date as bread-making.' One wonders what they would have made of automatic washing machines and bread-makers in today's homes. The organisation of the dyeing and dry-cleaning side of the business was similar to that of Pullars and by 1929 they too had over 4,000 agencies around the country operating under the brand name, 'Silver Tay.' By making the same use of the railway they offered a two-day service to all parts of Great Britain. They were as aware as Pullars of fierce competition and so reduced prices and offered 'suit fortnights' accordingly. There were also the veiled accusations in the press, such as the following in 1933: 'Unfortunately there are big and influential firms in the trade who are still determined to operate on a philanthropic basis and the price-war therefore shows no signs of abating. Until such time as good sense gains the ascendancy, the position of making money out of dry-cleaning is non-existent.' In the mid-1930s, frustrated by what they regarded as a slow and expensive service by the railway, which was making competition with English

firms impossible, they closed their southern English agencies and, focusing solely on Scotland and the north of England, began servicing their surviving agencies by road and post rather than rail. After the war they found themselves with plenty of work, both from the government and from the public who, in a time of rationing, had old clothes dyed instead of buying new. The long-term decline, though, as experienced by Pullars, was mirrored by Thomsons who finally closed in 1967 with the loss of 100 jobs.

Closely shadowing the fortunes of Pullars was another major Perth textiles firm, that of John Shields and Co. Founded in 1851, it was within 20 years producing great quantities of fine linen

A Pullars shop photographed in the pre-decimal currency age, possibly in the 1960s.
Courtesy of Perth Museum and Art Gallery, Perth and Kinross Council.

from the 300 looms housed in their new factory, the Wallace Works on the Dunkeld Road. Such was the reputation of the company that in 1893, on the marriage of the future George V and Queen Mary, the city of Perth chose to present the royal couple with an oak chest full of what was described in the local press as 'probably the finest linen damasks ever made in Scotland.' In 1900, as we have seen, the factory was further enlarged to accommodate the 900 looms then required to cope with demand. The company survived the war years in reasonable shape, having been forced through restrictions on the supply of flax to diversify into cotton weaving. After the war they were seriously affected by the high costs of raw materials and production, and by stiff competition from Ireland and Europe where wages were much lower. When American customers started buying from continental Europe as well, the management decided in 1936 to close the company and lay off its 300 employees. But they had not reckoned with Lord Provost Nimmo who tenaciously explored various ways of saving the firm. Ultimately A.K. Bell took over as chairman of a new company and wasted no time in revamping old practices: agents were established throughout the British Empire, machinery was updated, the range of manufactures broadened, and weaving with new materials tried. The results were rapid and increased orders from around the globe flooded in, but with the advent of war the turnaround was short-lived. After the war John Shields and Co went through a series of take-overs and name changes, eventually becoming part of the Forfar-based firm of Don and Low. The Wallace Works were finally closed in 1995 and demolished two years later to make room for a leisure park. This part of the Dunkeld Road now enjoys a much lighter and brighter appearance: many a city child will remember the high grey walls of firstly the barracks and then the Wallace Works and neighbouring factories which seemed to run interminably along the Dunkeld Road towards the swimming baths.

One such factory was the Balhousie Works of Coates Brothers and Co., jute spinners and carpet weavers. James and Henry Coates were well-known in the town as doers of good works though Henry gained a certain notoriety in later years for his less than acceptable interests at the Perthshire Natural History Museum. The story of the business was a familiar one of ups and downs, of problems caused by war and strikes, of its eventual take-over by a big Dundee carpet manufacturer in 1962 and subsequent closure in 1966.

An interior view of the Wallace Works taken in 1959.
Courtesy of Perth Museum and Art Gallery, Perth and Kinross Council.

Another of Perth's internationally known businesses was the North British Glass Works founded by John Moncrieff in around 1865. They were initially based in South Street before moving to a larger site in St Catherine's Road. By 1900 the firm had leased an additional 32-acre site by the harbour, but even so, notwithstanding the size of the operation, the glass works were not a major Perth employer. The company specialized in industrial glass and enjoyed a worldwide reputation for gauge glass which was used in steam boilers across the globe. The company prospered during World War One as much of the nation's glass for use in scientific experiments, which had previously been acquired from Germany, now had to be produced at home. After the war, though, cheap German products began flowing back into Britain and Moncrieffs found themselves facing serious competition. In subsequent decades, in spite of competition, local industrial problems and international difficulties such as tariffs, quotas, political crises, and the problems of getting payment from foreign companies, the firm kept itself afloat on the high reputation it had earned for the quality of its products. The 1930s were generally a lean time, but exporting was made easier when the country abandoned the gold standard and the value of the pound thus dropped. There was also a growing demand from Germany from 1934 and, in the immediate post-war period, a huge demand for gauge glass from the world over. In 1952 the Moncrieff family lost control of the company which by the 1970s, in spite of winning some substantial overseas contracts, was in financial difficulties. The end was avoided by redundancies and company streamlining in 1982. Ten years later a further change of ownership resulted in the company being renamed Monax Glass, an echo of the original founder's name respectfully being preserved. The St Catherine's Road works finally closed in 1995 and have since been replaced by a development of upmarket flats known as Hyalus Bank, a name which derives from the Greek word for glass.

Vincent Ysart creating a new piece of Vasart glass in around 1960.
Courtesy of Perth Museum and Art Gallery, Perth and Kinross Council.

The most famous non-industrial product from the Moncrieff factory was the art glass fashioned by the Ysart family. The Barcelona-born Salvador Ysart was taken on by the company in 1922 and together with his four sons produced some of the most sought-after art glass of the 20th century. Known as Monart, a marriage of the Moncrieff and Ysart names, the glass was characterised by vivid colours and swirling decoration and, in the shape of bowls, vases, table lamps and other items, commands a high price in antique shops today. Its attractions were obvious from the very beginning, the *Perthshire Advertiser* commenting in 1924 that 'this new type of glassware is surprisingly beautiful.' William Watson, of the High Street china shop, saw the potential immediately and was astute enough to acquire the sole selling rights in Perthshire, while in London it could be found on sale in high-class department stores such as Harrods and Liberty's. After World War Two, three of the Ysart brothers left the North British Glass Works to start their own business by the Shore making the similarly highly regarded Vasart ware. The fourth brother, Paul, remained with Moncrieffs and continued to make Monart until his move to Wick in 1962 to take up an appointment with Caithness Glass. It would have been he who made the Monart items which were presented by the city of Perth to the future Queen Elizabeth and Duke of Edinburgh on the occasion of their marriage in 1947. Further spin-offs from the production of Vasart include the companies of Strathearn Glass and Perthshire Paperweights. Caithness Glass, with its Ysart connection, opened a glass works on the Inveralmond Industrial Estate in 1979 where, until its closure in 2008 by owners Dartington Crystal, all that company's paperweights were once made. Moncrieffs and Perthshire Paperweights bitterly opposed the new glass works, objecting not so much to the added competition as to the substantial subsidy given by the Scottish Development Agency to a business rival. Such was the fragility of the local glass industry.

If the women of Britain were familiar with the Pullars of Perth brand then the men were equally at home with the whiskies of Perth. While the

Watsons High Street shop window in 1960, decorated with a display of Monart ware. The notice in the window reads: 'Sole agents in Perthshire for Monart glass.' Courtesy of Perth Museum and Art Gallery, Perth and Kinross Council.

connoisseur of Scotland's national drink might turn his nose away from anything less than a single Highland malt, the average man in the street, in this country and overseas, was more familiar with the blended whiskies which flowed out of the bottling plants of Perth. Of the five companies which spring to mind – those of Arthur Bell, John Dewar, Matthew Gloag, Peter Thomson and James and Thomas Currie – the names of only the first three still survive, though no longer independent. Bells and Dewars are well enough known by those names, while Gloags is better known through its most popular brand, the *Famous Grouse*.

The art of whisky blending originated in the second quarter of the 19th century, Dewars and Bells being among the first to develop successful blends and bottle them. The *Perthshire Advertiser* tells the story: 'The House of Dewar, amongst others, discovered that the heavy Highland malt whiskies, though palatable enough to those living constantly in the open air and taking plenty of exercise, was quite unsuited to the palates and digestions of the great majority of mankind, who perforce are obliged to lead a sedentary life. This heavy spirit, with all its peaty characteristics, was mixed with some of the lighter whiskies made in the south of Scotland, and the resultant blend was one which retained the flavour of the north country whiskies, and the palatability and digestibility of those of the south. After repeated experiments and trials, a blend was finally evolved at Perth as one likely to meet the taste of the average man, and the firm set about persuading the average man that Dewar's – and Dewar's only – was the whisky for him.' Alexander John Cameron was the firm's first master blender, a man of such skill – he blended as many as 40 individual whiskies into the *White Label* brand – and such importance to the firm that he was offered a seat on the board at the age of 40. When he died in 1928, aged only 57, the flags on the Dewars buildings flew at half mast. There was perhaps no better tribute to him than the company's advertising slogan, 'It never varies.'

The company focused initially on London, a potentially huge market in which whisky was relatively unknown to the gin and brandy drinkers of the south. In time, thanks to the efforts of Thomas Dewar, a son of the founder and a tireless business traveller, the company built up a network of offices and agents over large swathes of the British Empire and beyond. A symbol of the company's success – and one of Perth's best known landmarks until its demolition in the 1980s – was the huge red-brick bonded warehouse which was erected on the Glasgow Road in

1912 and which had an estimated storage capacity of 2,000,000 gallons of whisky. As with most other Perth firms which depended on exports, this building stood next to the railway line. The 1920s and 1930s were difficult times, when excise duty put a bottle of Scotch beyond the reach of an average wage. Prohibition in the USA had a similarly adverse effect on trade until its repeal in 1933, after which time and until the advent of war the company's future looked bright.

One of the most instantly recognisable landmarks in Perth was the Dewars bonded warehouse which stood close to the railway between Glover Street and Glasgow Road.
From the collection of the late Harry Chalmers, Perth.

The industry was heavily controlled during and after the war and the return to normality took a number of years. The demand for whisky was high but production in 1946 was down to 50 per cent of pre-war levels. This was partly due to restrictions on the supply of grain, as much of that which had been earmarked for distilling was sent to feed the hungry in Europe instead. The government was also desperately in

A photo of 1954 showing Dewars White Label being packaged and made ready for despatch to distant destinations.
Courtesy of Perth Museum and Art Gallery, Perth and Kinross Council.

need of hard currency and decreed in 1947 that only 25 per cent of production could go to the home market and that the remaining 75 per cent had to be exported. By the following year the ratio had stretched to 20–80, the main beneficiaries being the USA and Canada. At home, meanwhile, duty was again increased and by 1949 the Chancellor was pocketing over £10 on every gallon of whisky sold.

The immediate post-war years were tough but the focus on exporting stood the company in good stead in later years. Exports steadily increased after the move in 1962 to a state-of-the-art blending and bottling plant at Inveralmond and within four years the company had won the prestigious Queen's Award for Industry. In 1975, with almost 90 per cent of its output being exported, more than half of it to the USA, the company was ranked as the second-largest Scotch whisky business and became one of only three British companies to win the Queen's Award for a fifth time. Locally, the Inveralmond plant with around 750 staff was one of the major Perth employers and one of the biggest whisky operations in Scotland at the time.

Dewars underwent a number of mergers and take-overs in its long history, being a subsidiary in recent years of United Distillers, Diageo and Bacardi. The most infamous take-over occurred in 1986 when the Distillers Company (of which Dewars was then a part) was acquired by

The beginning of the end for a world-famous Perth company – the demolition of Dewars bonded warehouse in 1988.
From the collection of the late Harry Chalmers, Perth.

Guinness whose boss, Ernest Saunders, was later found guilty of financial fraud and jailed. In 1993 United Distillers announced the closure of the Inveralmond plant which resulted in huge protests from trade unions, politicians and even, perhaps surprisingly, clergymen. These were to no avail and shortly after midday on 21 June 1994 the final bottle of *White Label*, the last of an estimated 1.5 billion, came off the production line, was packaged and sent off to Canada. Dewars still has a big presence in Aberfeldy, where the whole story began, and *White Label* is still the biggest-selling whisky in the USA. But with the demolition of the bonded warehouse in 1988 and the bottling plant in the later 1990s there is no longer any visible sign of the long and fruitful link between Dewars and Perth.

In broad terms the history of Bells whisky is very similar to that of Dewars. Arthur Bell, like John Dewar, began in Perth in modest fashion in the earlier 19th century and, having established a successful business locally, depended on the business acumen of his offspring to make the Bells brand known throughout the world. Robert Bell was a little younger than Thomas Dewar but beat the same path to the Empire while his better known older brother, Arthur Kinmond Bell, concentrated on the home market. A.K. Bell, whose charitable deeds feature throughout this book, died in 1942 and was succeeded as chairman by W.G. Farquharson who took the company to new heights and who, at the end of his career, was awarded the freedom of Perth. He in turn was succeeded by the flamboyant Raymond Miquel who moved the company headquarters from Victoria Street to Cherrybank, bought Gleneagles Hotel and between 1974 and 1984 increased the company's pre-tax profits tenfold. It was his

A Bells lorry stands outside the company's premises in Victoria Street in 1954. 'Afore ye go', the slogan of their popular whisky, appears above the driver's cab.
Courtesy of Perth Museum and Art Gallery, Perth and Kinross Council.

misfortune, too, to come up against Ernest Saunders in a hostile take-over bid in 1985. Both companies took out full-page advertisements in the local press: Bells went for the managerial approach with graphs and diagrams showing how well the company had performed while Guinness simply stated, with a superbly positioned apostrophe, 'Guinness is good for you. Bells has lost its way. Accept Guinness' offer now.' The Guinness offer was indeed accepted and Miquel resigned from the board only to appear back in Perth, briefly, as chairman of the brewing company, Belhaven. With the transfer of jobs to London in the late 1990s and the subsequent purchase of the Cherrybank building by the Bank of Scotland, Bells, like Dewars, no longer has a presence in Perth. Thus the companies' histories were very similar, comprising periods of award-winning success and relative weakness when job losses and take-over threats were the norm. The main difference between them, apart from size, was Dewars' domination of the American market and Bells' of the UK market. Like Lord Dewar, and indeed his brother Lord Forteviot, A.K. Bell was a generous philanthropist, establishing the Gannochy Trust in 1937 which has since donated vast sums to charities and educational and sporting institutions in Perth and throughout Scotland.

Bordeaux House, the name of Matthew Gloag's premises in Kinnoull Street, and the sculpted bunch of grapes high on the frontage were indicative of the company's interests in wine as well as whisky. This photo was taken in c.1914.
Courtesy of the A.K. Bell Library Local Studies Department, Perth and Kinross Council.

There were other Perth businesses in the drinks industry, notably Gloags who, buoyed by the success of the *Famous Grouse*, were by the early 20th century situated in a prime position at Bordeaux House in Kinnoull Street. Highland Distilleries took over the firm in 1970 (they in turn were taken over by the Edrington Group in 1999) and in 1996 they moved from central Perth to new premises at Kinfauns where they continue to manage Scotland's best-selling brand. Dean of Guild Peter Thomson took over a whisky, wine and grocery shop in the High Street in the early 1900s which, under his son, David, the late lord provost, developed into a major business with the Beneagles brand of whisky as its flagship. In 1974 the company opened a blending and bottling warehouse on the Crieff Road which was further extended in the early 1980s. Corporate predators, however, attracted to the smell of success, mounted take-over bids and by 1985 the company was under the control of Waverley Vintners. The city was also home to the Perth Brewery, a firm owned by John Wright and Co. who for a long time were the only brewers in the city. Sales rose in the post-war period, thanks to the scarcity of whisky, and, despite the good quality of the beer, they were equally prone to falling when excise duty was high and the weather cold. Like Peter Thomson and Son they too had a distinguished lord provost at the helm in the shape of Sir Robert Nimmo. In 1961 the company merged with Vaux and two years later the brewing industry ceased in Perth, only to be revived in 1997 with the establishment of the Inveralmond Brewery.

A late starter compared with most of the firms already mentioned, but equally dominant in its own sphere of business, was the General Accident (GA), an insurance company which was set up in 1885 in response to legislation which made employers responsible for compensating their staff should they be injured in the course of their work. Initially based in an office in Tay Street, which later became home to the company's archive, the firm moved to a prestigious new headquarters on the southern corner of the High Street and Tay Street in 1901, replacing the General Post Office which had moved to its own equally prestigious new building further up the High Street. By this time it was already providing burglary, fire and motor cover, was a quoted company on the London Stock Exchange, and had successfully resisted a take-over attempt by Norwich Union. And six years before the town council acquired its first typewriter the GA already had two. Such a dynamic start was

A collection of labels for the range of beers made by the Perth Brewery.
Courtesy of Perth Museum and Art Gallery, Perth and Kinross Council.

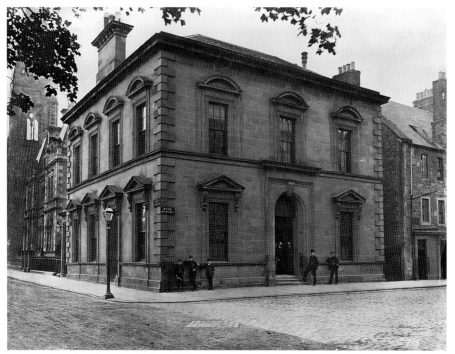

The short-lived General Post Office on the corner of Tay Street and High Street.
Francis Norie-Miller built his General Accident headquarters on this site when the
GPO relocated to the High Street-Scott Street corner.
Courtesy of Perth Museum and Art Gallery, Perth and Kinross Council.

due to the efforts of the first general manager, a young Francis Norie-Miller who, like the managers of other big Perth businesses, established a network of branches and agents across the country and overseas which allowed the firm to expand rapidly. Within 18 years he had offices in America, Europe and Australia.

The company's particular speciality was motor insurance and through insuring the royal cars it was awarded a royal warrant by George V. It received a huge boost when the *Road Traffic Act* of 1930 made the insurance of motor vehicles a legal requirement and within two years it was firmly established as the UK's leading motor insurer. By the time of the firm's Jubilee in 1935 it had 130 offices throughout the country which generated one third of the company's total income, another third coming from the USA and the remaining third from the Empire and other foreign countries. Sir Francis Norie-Miller, having presided over an extension to the High Street headquarters and the opening of a new sports ground and pavilion at Rodney, across the river, and with a baronetcy in the bag, had stepped up as chairman and managing director of the firm leaving his son, Stanley, to take over as general manager. Stanley took on the managing directorship in 1938 but Sir Francis stayed on as chairman and by 1940 was able to state that the General Accident in just over half a century was in 'the first rank of the Empire's great insurance companies.' Sir Francis died in 1947 though one wonders how the company might have fared had he not cancelled his booking on the *Titanic*, a mere three weeks before its fateful voyage in 1912. As it was, the company lost £2,500 in the disaster, having insured both the purser and chief engineer. Francis escaped a watery grave but his elder son, Claud, did not. He died in 1917 when the troopship *Transylvania* fell victim to a German torpedo in the Mediterranean, his brave death redeeming an unfortunate period as an employee of the GA in North America.

The post-war years under Sir Stanley's leadership saw further developments. The growth of business from America over half a century, at a time when hard currency was desperately needed, made the GA the second-biggest dollar earner for the UK. In 1958 a further extension to the headquarters building, as far as the Watergate, was opened with the ground floor being given over to a new Perth branch office. 'One of the premier buildings of our city,' said Lord Provost John Buchan at the opening. The architect was Graham Young, son of G.P.K. Young who had designed the original 1901 head office. Further local expansion occurred in the 1960s when the company demolished Sir Robert Pullar's former home, Tayside, on the Isla Road and built its new computer

The new General Accident headquarters was completed in 1901 and in this photo appears to be decorated for the coronation of Edward VII in 1902. As the company grew so did the building which was extended on two occasions.
Courtesy of Perth Museum and Art Gallery, Perth and Kinross Council.

department there, and also at Viewlands House which became a hostel for staff who came from all over the country for training. Sir Stanley had by this time retired as managing director but was still chairman. He seemed reluctant to sever his connection with what must have felt like his family business and so, shortly after the acquisition of the Yorkshire Insurance Company in 1967, he retired as chairman and instead became governor of the company. He died in 1973, having had the satisfaction of seeing the new riverside walk named in his honour and of seeing a plaque to his memory erected on the wall of the Queen's Bridge (which was subsequently repositioned in a more visible location near the Riverside car park). By the time of his death, father and son together had created the third biggest composite insurance company in the UK which employed 15,000 staff worldwide, was Perth's largest employer and which took in around £500 million annually in premium income.

A respectful few months after Sir Stanley's death the company announced radical plans to leave its historic High Street headquarters and relocate to Pitheavlis on the south-western edge of the city. In a further break with the past, the company also decided to end its dowry scheme whereby female employees were given a sum in the region of £500 to £1,000 on marrying. This was a highly unpopular move among

Claud Norie-Miller was the older of Francis's two sons and might reasonably have expected to take over from his father as boss of the General Accident. His death in World War One allowed his younger brother Stanley to take over instead. Claud's body was never found, following the sinking of the troopship *Transylvania*, but he is remembered in Savona, Italy, in this sunlit Ligurian war cemetery close to the Ventimiglia-Genoa motorway.

the many women who worked for the GA but the firm felt they had no option under the terms of the *Equal Pay Act*. However, equality of the sexes was perhaps a difficult concept for what was no longer a young company. The press gleefully recounted the story of how Provost John Mathieson, addressing the annual general meeting of 1980, praised the company's forward-looking management, quite unaware that a woman reporter had been asked to leave as the meeting was 'a male-only gathering.' Work on the Pitheavlis site got underway in 1979 and was reckoned to be Perth's biggest and most expensive building project. The new world headquarters was opened in 1983, complete with a sports complex, and cost a massive £30 million, three times the estimated figure in the mid-70s, though runaway inflation would have accounted for much of the increase. Meanwhile, in order to keep a presence in central Perth, the GA opened a new branch in an attractive modern building in South St John's Place.

In its new flagship the GA set out on the turbulent seas of Thatcherite Britain and it turned out to be a rough voyage. Buffeted by industrial action, rocked by fears of job losses, and taking high-profile hits such as a £100,000 loss when Shergar disappeared, they nevertheless produced a string of year-on-year record profits. London, however, had become

The Pitheavlis premises of Aviva, formerly Norwich Union, were originally built as the General Accident's new world headquarters. The extensive building was designed to sit gently within the landscape rather than dominate it, which, now that trees and plants have matured, it does very successfully.

one of the world's premier financial centres after the Big Bang of 1986, and the GA found it increasingly difficult to remain aloof 400 miles away in Perth. Staff and company funds were drawn inexorably southwards and by the mid-1990s only a small proportion of the £26 billion being managed by the company was done so in Perth. In 1998, despite a huge profit of £500 million, the company merged with the Commercial Union to form CGU Insurance, and in 2000 a further merger with the Norwich Union resulted in the final disappearance of the respected name of the General Accident. Now a member of the Aviva family, the company's workforce has waxed and waned in recent years but nevertheless is still one of Perth's biggest private sector employers.

CHAPTER EIGHT

Unemployment and the New Industries of Perth

IN THE 1960s the council woke up to the fact that, as in the 1920s and 1930s, they were about to have another unemployment crisis on their hands. With the textile industries in a long slow decline and others dependent on a railway infrastructure whose future was suddenly in serious doubt, plus the post-war population 'bulge' just about to leave school, there was a double whammy coming of more unemployed workers competing for fewer available jobs. After two decades of low unemployment, thanks to the war and its aftermath, the spectre of 1930s queues at town centre employment exchanges was once again haunting the minds of local councillors.

There had been precedents for council intervention in local industry. Lord Provost Nimmo's attempts to save the Wallace Works was one example and even as far back as the first decade of the century the council recognised the need to promote Perth as a good place for starting up new industries. In the Great Depression of the early 1930s when unemployment was rising, particularly among dyers and textile workers, the Perth and District Development Council, a spin-off from the Scottish National Development Council, made strenuous efforts to attract new businesses to Perth. Its chairman, Lord Provost Dempster, and his

The Labour Exchange in King Edward Street in c.1924. Courtesy of Perth Museum and Art Gallery, Perth and Kinross Council.

committee of representatives of many of Perth's major companies, contacted businesses south of the border as well as in the United States and Europe, some as far away as Berlin and Vienna, and highlighted the excellent transport links – railway, roads, the harbour, and a proposed airport – plus some of the lowest rates and cheapest gas and electricity in Scotland. A number of enquiries were received but the campaign resulted in little if any actual practical benefit. As the *Perthshire Advertiser* wistfully commented: 'A few more factories would be a pleasant sight for eyes which have tired of scanning the *Situations Vacant* columns in the newspapers.' In this same period the town council also held well-attended trade exhibitions in the City Hall in which around 60 stands were occupied by local firms. They also considered job creation schemes, much as their predecessors had done in the earlier 19th century when the council used the unemployed to lay footpaths on the North and South Inches. Thus, with the financial help of the government, public works such as repairing river banks and improving the dangerous corners at the junction of Perth Bridge, Tay Street and George Street, were carried out. The council's concern continued through the 1930s after which the advent of war put a temporary end to the problem of unemployment.

A letter from the Perth and District Development Council attempting to attract Guinness to Perth during the Depression of the 1930s.
Courtesy of Perth and Kinross Council Archive.

The 'bulge' in 1962 manifested itself in 28 per cent more school leavers than the previous year, many of whom found themselves without a job. Nevertheless, despite the lack of new business enterprise, attempts were at least made to train a willing and waiting workforce. The embryo Perth College, then known as the Further Education Centre and operating from the former Southern District School, began pre-apprenticeship day classes in engineering which achieved such good results in placing

The gently rounded corners at the western end of Perth Bridge, which replaced the original sharper and more dangerous angles, resulted from an employment creation scheme in the 1930s. Courtesy of Iain McDonald, Glossop, Derbyshire.

students in employment that similar classes were started for the building trades, electrical workers, vehicle mechanics and others. These in turn were so successful that pressure began to mount for a purpose-built centre and by 1965 land at Brahan, which had been earmarked for housing, was instead designated as the site for the new Perth Technical College. The youth employment service also found itself under considerable pressure, frustrated equally by the lack of engineering and electrical apprenticeships for boys and by the reluctance of girls to undertake shop work because of Saturday working. The education authority recruited a careers adviser while a growing number of pupils simply stayed on at school beyond the age of 15 to take further qualifications.

A more radical solution to the problem of finding work, and one which many more families were resorting to, was to go to where the work was, even if that meant uprooting to England or emigrating abroad. Emigration had featured in Perth life for many years and high levels were recorded in the years preceding World War One when, for example, the Canadian Pacific Railway placed advertisements in the Perth newspapers offering 'Information for Emigrants – Winnipeg and Beyond' and the Royal Bank of Scotland offered facilities for transmitting money to

Canada and the USA. In 1913 the Winnipeg Perthshire Association was founded to help new immigrants settle in and find work. Britain was described at that time as a country 'drained of hundreds of thousands of its workers who have emigrated.' In 1927 the advertised fare 'for approved settlers' from Glasgow to Quebec was a mere £2. The 1960s saw this phenomenon peaking again and the local press would regularly feature smiling families on the point of departure to distant parts of the Commonwealth, leaving behind them, unseen, heartbroken parents and sad friends. The author well remembers the sadness of losing two childhood friends on the same day in 1965, one heading for Australia and the other to New Zealand. A decline in numbers leaving was noticeable in the later 1960s, so that while the *Perthshire Advertiser* could lament the departure of 29,000 Scots in 1966–67 it could also say in 1970 that 'the dark days of the '60s, when many thousands of young Scots could not get out of the country fast enough, have passed – for the time being.' One reason why the population of Perth did not grow as expected (in 1969 Lord Provost David Thomson predicted a population of 70,000 by 2000) is that too many young men left the area to find work elsewhere. A major report of 1970 on the future planning of Perth confirmed what the press had already made obvious: that job opportunities for men had been dropping, that they would continue to drop unless jobs for men were created, and that the population of the city would grow hardly at all in the next 20 years.

An advertisement in the *Perthshire Advertiser* in the mid-1960s, at the height of the emigration boom.
Courtesy of the A.K. Bell Library Local Studies Department, Perth and Kinross Council.

The unemployment rate in Perth in the early 1960s stood at around two per cent, well below the Scottish average, though the true extent must have been hidden to some degree by emigration. The council tackled this problem initially by offering assistance to local firms wishing to expand and by making renewed attempts to bring new industry to the city. The Glasgow overspill, for example, was spreading beyond the confines of that vastly overcrowded city and the council hoped to entice employers as far as Perth, but in the days before the A9 was upgraded it was seen as too far away. As the 1960s progressed the council became increasingly concerned not just about high levels of emigration and rising unemployment but also about the lack of employment opportunities for able and ambitious young people in technology and industry. They therefore made strenuous efforts to inform business and industrial leaders of the benefits of relocating to the city, while at the same time arguing for industrial fairness as Perth was considerably disadvantaged by not being within a targeted growth area. The policy began to pay off. In 1966 the whole of Scotland, with the exception of Edinburgh, was re-designated a development area and towards the end of that year it was announced that G.R. Designs of Surrey would establish a factory in Perth for the production of electronic equipment. There was a great sense of relief when the factory opened in 1967, as Perth had been reeling from a succession of unemployment blows, ranging from the railway cuts and the closure of the Infantry Records Office, to the end of carpet weaving at the Balhousie Works, the demise of Thomsons the launderers and drycleaners, and the collapse of Dorran Construction. All these events added to the urgency of the situation and the warmth of the welcome given to G.R. Designs. In that same year the lord provost, after a civic visit to Ontario, travelled on to Chicago with a view to attracting American business to Perth and also, with other Scottish civic chiefs, toured the English Midlands with the same purpose in mind. Government departments were also targeted, making it the biggest campaign to attract new industry yet mounted by Perth. In 1968 the council sent 3,000 brochures outlining the merits of the city to named industrialists in the south and midlands of England while in the same area a further 9,000 were distributed in railway carriages, first class only, all of which resulted in a grand total of 15 enquiries.

The council realised that companies would be more easily tempted to Perth if industrial accommodation were readily available and set about providing it. An industrial estate was included in the plans for North Muirton which were announced in 1966 and in that year the council extended the burgh boundary northwards to allow the development to proceed. The North Muirton Industrial Estate was open by 1968 and, with several companies showing an interest in its facilities, the council began looking for other suitable sites. Sensing that rail transport had no future and trusting that the city bypass would one day be built they plumped for what would shortly become the Inveralmond Industrial Estate and in 1969 extended the burgh boundary even further north. These were desperate measures as the council was well aware that the city, compared with the new towns in the central belt, was becoming an industrial backwater. But the will to work was there and the first Scottish workers to join the 'I'm Backing Britain' campaign were five office girls in the Perth Garage in York Place who decided to work an extra hour a day for nothing.

The quiet urgency of the 1960s continued into the next decade. The lord provost fired off another 2,500 letters to English industrialists and received no response whatsoever. The snappily named Tayside Economic Planning Consultative Group was formed with the same purpose in mind, and the Tayside Development Authority vainly urged the government to put the area on an equal footing with Glasgow and the west of Scotland by granting it special industrial development status. Meanwhile emigrants were still leaving, though at a slower rate, and companies were closing or laying off staff, pushing the city's unemployment rate to over three per cent which, while not high, was still a 50 per cent increase in ten years. Then in 1972, a dark year of a miners' strike and power cuts, there was a glimmer of light when Michelin applied for permission to build a tyre factory at Huntingtower and promised to create around 500 jobs. Apart from the understandable

A photo of the ceremony in 1960 to mark the laying of the foundation stone of the new Dewars factory at Inveralmond. Its success would have encouraged the council to proceed with developing edge-of-town industrial estates.
Courtesy of Perth Museum and Art Gallery, Perth and Kinross Council.

protests from nearby residents there was also a problem with the proposed site which had previously been zoned for agriculture. After a long public enquiry, to which even archaeologists had been summoned to try and stop the development, and a subsequent appeal, the Secretary of State for Scotland finally snuffed the light out by decreeing that the factory should not be built, a decision that outraged many individuals and organisations in the city.

In 1973 the tide began to turn. A London company, Morganite Electroheat, announced its decision to relocate to Perth where around 100 jobs, mainly for men, would be created. Later that year the British Gas Corporation named the old gas works site at Friarton as the proposed headquarters of a huge North Sea gas development throughout Scotland. And with the council building a number of advance factories at North Muirton and Inveralmond, adding to the industrial attractiveness of the city, new businesses began to pour in. Such developments, together with the raising of the school leaving age to 16, resulted in a big drop in local unemployment. Finally, in 1975, the chairman of the General Accident announced in a speech that the exodus from the city of young men looking for work had largely been halted.

The establishment of the industrial estates, though seen as almost a last resort at the time, proved to be a highly successful policy and many significant Perth employers have been, or still are, based there. These include Kleinerts, later taken over by the babywear manufacturers Lawtex, Caithness Glass, Scottish Hydro-Electric, and even a helicopter company. The success of the industrial estates led to the creation of others such as at Whitefriars and of business parks and centres set up by the likes of Perth Partnership, the SDA and private enterprise.

The survival of the fittest was the ethos of the Thatcher years and in the recession of the 1980s many businesses found themselves in trouble. Some adapted, some lay down and died and some were swallowed whole by the big beasts prowling the jungle. In June 1979, just after Mrs Thatcher became prime minister, the combined Perth-Crieff unemployment rate stood at 5.2 per cent but by January 1983 this figure had more than doubled to 11.5 per cent. Times were tough but it was the new government's policy of giving free enterprise its head, rather than any of the council's efforts over the years, that gave rise to one of the great local success stories of century.

Stagecoach today is a giant in the world of transport, having extended its field of interest from bus and coach travel to rail and aviation, and in the process making the brother and sister partnership of Ann Gloag and Sir Brian Souter two of the richest people in Scotland. The story began, though, with the deregulation of inter-city coach travel, one of the Thatcher government's earlier pieces of legislation, and a couple of second-hand coaches. The *Courier and Advertiser* ran a brief article in October 1980, just three days before the legislation came into effect, stating that 'a Perth firm is to run a regular coach service to London from Dundee for £9.50.' The first coach set off at 8.15 pm on the following Thursday and called at Perth, Stirling and Glasgow before arriving at King's Cross at 7.30 am the following morning. Cheap and cheerful though the service may have been the company quickly began to focus on expansion and quality and within about a year of starting had bought several more coaches, including a brand new £60,000 50-seater, and were advertising daily services from Perth to Paris for £43 return and also to Athens, Barcelona and Portugal. While European coach services never materialised they at least show how ambitious the company was from its earliest days.

Stagecoach had a reputation for employing aggressive business tactics which is hardly surprising as they met with pretty aggressive opposition when they first started up. The press charted the progress of the

An early Stagecoach bus brought out of retirement and spruced up for a special occasion.
From the collection of the late Harry Chalmers, Perth.

company as it invested in expensive new double-decker coaches, waged fare-cutting wars with rivals, took over smaller companies including a local favourite, A & C McLennan of Spittalfield, and gradually spread south of the border. Further deregulation of in-town bus services in 1985 saw Stagecoach moving into that sector too. That first coach journey would have made the fledgling company a few pounds profit by the time staff wages, fuel and bus station fees had been paid. Yet by December 1999, having been floated on the Stock Exchange and within 20 years of that first tentative overnight journey to London, Stagecoach had achieved a turnover of £1 billion. Earlier that year it had acquired Coach USA in a $1.2 billion deal. It had business interests as far afield as New Zealand, China and Africa, employed 37,000 staff worldwide, and had 16 per cent of the UK bus market with 7,500 vehicles. It had acquired the South-West Trains franchise in 1995, bought into Virgin Rail and bought Prestwick Airport in 1998. It was doing, in fact, exactly what Guinness, Norwich Union and others were doing to Bells, Dewars and the GA. By 2012 the Stagecoach Group had become the second-largest transport firm in the UK with around 35,000 employees world-wide and a turnover in excess of £2 billion. Ann Gloag stood down as an executive director in 2000 in order to concentrate on charity work (for which she was later awarded the OBE), and in the summer of 2012, having been knighted the previous year, Sir Brian announced his intention of retiring as chief executive of the Stagecoach Group though staying on as chairman.

At the end of the 20th century the biggest income generator in Perthshire as a whole, and one in which Perth itself played a major part, was tourism. In a sense it is also one of Perth's oldest surviving industries in that the city regularly featured in the itineraries of the many travellers to Scotland from south of the border and further afield in the 18th and 19th centuries. Some of the published accounts of these early travellers describe with great admiration the architecture of the town and the beauty of the Perth Bridge. One or two mention the activity which most early tourists undertook, that of looking through the window in the Gowrie House (prior to its demolition in 1806) through which James VI shouted for help during the event known as the Gowrie Conspiracy. The first guide books aimed specifically at visitors to Perth were published as early as the 1820s.

At the dawn of the 20th century Perth thus considered itself to be

The Pavilion Theatre opened in 1928 on a corner of the South Inch beside the
Marshall Place and Edinburgh Road junction. The owners aimed to put on a series
of twice-nightly summer shows, particularly for tourists to the city. The Pavilion was expected
to be 'a permanent place of entertainment where "Pierrot" shows can be enjoyed',
Pierrots having hitherto performed in the open air on the North Inch behind Charlotte Street
and near Barossa Place. In the post-war period the theatre became a transport café which
finally closed in 1968. It was demolished five years later.
Courtesy of Perth Museum and Art Gallery, Perth and Kinross Council.

something of a tourist town. The local press would regularly comment
on the number of holiday-makers in the streets and the council were
well aware of the need to make the town as attractive as possible for
both residents and tourists. By 1924 the council had an Advertising
Committee whose efforts in highlighting recreational activities such as
putting, tennis and listening to band concerts on the North Inch had
been quite successful in attracting visitors to the city. On the eve of
World War Two the council, having failed to attract new industries,
decided instead to focus rather more on tourism. With the advent of
war, though, the implementation of this policy was delayed by 30 years.

In the 1960s, a period when the council was desperately trying to
tackle the growing problem of unemployment, the tourist industry was
rapidly expanding. This was due to those many visitors who were still
in work, the 'never had it so good' generation with higher levels of
disposable income who, thanks to foreign exchange restrictions, were
discouraged from yet discovering the delights of Benidorm. In the middle

of that decade Lord Provost Ritchie stated that out of the whole of
Scotland Perthshire was second to only Edinburgh in terms of numbers
of visitors. Realisation struck the local press first. The *Perthshire Advertiser* stated in 1966: 'We should recognise that Perth is essentially a tourist
centre and that tourism is now our largest and most rapidly growing
industry.' It then urged residents to plant flowers, create floral displays
and generally welcome visitors to Perth with colourful front gardens,
window boxes and hanging baskets. This coincided with the formation
of a committee to encourage the floral decoration of city buildings as
part of the national tourist industry's Britain in Bloom campaign. Such
was the power of the press that within three years Perth had won the
large burgh category of the Scottish section of Britain in Bloom.

The council agreed in 1968 to invest more in tourism and appointed
25-year-old John Grainger as the city's first tourist manager. 'Given a lot
of money and a fair bit of time,' he said, 'wonders could be worked,'
and how right he turned out to be. Not only did he start with a major
advertising campaign but made sure that those attracted to the city

The city's floral displays have become increasingly interesting and topical since
the early drive to promote tourism in the 1960s. This display at Dewars Corner,
close to the ice rink, focused on curling.

would be inspired to stay through the provision of wide-ranging entertainment and activities. There then followed a series of events new to
Perth, all designed to appeal as much to visitors as to residents. The first
Fair City Week was held in 1968 and featured, among others, a parade
of floats through the city streets, a boat race on the Tay and a gymkhana
on the South Inch. The following year's event also included a race from
the top of Callerfountain to the top of Kinnoull, a distance of almost five
miles, which attracted around 100 competitors, several of whom were in
fancy dress and one even on a unicycle. The 1971 and 1972 events also
included Beat Festivals which, in a city already well patronised by big
names in pop, proved to be some of the best attended events in the City
Hall in many years. Even local skinheads behaved themselves and did
not draw attention away from the Bay City Rollers who were the main
act in both years. A Perth Festival of Sport was also inaugurated which
included a Dunkeld to Perth canoe race. A 40 per cent increase in visitor
numbers in 1969 and an industry worth £1.2 million to the Perth
economy in 1971 showed how effective the new appointment had been.

Grainger's concerted drives to attract more tourists were highly
successful and after the biggest-ever campaign in 1972 the Perth Tourist
Association received around 25,000 enquiries from interested holiday-
makers. There was something of a lull while he took a regional tourist
appointment in the later seventies but he returned in 1982 as manager of
the newly formed Perthshire Tourist Board. This coincided with a letter
in the *Perthshire Advertiser* from a disgruntled tourist, complaining about
dilapidated buildings, shabby shop fronts, potholed roads and even unwashed curtains. Such views were compounded in 1988 when a consultants' report, commissioned by the district council, concluded that Perth
had a low level of recognition outside Scotland and had an air of 'shabby
gentility.' There was worse the following year when an American film
director very publicly declined to film in Perth because of litter and dog
mess. This was the challenging background against which Grainger had
to work. He continued to press the case for investment in tourism as a
major local industry and proved his point in the mid-80s when a £15,000
promotional campaign netted an estimated £7 million return.

The district council took heed of the negative comments and in tandem
with other organisations, such as Take a Pride in Perth, Perth in Bloom,
Perth Enterprise Company and Perth Partnership, set about the task of
cleaning and beautifying the city. Plaudits quickly rolled in, the most

Perth's tourist information centre has had a somewhat nomadic existence,
wandering from one desert area at the old waterworks to another at the Lower City Mills.
Its sojourn in the busy High Street was brief.

eye-catching when the residents of Perth and Kinross were named as
enjoying the best quality of life in Britain (well OK, among 145 medium-
sized local authorities), an accolade which the council dined out on for
a number of years, while conveniently overlooking the fact that the area
had later slipped down the rankings.

After the initial success in floral competitions there was again a
fallow period in the seventies, though local guides and junior members
of the Royal Horticultural Society of Perthshire laid the foundation of a
floral revival when between them they planted almost 50,000 crocus
bulbs on the South Inch beside the Edinburgh Road and along Marshall
Place. The renewed vigour of the 1990s gave Perth a string of successes
in Britain in Bloom, the pinnacle of which was reached in 1994 when
the city, representing Britain, came third in the European event, the
Entente Floriale. Tourist statistics showed record numbers visiting the
city and there was even talk of Perth becoming Scotland's 'leisure
capital', a title it surely deserved in 1991, if only briefly, when Perth won
the title of 'Scottish Tourism City', beating Edinburgh into second place
and winning particular praise for its leisure facilities, the welcoming

As visitor numbers began to increase so too did the bed and breakfast establishments
which now line the main routes into the city. These, in Pitcullen Crescent,
illustrate the importance of being near the top of the Yellow Pages list. For anyone seeking
a business opportunity there is not, as yet, an Aardvark Guesthouse.
Courtesy of Iain McDonald, Glossop, Derbyshire.

attitude of the people, and the efforts of the 'Take a Pride in Perth'
campaign.

This same decade also witnessed a revival of tourist-orientated events,
though on a more sophisticated level than Fair City Week of the late
1960s. These included the Scottish Food Proms, which developed into
the Perth Food Festival, and the Perth Motor Festival which was centred
on the Dunkeld Road's string of car dealerships, the celebrated motor
mile. The latter attracted as many as 35,000 visitors in 1998, one of the
main attractions being *Thrust SSC*, the vehicle which had won the world
land speed record earlier that year. The biggest festival of all, of course,
was the Perth Festival of the Arts which began in the early '70s and gave
a tremendous boost to the city's cultural reputation.

Grainger's talent for attracting visitors to Perth was not restricted to
tourists only. National organisations including the Scottish political
parties had been holding their annual conferences in Perth for many
years, attracted by its central position in Scotland and by the capacity of
the City Hall. By mid-century the city was gaining a national reputation
as a conference centre. Perth's tourist chief quickly appreciated the value
of such events to the town coffers but even he would have been
surprised by the estimated £100,000 spent in Perth, not by wealthy Tory

delegates but by the trade unionists of the STUC at their 1976 conference – 'the biggest-ever conference bonanza' said the press. A developing and prosperous conference industry throughout the 1980s nevertheless suffered some setbacks. In 1981 there were adverse comments about the City Hall from the SDP after their conference and in 1989 there was a real sense of shock when the Scottish Tories, after 13 years in Perth, decided to hold their 1990 conference in Aberdeen. The district council very quickly pushed through plans to update the City Hall's facilities which in turn prompted declarations by both the Tories and the SNP that they would return to Perth on a regular basis. By 1992 conferences accounted for ten per cent of Perthshire's tourist industry though there was continuing disquiet about the suitability of the City Hall for an increasingly sophisticated and demanding clientele. The council continued in piecemeal fashion to update and improve the building throughout the 1990s but its days were numbered and it was eventually replaced as the city's premier gathering place by the Perth Concert Hall.

By the time John Grainger retired in 2001, as chief executive of one of the most successful tourist boards in Scotland and with a well-deserved MBE to his name, the industry was generating around £377 million to the local economy, equating to 36 per cent of the Perthshire GDP, and was supporting around 11,500 full-time jobs. But even then he was only too aware how fragile a flower tourism could be and how numbers could suddenly drop because of external factors such as bad weather or a strong pound. Right to the end of his career, with a decline in the industry in the offing, he continued to argue for urgent action and extra investment.

The previous two chapters have focused predominantly on the management of Perth's main businesses and industries, and in what is generally perceived as a genteel middle class town it is hard to imagine any significant level of industrial unrest. But we have already seen how tempers flared during the strikes of painters and printers in 1900 and how violence erupted during the strike at Pullars in 1917, and many other examples were to follow. That first year of peace after World War One was, in fact, decidedly unpeaceful with almost all workers demanding higher wages. They had genuine grievances in that unemployment was rising and pay had not kept in line with the huge price increases caused by war. They now had a voice locally through the Perth Trades Council which was doing much to foster trade unionism in the city, and also at both local and national level through the Labour Party which was making

its presence felt through rallies on the North Inch. 'Street orators', preaching the politics of the left in the city centre, would have aided the
Labour and trade union causes. By 1926, the year of a lengthy and
crippling coal strike as well as the short-lived General Strike, the unions
had become a force to be reckoned with, though they were also gaining
an unwelcome reputation for comments such as 'my union says I must do
as little work as possible' which, though reported in 1921, is associated
rather more with the restrictive union practices of the 1970s and 1980s.

Industrial unrest simmered again in the 1960s and boiled over
completely in the 1970s. Although the staff of some local companies
such as Dewars took industrial action it was predominantly a decade of
national dissent with significant local consequences. Some will still
remember the panic-buying of bread when bread van drivers went on
strike. There were strikes also by printing and postal workers, by brewery
and bus workers, and by dockers, whose action, or rather inaction, led
to shortages of imported fruit and vegetables in the shops. The miners'
strikes of the early 1970s brought power cuts to all areas of the city by
rotation, caused the cancellation of evening entertainments and an early
Epilogue on television, restricted the heating of offices and shops, and
even resulted in the switching off of the 1973 Christmas lights in the
High Street, a mere half-hour after they had first been switched on. A
couple of weeks later an editorial in the *Perthshire Advertiser* described
the country as staggering and stumbling 'like a Hogmanay drunk over
the threshold of 1974 into a new year whose prospects look as bright as
the blackest piece of coal.' The biggest casualty of the miners' strike was
Ted Heath himself who with his piano was ushered unceremoniously
out of Downing Street. The late 1970s saw strikes by firemen, petrol
tanker drivers and hospital workers, among others, a period better
known as the 'winter of discontent.' The infamous miners' strike in
1984–85 led to a few arrests at Perth Harbour when flying pickets tried
to prevent the unloading and distribution of coal from Europe and, at
around the same time, teachers also took industrial action.

CHAPTER NINE

The Shopping Experience

SUPERMARKET GIANTS whose names are familiar across the country have transformed the way in which we shop. Sixty years ago the idea that we could help ourselves to whatever we wanted from the shelves and just pay – with a bit of plastic – on the way out would have had most city centre grocers shaking their heads in incomprehension. Ten years ago the notion of continuous twenty-four hour opening, of buying insurance at the checkout, or of asking the checkout girl to give you cash, instead of vice-versa, was almost as alien.

The buying power and global reach of the great supermarket chains ensures that today's public has access to an enormous range of goods from around the world. Even so, the range of foodstuffs available in Perth in the later 19th century was much wider than many of us perhaps realise. Try, for example, a gastronomic tour through the August 1885 catalogue of Robert Smith, 'Italian warehouseman, family grocer and wine merchant' of 70 St John Street. There was a wide choice of teas for the early morning brew, as well as detailed instructions – actually in the catalogue – about making the perfect pot: heat the teapot, use boiling water, and allow to infuse for between 20 minutes and half-an-hour, 'the finer grades requiring the longer time.' Bacon for breakfast, of course, with toast and a choice of butter from cows fed on grass or stubble, or perhaps just the finest, richest butter from Denmark. Come mid-morning there were several varieties of coffee bean on offer, all roasted on the premises by the 'New Patent Roaster', and by way of accompaniment 30 types of biscuit on sale, ranging from Bath olivers and ginger nuts to almond and lemon rings and Niagara wafers. And for lunch, why not open a tin of boiled rabbit? Well, perhaps not, but you get the general idea.

Perth's principal shopping street, the High Street, was very different at the beginning of the 20th century. Superficially still recognizable with its gentle curve, the river at one end and St Paul's Church at the other, the everyday sights, sounds and scents from that time have long gone. The enticing smells of coffee, cheese, apples and fresh bread, free from plastic wrapping, would have wafted from the open doors of grocers,

The High Street in c.1900 with a horse-drawn tram in the distance and the Red Lion Inn on the right. Friends converse, a child pushes a baby in a pram, a dog wanders around and on the left a little girl wonders what that funny man with the camera is doing in the middle of the street. The Calderwood shop would later be demolished to make way for Woolworths.
Courtesy of Perth Museum and Art Gallery, Perth and Kinross Council.

greengrocers and bakers, and the scents from florists would vie with the less pleasant odours from drains, unwashed bodies and herds of farm animals on their way to market or to the abattoir at the Shore. There were the sounds of horses, clip-clopping on the High Street setts, of the wheels of the trams they pulled, the hammering of hot metal on the anvil of the blacksmith at 129 High Street, the gentle murmur of conversation, the squeals of the city's children playing, the raucous shouting and singing from public houses such as the Red Lion at 123 High Street, and the more melodious sounds, perhaps, from the pupils of Henry Wallace, the music teacher at the top end of the street. In appearance the street would have looked more enclosed than it does today, with the dominating presence of the General Post Office, opened in 1898, at the corner of the High Street and Scott Street and the absence of the wide opening into King Edward Street. Neither were there the wide shop fronts which major chains like Boots and Marks and Spencer now have.

Striped and coloured awnings over shop windows featured on sunny days and whatever the weather there were the many shop signs along the street at first-floor level; the open umbrella to indicate the premises of umbrella maker John Black, the pub signs, and the bronze fish outside Stobie's premises near the top of the High Street. The presence of early chain stores, such as Liptons and Maypole Dairy, which sold a limited range of groceries and dairy products at low prices, was a pointer to how the High Street would develop during the course of the century.

The street today, free of traffic and with shops closing at 5.30, is generally quiet in the evening. Not so a hundred years ago when shops stayed open for much longer. They had plenty of passing trade as the occupants of the city's many substandard and overcrowded dwellings, without the attractions of television and radio, chose to spend free time outside. Even the Post Office was open between 7.00 am and 9.00 pm, Monday to Saturday, and for couple of hours on Sunday as well. One little cameo from 1912 illustrates this very well: ten Perth confectioners with tea-rooms objected to a proposed new by-law compelling them to close their doors at 10.00 pm, as 'by far the greater proportion of their business... is

Liptons High Street shop in the late Victorian period. Bacon and smoked hams line the shop front beneath the royal coat of arms. Staff are impeccably dressed, though less so the street urchins who nevertheless seem to have been welcomed into the photo.
Courtesy of Perth Museum and Art Gallery, Perth and Kinross Council.

done on a Saturday night... between the hours of 9 and 11.30, up to which last-mentioned hour the objectors state the streets of Perth are busy with people returning from business, places of amusement and the like.' The trend in the past century, thanks partly to the early closing movement, has been towards shorter days for those serving behind the counter, though in contrast lunchtime and Wednesday afternoon closures, with a very few exceptions, are now a thing of the past. Two traditional shop holidays also disappeared in the 1970s after tourist industry pressure finally overcame shop-worker resistance. These were Midsummer Saturday at the start of the trades fortnight in early July and Inauguration Day in late August which commemorated the unveiling of the Albert Memorial on the North Inch in 1864.

Advertisements in Leslie's *Directory for Perth and Perthshire, 1901–1902* provide an amusing glimpse into the shops of Perth at that time and the products they sold. To take a few at random: William Morrison, builder and contractor of Bridgend, who had the largest selection of curling stones in town; Alexander Clyne, on the corner of South Street and Princes Street, who was advertising old Highland malt whisky for 17 shillings (or £0.85) per gallon; the Victoria Carriage Works at 219–221 South Street where carriages of all types – from Landaus and Broughams to omnibuses and dogcarts – were built; Charles Gruber, a pork butcher and sausage maker of 91 High Street; James Thomson, a sculptor at 4 Princes Street, who carved mantelpieces and coats of arms; the Perth Creamery Company of York Place who supplied butter, cream and milk; James Chalmers' Ham-Curing Establishment at 58 Victoria Street, where owners of pigs for curing were asked to send them in early in the week; the Strathmore Hotel in Bridgend, where cyclists seemed to be particularly welcome and where funerals were also undertaken; the Grand Temperance Hotel on the corner of High Street and Kinnoull Street, offering 'commercial dinners' for two shillings, as well as 'every comfort for cyclists' (except, presumably, beer); and John Campbell of Mill Wynd who sold 'home-brewed ginger beer of excellent quality, in stone bottles.'

Such advertisements paint a picture of an abundance and variety of food and commodities, all of which was to change during World War One. Food became scarce, prices rose and rationing was introduced. There was no speedy return to normality at the end of the war and as unemployment began to soar, so there was less money to spend in shops. In an attempt to stimulate British trade and thus reduce unemployment, the Government announced an Empire Shopping Week in May 1926, though it is perhaps ironic that the General Strike followed only days later. One can still hear the jingoistic echoes of World War One in newspaper advertisements such as 'British mowers for British lawns' and 'British bread for British people' which were trumpeted respectively by Garvie and Syme, the ironmongers, and Kennaway the baker, both

The interior of Montgomery's bake house at 279 High Street in 1934. The owner probably would not have won many food hygiene awards today though some would swear that the bread tasted better.
From the collection of the late Harry Chalmers, Perth.

well-known firms in the city until recent years. Another prominent business excelled itself with an advertisement for Fitu corsets which were 'made by British workpeople, owned by a British company, financed by British money, designed by British corset artists in Bristol, and obtainable in Perth at Cairds only.' Others spelled out the message very carefully, leaving no room for doubt as to where the loyalties of the Perth shopping public should lie: 'Wright's Perth-brewed ale. Keep your money circulating in Perth. Every time you order the product from an 'outside' firm you send money out of Perth, leaving less for Perth people to spend on your goods or labour.' Even the *Perthshire Advertiser* proudly stated in 1930 that the newspaper was printed on British paper on British machines with ink from British firms.

The move away from one man and his shop towards present-day supermarkets and department stores perhaps began with the establishment of the City of Perth Co-operative Society in 1871, though its founding principle, in contrast to today's temples of consumerism, was distinctly anti-capitalist. Indeed with the regular dividend for members and the fact that purchases could be made on account and paid for at the end of the week when the pay packet came home, it was particularly appreciated by the less well-off. From small beginnings the Co-op developed into one of the biggest commercial organisations of 20th-century Perth. With its main premises in Scott Street, there were at one time 20 other trading outlets in the city employing a staff of well over 400 and attracting members in their thousands. There was nothing, it seemed, that the Co-op could not supply: grocery, meat, fish, poultry, drapery, furniture, books, joinery, decorating, evening classes, housing, milk from their own cows, and even funeral undertaking. It is not difficult to see how entwined the townspeople of Perth became with the Co-op. It survived and prospered for over a century, though its decline and ultimate merger with the Co-operative Wholesale Society (CWS) in 1985 went hand in hand with the brave new world ushered in by the Thatcher government. Perhaps its dusty image and associations with the Labour movement were too much at odds with a period of rampant and glossy capitalism. Nevertheless while the familiar Co-op shops have all but disappeared from the streets of Perth the CWS was adapting to new commercial realities. At a time when shopping malls and retail parks were being proposed for the city the firm put in an application to transform its former Scott Street premises into a huge retail complex. The site was ultimately used for housing though the CWS for a number of years maintained a more fashionable presence in Perth through its home furnishings store, Concepts, in the St Catherine's Retail Park.

We have the Co-op to thank for introducing two major developments to Perth shopping, the self-service shop and the supermarket. What was probably Perthshire's first self-service enterprise opened in the Co-op's premises in York Place in December 1956. The *Perthshire Advertiser* commented on this new style of shopping which was coming over from the USA where it was already very popular. The same goods were available as before, it announced, though without the inevitable waiting in a queue. The self-service process was described, beginning with the checking in of the shopper's bags in exchange for a carrier bag. The shopper then helped herself to items from the shelves, paid the check-out girl and received her own bags back. The only disadvantage to this new way was that 'the shopper tends to take things she wants but does not really need.'

Perth's first supermarket was opened by the Co-op in June 1963 on the site of their former central grocery store in Canal Street. Customers now had access under one roof to meat, fish, fruit, vegetables, spirits, groceries, bread, cakes and even hardware goods. Large glass windows

A Co-op shop window in 1951 piled high with goods. Take a closer look, though, and admire the way the packets of breakfast oats, desiccated cocoanut [sic] and Semola have been carefully arranged and balanced. Little wonder they called in the photographer when the display was finished.
Courtesy of Perth Museum and Art Gallery, Perth and Kinross Council.

fronted the store and inside were mirrored walls, brilliant lighting, refrigerated units and three check-out points. In the wake of the Co-op came other supermarkets such as Masseys which opened in December 1965 in a brand new building on the corner of the High Street and Kirkgate, a site formerly occupied by Garvie and Syme. The store's advertisements placed great emphasis on the range of stock and the cleanliness of the premises. 'We are more than hygiene-conscious,' said the new general manager. 'We satisfied the most hygiene-conscious town in Britain [referring to Aberdeen] and I think we will do the same here.' Cooper Fine Fare, Templeton, William Low, Presto and Tesco also set up supermarkets in the central area but with the exception of Tesco none survived the advent of the larger edge-of-town stores.

The council, meanwhile, were themselves considering the shopping facilities in central Perth and were aware that Dundee and Stirling were

The western end of the High Street in 1963 at a time when coal was still being delivered to city centre flats. The Louis Flood Collection. Courtesy of Perth Museum and Art Gallery, Perth and Kinross Council.

even then enticing shoppers away from the Fair City. In 1956, with the Meal Vennel slums in the process of being cleared, they held an architectural competition to design a new city centre to fill the vacant space. A Glasgow firm of architects was successful and in 1961 the new St John's Square, consisting of shops, offices, housing and a garden of remembrance, was completed and opened at a cost of just under £250,000. It was described at the time as 'a scheme of considerable architectural value and a good business and economic proposition.' One of the most popular businesses here was The Music Shop, partly owned by the late Sir Jimmy Shand. It was taken over in 1967, renamed Concorde, and became the main source of records for the pop-loving youth of the city for many years. In time, however, the modern 1960s architecture became somewhat old-fashioned in appearance, and the dimly lit arcades, shaded by wide pillars, provided, as one shop proprietor described it, 'a haven for skinheads and layabouts.' Another small shopping development was built in Scott Street in the mid-1960s on the site of the Wilson Church.

As supermarket shopping became the norm the companies themselves sought ever-larger premises with additional land for car parking and, as suitable sites were hard to come by in the city centre, they began to look for edge-of-town sites. It was obvious to many, however, that if such developments were permitted to proceed unregulated the whole focus of city shopping would move away from the centre to the outskirts, to the detriment of existing city centre food shops. The first clash between the town council and the supermarkets came in 1971 when Asda were refused permission to build a store at Inveralmond. This refusal hardened into

The St John's Square shopping and housing development looking somewhat down-at-heel.
This photo may have been taken just prior to its demolition. The several coats of arms
of the royal burgh decorating the square at first floor level are a measure
of the civic pride felt when it was first opened in 1961.
Courtesy of Perth Museum and Art Gallery, Perth and Kinross Council.

firm policy in 1974 when the council decided in principle to refuse any development over 1,000 square metres outwith the central area. Tesco, however, were given permission for a supermarket on the Edinburgh Road in 1975 on the grounds that it was serving the Moncreiffe and Friarton areas. When this store opened two years later the promotional material referred to a 'fabulous new discount store' with 17-inch colour televisions on sale at £190 and digital clock radios for £20 (which nowadays probably come free with a packet of cornflakes). Other big supermarket names put in applications for edge-of-town developments but the district council resolutely followed the policy of its predecessor and turned them down.

Supermarkets were not the only ones eyeing up Perth. In the same period the big national chain stores flooded into the High Street, following the few such as Boots and Woolworths who had blazed the trail in the 1920s. Boots had a High Street shop by 1923 and Woolworths had already demolished their original store and were building a second, a brand new two-storey shop, by the time Marks and Spencer opened their first in the mid-1960s. Marks and Spencer vacated this shop, adjacent to Meal Vennel and backing onto St John's Square, and moved to their present site in 1979 whereupon British Home Stores, and later Primark, took over their old store. A Wimpy Bar opened in 1968, and many other national names, familiar from High Streets around the country, fought for prime central locations. In 1974 Mothercare acquired the prestigious corner site formerly occupied by the General Post Office. Everywhere there were new building societies, prompting complaints as early as 1976 about their proliferation. By 1980 there were only six privately-owned family shops left in the High Street.

The shopping revolution continued on an even larger scale in the 1980s. A harbinger of the change to come was the announcement in January 1980 that House of Fraser was to build a huge four-storey department store on the site of the old fire station in King Edward Street and extending into the High Street. Later that year plans for three separate massive shopping complexes were announced, the first by Littlewoods who hoped to develop the area between Meal Vennel and Scott Street,

A site being cleared in the High Street for Perth's first Woolworths store in the 1920s.
Courtesy of Perth Museum and Art Gallery, Perth and Kinross Council.

including the site of Central District School, the second by Grampian Properties (a wholly-owned subsidiary of the GA) who proposed to create a shopping mall between High Street and Mill Street, and the third by the firm of G. Percy Trentham who had another part of the High Street in their sights. Littlewoods dropped out the following year on account of the deepening recession but this did not deter Grampian Properties whose plans for three large stores, 44 smaller shops, housing and extensive parking were given permission in principle. Entry to the huge scheme, however, hinged on the willingness of Boots to sell their shop, and when the council approved a major extension to their store Boots announced that they were going to stay, thus putting an end to the High Street-Mill Street mall in that format.

Meanwhile G. Percy Trentham was taking a closer look at the area which was no longer of interest to Littlewoods. They quickly made successful offers for both the Central District School site and Rattray's High Street shop and by the end of the year had announced plans for a £20 million shopping mall on the site of St John's Square. In 1982 another developer took over the scheme for High Street-Mill Street and having devised another entrance to it, not dependent on Boots, it was back in the running again. That summer, however, the council considered both proposals and finally opted for Trentham, a decision – 'one of the most momentous in Perth's recent history', according to Provost John Mathieson – which marked the end of the debate.

Inevitably the protests soon started. Councillors Jean Hamilton, a rebel without a cause since the closure of the steamie, and Willie Wilson took up cudgels on behalf of the St John's Square residents who faced rehousing, and Perth Civic Trust argued that Meal Vennel, one of the city's most historic – and least attractive – streets, should not be allowed to disappear under the new mall. The decision went to two public enquiries, at which appeared the eminent historian Archie Duncan to back the Civic Trust line, before the mall was given the final go-ahead. Eviction notices were issued and the demolition of St John's Square started in the summer of 1985. The mall, now named the St John's Centre, was officially opened by the Duke of Westminster in 1988 and at the time of writing, approaching its 25th year, is as integral a part of the city centre as ever. Its continuing success, perhaps, is due to the minimal architectural impact on the High Street and South Street façades, which has prevented the mall from appearing dated, and to the demands of

Meal Vennel, or simply The Vennel as it was often called, in the 1930s. Much of this characterful thoroughfare was demolished in the 1950s and replaced with soulless back entrances to shops and goods areas for servicing the St John's Square development. Its final date with the demolition men in the 1980s was a controversial issue.
Courtesy of Perth Museum and Art Gallery, Perth and Kinross Council.

modern retailing which have ensured that the shops inside look as attractive and appealing to the shopper as they did 25 years ago.

While this was going on in central Perth the district council's ageing edge-of-town shopping policy was suffering more and more blows from the supermarket chains and big retail stores trying to hammer their way in. William Low tried for a Crieff Road site but had to settle for the former Bells headquarters in Victoria Street, and Queensway and B&Q were similarly rebuffed. By the mid-1980s the council was virtually under siege, encircled by commercial giants tossing dozens of flaming multi-million pound planning applications over the defences. When the regional council, like the cavalry to the rescue, suddenly took the responsibility for shopping matters out of the district council's hands and into their own, the district council was outraged and subsequently appealed, in vain, to the Secretary of State for Scotland to reverse the decision. The upshot was that the regional council finally approved the William Low development on the Crieff Road, rejected Asda's plans for a store at Broxden and

St Catherine's Retail Park near the city centre with its strongly angled blue roofs and acres of parking. Major improvements were proposed in 2010.

formulated a new shopping policy which envisaged a retail park on the fringe of the city centre. Even this development, approved by both region and district, underwent a series of planning refusals and appeals before receiving the final rubber stamp. The development site, later named the St Catherine's Retail Park, extended to 28 acres and included the mart which was about to be vacated by United Auctions. MFI was the first to announce a presence in the retail park in 1989, Safeway successfully bid for the site of the former mart and firms such as Halfords and Currys, which had previously squeezed into small city centre shops, relocated to the much larger and more suitable warehouse-style premises where they were joined by several other major national firms such as B&Q and PC World.

While national names are now familiar in the High Street there have been instances when the converse was true, when local shops could boast customers the length of the country. The firm of Charles Rattray, tobacco blender, dated back to around 1912 and became known as one of the finest cigar and tobacco shops in Britain. Pipe-smoking premier Harold Wilson had long been a connoisseur of Rattray's blends and visited the shop when he was in Perth for the Scottish Labour Party conference in 1971. The oak-panelled High Street shop with its cedar-lined tobacco room was better known to most locals for its carved wooden figures, including one of a kilted highlander (for those who mourn its passing it can still be seen, if you ask, in the collection of Perth Museum and Art Gallery), and for its range of 17th- and 18th-century Dutch tobacco jars. Rattray closed in 1981, as did Alexander and Brown, a firm of seedsmen who owned large premises in South Methven Street. In 1929, around 30 years after the establishment of the business, they had thousands of customers throughout Britain, including the royal family, and were exporting seed to countries as far as Canada, the USA, Kenya and India. Malloch of Perth was established in 1875 by the great angler, P.D. Malloch. The firm made fishing rods, importing wood for the purpose from British Guiana, had a taxidermy department, made and exported salmon and trout flies all over the world and acted as agents for landowners wishing to let salmon beats and grouse moors. The name still survives in a shop in the Old High Street but the business has no other connection with the original firm.

A nocturnal view of Norwells High Street shoe shop in 1955. The Norwells were a respected family of shoemakers whose advertising slogan was 'Trust the man behind the boot.'
Courtesy of Perth Museum and Art Gallery, Perth and Kinross Council.

Old established businesses with a predominantly local reputation include Banks in St John Street, which began life in 1831 as the St Catherine's Ropeworks, and is now more concerned with ski-ing and outdoor sports equipment. Cairncross the jewellers, also in St John Street, dates back to 1869 and remained in family ownership until 1988, having been run by the most gentlemanly grandsons of the founder. There are several other shops in Perth which have been a part of city life for many decades: those still trading include Holdgates (fish and chips), Dunns (art supplies), Peddies (ironmongers) and Watsons (china). Those which have ceased trading include Woods (bakers), whose first-floor tearoom was a favourite of General Accident staff across the

The interior of MacFisheries High Street shop in (probably) the 1960s.
Courtesy of Perth Museum and Art Gallery, Perth and Kinross Council.

road, the craft shop which occupied the Fair Maid's House, Humes (ironmongers), Norwells (shoes), Joe Anderson (sports goods), R.A. and J. Hay (stationers and booksellers), Bob Croll (toys), and Cairds (clothing). Even Woolworths, a focal point in the High Street for over 80 years, finally closed its doors in 2009.

One of Perth's best loved shops is McEwens which still occupies its original site in St John Street and can boast a wide and loyal clientele, some of whom have been patrons of the business for over half a century. Established in 1868 as a drapery store it gained a reputation as *the* place to shop when James Brough, one of the owners, began travelling to Paris and returning with the latest designs from the capital of fashion. More recently, under the ownership of the Bullough family, the shop has expanded into neighbouring properties in South Street and Watergate and is now one of Perth's largest independently owned businesses. Even now it caters primarily for women though 50 years earlier it did so almost exclusively, and many an elderly Perth male will recall the feeling of discomfort when required by his wife to enter the dreaded portals of McEwens.

The stylish interior of Noel Hamilton's St John Street fashion store in 1960.
Courtesy of Perth Museum and Art Gallery, Perth and Kinross Council.

At the beginning of the 21st century the city centre was dominated by the big national chain stores, by banks and building societies and by those few remaining local shops which could afford the business rates on prime properties. The continuing financial crisis of recent years and the double-dip recession, though, have taken their toll and a number of prime retail properties – including a few units in the St John Centre – are lying empty. The majority of purely local shops tend to be found just off the High Street, or in the Perth suburbs such as Bridgend, Letham and Craigie. Supermarkets have come and gone, sweeping into the centre in the 1960s and just as quickly retreating. The city centre of the early 20th century, with its myriad grocers, butchers, bakers, greengrocers and fishmongers, has gone for ever, leaving only a handful of their number still surviving.

CHAPTER TEN

Housing: The Building of Greater Perth

WHEN JOHN PENMAN retired in 1960 after 21 years as burgh surveyor for Perth, a post which would now equate to a local authority's director of planning, he was described in the press as the 'architect of Greater Perth.' This phrase might raise an eyebrow today but almost half a century ago it was an apt description of what was outwardly a new city.

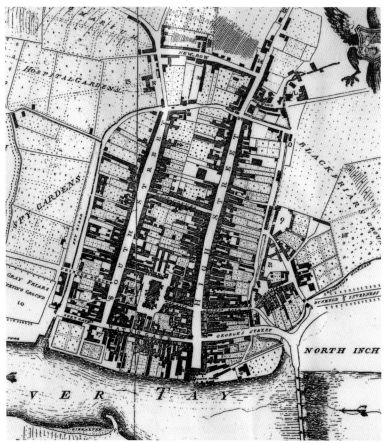

This extract from Rutherford's map of 1774 shows just how compact the city was at that time.
Courtesy of the A.K. Bell Library Local Studies Department, Perth and Kinross Council.

Until the mid-18th century Perth had spread little beyond its mediaeval boundaries which could be considered as a rectangle bounded by the Tay, Canal Street, Methven Street and Mill Street. Maps of around 1800 show that new building was either planned or underway to the north and south of the town, generally bordering the Inches, which in time was followed by the villas in Craigie, in the Balhousie Street area, along the Glasgow Road and on the lower slopes of Kinnoull. Almost all of this new housing was for the middle classes. Most of the working class population, which had greatly increased in the late 18th and early 19th centuries in the wake of agricultural reforms in the country, were still crammed into ancient and poor housing in central Perth and Bridgend, some of which had been described in 1898 as worse than the slums of Edinburgh and Glasgow. These twin social problems of slums and overcrowded dwellings were the principal spurs to the rapid growth of housing in 20th-century Perth, which in turn led to the concept of a 'Greater Perth.'

In the later 19th century several Scottish cities were given powers, by local Acts of Parliament, to knock down slums and build new streets and houses. Perth's turn came in 1893 with the *Perth Improvement Act.* The preamble starkly states the facts: '...Many of the dwelling houses in certain districts of the burgh are old and dilapidated, and in ruinous condition, and unfit for human habitation, and such districts are so densely populated as to be injurious to the moral and physical welfare of the inhabitants... and it would effect a great public improvement and be conducive to the public health if various houses in such districts were taken down, and the said districts reconstituted...' The Act went on to specify five separate 'works', the main ones resulting in the linking up of Kinnoull Street and Scott Street and the creation of

The junction of Mill Street and Castlegable, a quaint corner of Perth which has gone for ever.
Courtesy of Perth Museum and Art Gallery, Perth and Kinross Council.

King Edward Street, all of which were duly completed within the specified ten years. Not all the evictions went smoothly, though, some being described in the press as 'lively.'

The clearance of slums and demolition of poor quality and derelict housing continued through much of the century. In the years immediately preceding World War One the council put a number of closing orders on 'unsavoury-smelling dwelling houses' in Meal Vennel, Thimblerow, Skinnergate and Castlegable, and others were 'put into a proper sanitary condition' with the provision of lavatories and water. Major clearances included firstly Thimblerow in the 1920s, which was laid out as a children's playground, and then Castlegable in around 1930, on which was subsequently built the new art gallery. Pomarium, or the Pow or Powmarry as it was called, and parts of Meal Vennel and Stormont Street went in the 1950s, and Commercial Street and other properties in the Old High Street area in the 1970s.

The council's first attempt at house-building was triggered by the *Perth Improvement Act* which required them to build 'working men's

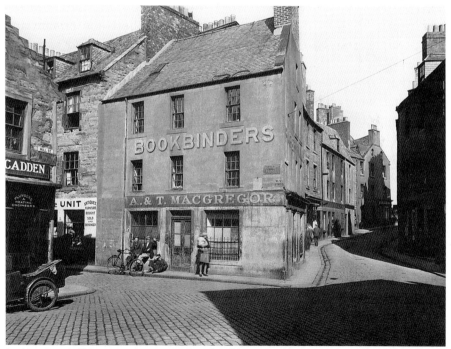

Looking from Mill Street, at the corner of Castlegable, up into Bridge Lane. A photographer today, standing in the same spot, would be looking towards Perth Museum and Art Gallery. Courtesy of Perth Museum and Art Gallery, Perth and Kinross Council.

housing' for those who found themselves homeless as a result of the improvement works. Thus in around 1900 they erected a tenement block in the Old High Street, now St Catherine's Court, and another, St Johnstoun's Buildings, on part of the site of the old gas works on the corner of Victoria Street and Charles Street. Tenements in South Street and at the Shore were also built at this time. As new tenants subsequently found to their cost, though, the rent for a 'working man's' flat was rather too high for the average 'working man's' wage. The true era of council housing was kick-started by the publication in 1917 of the report of the Royal Commission on the Housing of the Industrial Population of Scotland which highlighted the shameful reality of poor quality housing, slums and lack of sanitation, together with the failure of both the private and public sectors to do anything about it. The Commission estimated that almost a quarter of a million new homes, houses not tenements, were required throughout Scotland and put the onus firmly on national government, working through local authorities, to bring this about. Lloyd George took up the cause, uttering his much-quoted phrase before the 1918 general election that Britain must be 'fit for heroes to live in', and after the election enacted the necessary legislation to allow the housing crusade to begin.

St Johnstoun's Buildings were one of the first blocks of 'working men's' housing built by the council for those displaced by the Perth Improvement Act.
From the collection of the late Harry Chalmers, Perth.

The local response was fast, the lord provost acknowledging at the end of 1919 that 'the housing problem demands our immediate attention.' The following year work began on 16 houses at Darnhall Drive and another 40 in Dunkeld Road, though progress was hindered by the post-war difficulties of sourcing materials and labour unrest. Residents from the condemned Thimblerow moved into the completed Dunkeld Road scheme in 1925 whereupon the council embarked on another 150 houses on various sites. In 1926, for example, 84 three-apartment houses were underway at Murray Crescent, consisting of living room, two bedrooms, bathroom and kitchen, complete with sink, wash tub,

Some of the city's first council houses were erected in Dunkeld Road in the early 1920s,
before Muirton Park was built.
Courtesy of the A.K. Bell Library Local Studies Department, Perth and Kinross Council.

boiler, cooker and space for a larder and coal store. The rent was to be
£25 a year. In spite of a flurry of new building the demand for housing
was still depressingly high with 370 applications for 56 new houses in
the Crieff Road-Dunkeld Road area. This was hardly surprising, considering there were still instances of chronic overcrowding where families
of seven shared only one room. To ease the situation the council in 1926
bought 50 Atholl steel houses, named after the 8th Duke of Atholl who
after World War One had the bright idea of bringing together the twin
problems of a steel surplus and a housing shortage. Although no
cheaper to build, these houses with steel panel walls could be put up
more quickly than conventional bricks and mortar. They were erected in
the Crieff Road and Craigie areas. In 1930 a total of 226 traditionally-
built houses were planned for Friarton, mainly for Castlegable slum-
clearance purposes, and in 1935 a similar number were announced for
Tulloch. By 1936, after 15 years of intensive building, there was still talk
of a housing crisis and to tackle it the council announced further large
schemes to be undertaken by them and private developers, particularly

at Muirton where the burden of building 600 new houses was to be shared by the council, Perth Housing Association and by developer David Beat. World War Two put a temporary stop to the building programme though schemes already underway, such as the final phase of the 600 at Muirton, were allowed to be completed. By this time the council had built a total of around 2,000 houses which over a 20 year period averages about one every three days. It is little wonder that unemployment was almost unknown among the building trades at that time.

In 1943 the council began to look ahead to a post-war Perth where they reckoned housing would once again be in desperately short supply. There were already 1,800 on the waiting list in 1939 and it was expected to get worse. In the four years up to June 1943 there had been over 2,000 marriages in Perth, the majority of them with at least one spouse serving in the Forces, and these new couples would expect to be housed on their return from war. Continuing problems of unfit dwellings and overcrowding also still needed to be addressed, all of which contributed

An aerial view of the 1930s showing the construction of the Friarton estate.
The Edinburgh Road is in the background.
Courtesy of Perth Museum and Art Gallery, Perth and Kinross Council.

to an estimated shortfall of 3,000 houses by the end of the war. With commendable foresight the council acquired land for between 400 and 500 houses in 1943 and more sites were being considered. Further thought was also being given to improving the quality of council housing by way of better soundproofing, more storage, central heating (in spite of most people's preference for an open fire) and the provision of utility rooms to make kitchens more attractive for eating in. In 1947 the council's approach to housing was singled out as one of the most progressive in Scotland.

A superb aerial view of 1947 showing a mix of sport, industry, transport and housing old and new. The Muirton council estate is in the foreground, Muirton Park behind and the Dunkeld Road diagonally bisects the photo.
Courtesy of Perth Museum and Art Gallery, Perth and Kinross Council.

To alleviate the crisis in 1945 the council sought to acquire temporary prefabricated houses from the Government but such was the demand from all over the country that only 100 of the 500 requested were received. Nevertheless these were ready for occupation by the following year. Dorran prefabs were also being produced locally at Robert Tarran's works at Tulloch where they were aiming at producing 50 houses a week. The fact that the first Dorran bungalow was officially opened by the Under-Secretary of State for Scotland, with the local MP and the lord provost in attendance, underlines the important role of prefabs in relieving the post-war housing crisis. Dorran flourished, if only briefly, in these years and by the mid-1960s was providing prefabs for use all over Scotland, Ireland, the north of England and even in Antarctica. The Perth prefabs were gradually replaced over the years, the last ones to go being those in Dunsinane Drive and Birnam Crescent in 1984.

In the ten years up to the end of 1955 the council had built around 2,450 of the 3,000 houses they had estimated would be required. Of these, 350 were temporary houses at Tulloch and Potterhill, 514 in Moncreiffe, 1,300 in Letham, and a further 160 were built at Darnhall and Muirton

A bleak view of Dorran prefabs at Hillyland in 1963, with Anderson shelters still in the back gardens. Designed as temporary housing only they were at this stage well past their prime. Courtesy of Perth Museum and Art Gallery, Perth and Kinross Council.

to complete those pre-war schemes. A further 700 houses were still planned for Letham which, as Perth's biggest estate with several thousand inhabitants, was also a showpiece where the council attempted to put at least some of their earlier aspirations into practice. Kitchens here were all-electric and bills paid quarterly, not by a penny in the meter. Rents, on the other hand, were relatively expensive at over one pound and three shillings (or £1.15) a week, compared with only eight shillings (or £0.40) in the condemned Pomarium. The scheme was finished in the early 1960s, complete with church, primary school, community centre, old people's club, and a widened Jeanfield Road for access.

Post-war council thinking had been taken to a new level by a major report on the future development of Perth by Sir Frank Mears, one of Scotland's leading planners in the 1930s and 1940s, who had a family connection with Perth through his marriage to the daughter of Sir Patrick Geddes. Letham was thus intended to be the last big estate to go up on the outskirts of the city, with inner city redevelopment being the new focus. This resulted in 1961 in the replacement of the Meal Vennel slums with the new St John's Square development and also in the new Pomarium, Perth's first multi-storey blocks of flats, for which a high demand was anticipated because of the views. The council continued to press on: with housing at Tulloch, with plans for another eight-storey block at Potterhill, and with plans for the redevelopment of the Old High Street area and Thimblerow. One of the more ambitious proposals was to redevelop the barracks area, The Black Watch having finally left its old home in 1961. The estimated timescale for this project was 20 years and the costs £1.5 million.

In the mid-1960s the council was again aware of an imminent shortfall in housing, a figure which was put at 4,300 houses by external consultants in 1969. This was due to a number of reasons, not least of them an increasingly ageing population and households with fewer people. To meet some of the demand the council acquired a tract of over 300 acres of farmland to the north of the city, incorporated it within the burgh boundary and announced plans for a major new housing estate together with a new golf course. Detailed plans for the first phase of housing at North Muirton were approved in 1969 with the whole scheme expected to include 1,500 homes and take a further three or four years to complete. The first tenants moved into North Muirton in 1970, paying a weekly rent almost double that of the first Letham tenants. Characterised by

Commercial Street prior to its demolition and replacement with the
award-winning new housing scheme.
From the collection of the late Harry Chalmers, Perth.

trees, grass and curving roads, and distinguished by having Perth's first
metrically measured house, it was the last and perhaps most successful
of the large schemes built by the council. The golf course, though, never
saw the light of day.

The council's most controversial scheme concerned Commercial Street
in Bridgend, an historic and for many years desperately run-down area
where flats in the 1930s were auctioned off for double-digit sums little
more than a teenager's pocket-money today. The replacement of its 88
houses, some dating from the 18th century and most below the 'tolerable standard', was first proposed in 1967 and was financed in part by
a grant from the Gannochy Trust. There was, however, considerable
opposition to the scheme, mainly from the newly constituted Perth Civic
Trust, who tried in vain to save at least some of the most historic
buildings, such as the Old Ferry House. Further opposition came from
the Scottish Georgian Society and the Scottish Civic Trust and there was
little surprise when the whole matter went to two public enquiries, one
of which at least resulted in the saving of the Cross Keys Hotel. The
objections were ultimately withdrawn when it was recognised that it
was too late to save the street and the Perth Civic Trust endeavoured
instead to ensure that the new scheme would be architecturally worthy of

Paul Street, taken in 1967, was demolished as part of the redevelopment of the
Old High Street area. The name survives only as the road leading to the Thimblerow car park.
From the collection of the late Harry Chalmers, Perth.

the old. And indeed it was, winning a clutch of commendations ranging from a Saltire Society award in 1980 to a European award for its outstanding use of concrete in 1984. The ultimate in national recognition, however, was its appearance on the 31p postage stamps of 1984.

Marginally less controversial was the massive (for Perth) 12-storey tower block proposed for Thimblerow to which the Civic Trust objected on the grounds that such a development would be utterly incompatible with neighbouring buildings such as the 18th century city mills. The council responded by suggesting and then approving a nine-storey block instead, which the Civic Trust, not beating about the bush, described as 'a wanton act of civic vandalism.' The Royal Fine Art Commission for Scotland threw its weight behind the Civic Trust, after which, in 1973, the council backed down and Thimblerow has remained a car park ever since.

The whole area around the Old High Street had been branded 'a sheer disgrace to any town' by Councillor Norman Renfrew in 1970 and was ripe for redevelopment. The council had more success with this and demolished 268 houses in the Milne Street-Market Street area, replacing them with three nine-storey tower blocks. This, their biggest-ever redevelopment up to that time, was completed in 1975. The later 1970s saw work begin on redeveloping the barracks and the area behind

North Methven Street. Financial stringency resulted in some delays to the scheme which, along with the new Drumhar Health Centre, was finished in the early 1980s.

In spite of these developments the housing situation was steadily worsening in the 1970s. House prices were rocketing, old houses were being demolished for the new inner ring road, Ugandan Asian refugees were arriving in Perth and the council house priority waiting list, which stood at almost 500 names in 1975 had soared to 1,100 two years later. In 1977 over a quarter of Perth homes were still below the 'tolerable standard', a term which could mean a number of things including the inconvenience (no pun intended) of having to share a lavatory. One very visible sign of the council's desperation were the flats and houses in Main Street in Bridgend which had been long discussed and which were finally given approval in 1971. They were built on the site of Bridgend Church and of Bridgend House where members of John Ruskin's family used to live. The flats are doubtless in keeping with Main Street but it is somewhat ironic that the houses by the river, which spoil the setting of the eastern end of Perth Bridge, were built where one of the world's most influential art critics used to play as a boy – he whose first published work argued that buildings should accord with the local environment.

Compounding the housing shortage was the developing problem of the deterioration of the original housing estates, in particular at Muirton and Hunter Crescent. As early as 1963 one writer had noted that 'there

The unfortunate over-development of a highly attractive site beside the river, close to the bridge. John Ruskin would not have been amused.

are streets in the inter-war housing areas which are already as grim and forbidding as 19th century slumdom, where vandalism is prevalent and humane manners are hard to seek.' In 1972 Hunter Crescent was given a facelift: houses were modernised with new kitchens and bathrooms, the area was landscaped with trees, and car parking, improved street lighting and play areas were provided. Houses in Cromlix Road and Muirton were later treated in a similar manner. But the Hunter Crescent improvements did not last long and within three years the residents, some of whom had been remarkably public-spirited by building themselves their own community centre, were calling for further action and a change of name. In Muirton, meanwhile, glue-sniffing, anti-social behaviour and vandalism, to the extent of several deliberately started major house fires within a few months, were literally destroying the community as well as any sense of community spirit. As one resident commented in 1982, 'I've never lived in a place like this in my life before.' It wasn't long before it was officially designated an 'area of multiple deprivation' and described as one of the worst housing estates in Scotland. The council and the Scottish Development Agency, armed with a multi-million pound campaign chest, began the fightback in the later 1980s, focusing initially on Hunter Crescent. With significant input from the residents it resulted in a revitalised area, complete with the new name of Fairfield, which on completion was described as an 'outstanding example of housing-led urban regeneration.' A massive project to transform Muirton, described as Perth's biggest-ever urban regeneration programme, was announced in 2004. Work on the £40 million scheme began in 2007 and the new street of Lark Avenue was the first to be completed. The depressing sight of boarded-up flats, burnt-out houses and forlorn stretches of wasteland, which once characterised Muirton and Hunter Crescent, have now been replaced with bright modern housing (some owner-occupied), pleasant gardens and tree-lined streets.

One contributory factor to the shortage of council housing was the right of tenants to buy their own council homes, a controversial piece of legislation which was brought in by the Thatcher government in 1980. Before then, though, councils had had the right to sell council houses to sitting tenants if they so wished and Perth Town Council first exercised that right in 1971. When the district council announced in 1979 that they would do likewise, and with discounts of up to 50 per cent depending on the length of tenancy, they were besieged with enquiries. Between

Some of the red-stone bungalows which form the Gannochy estate, Perth's 'sunshine suburb', which was begun by A.K. Bell in the 1920s.

1979 and 1982 the council sold 1,000 houses, this at a time when their rate of building was 1,000 every ten years, and by 1988 they had sold more than half their total housing stock, much of it to tenants in Letham and North Muirton. It must have seemed like a losing battle.

Building homes for rent has never been the sole preserve of the council. Individuals and organisations, some taking advantage of subsidies offered in the 1920s, responded to the housing crisis in various ways. A.K. Bell, for example, purchased the lands of Gannochy from the Earl of Kinnoull and between 1924 and 1931 built around 150 detached bungalows. Though far from complete in 1926, it was described at that time as 'a new and charming garden suburb'. High praise later came from Neville Chamberlain who said, 'I have visited many housing schemes but this one is unique in character and certainly the best I have seen.' In recent years the Gannochy Trust has built over 60 sheltered housing units in that still most attractive of suburbs. Whisky rival Lord Forteviot, whom we came across earlier as Lord Provost John Dewar, built cottages for his workers at Necessity Brae and after his death the Forteviot Trust built homes at Pomarium. Church Army Housing was busy at both Windsor Terrace and Carlile Place, the latter named after the Rev. Wilson Carlile, the organisation's founder. Perth Housing Association was similarly active at Florence Place and Muirton, while the City of Perth Co-operative Society focused on the Feus Road area. The work is carried on today by, amongst others, the Caledonia Housing Association which since 2011 has been the successor body to the Perthshire Housing Association. It not only provides hundreds of homes for rent throughout the area but has an ongoing construction programme including, at the time of writing, the latest phase of the Muirton regeneration programme.

The subsidies offered to private developers had a marked effect on Perth, not only in the number of houses they built but also on the appearance of the city. David Beat was one of the first large-scale developers in Perth and even in today's property pages the description 'Beat bungalow' will conjure up an immediate mental image of a neat, light stone bungalow with a central front door and a bay window surmounted by an archly pointed eyebrow of a roof. He was also a pioneer of the modern trend to restore old property: in the later 1920s he acquired Rosebank, an old mansion house on the lower slopes of Kinnoull, and subdivided it into three flats, each with electricity and 'every modern requirement.' Beat advertised extensively in the 1930s, describing his houses at Muirton Bank and Burghmuir as in 'undoubtedly the best residential areas in Perth,' while those at Viewlands were convenient for the new Academy and came complete with tiled bathrooms and power points in every room. Later he completed a scheme at Pitheavlis, on land he had acquired before the war, and by 1957 was advertising sites at Rhynd Road, Pickletullum, Bridgend and Scone: 'Our name your guarantee! Your house planned to your liking. Completely finished, ready to live in. Front wall and double gate with nine-foot wide path. Fences, clothes poles etc.'

The press noted in the pre-war period that 'large numbers of bungalow buildings which are being erected in the suburbs are indicative of an increasing desire on the part of householders to become owner-occupiers.' Another private developer, Neil S. Sutherland, whose houses in the Oakbank area and elsewhere are still much admired, took up this theme in his own advertisements. 'You can become your own landlord!' he said and outlined a hire-purchase arrangement which made a total price of £475 for one of his houses. There was clearly a desire to improve living standards across all areas of society, from those who dwelt in the overcrowded and poor quality houses at Pomarium to those who saw home owning as the next step up the social ladder.

The 1960s saw the further development of schemes at Burghmuir and Oakbank with building firms such as Thain, Wimpey and A. & J.

A row of typical Beat bungalows in Muirton Bank. David Beat was a prolific builder who left his mark not just on Perth but on places such as Dundee and Cupar as well. He was a keen traveller and survived the great San Francisco earthquake of 1906. He died in 1943.

Stephen to the forefront. In 1970 over 150 houses in Oakbank Road were approved, as were over 100 large houses set in large gardens on the lower slopes of Kinnoull Hill, in the triangle between Mount Tabor Road and Hatton Road. This latter decision was controversial, one objector describing it as the 'rape of Kinnoull Hill' but as we have seen the council were under tremendous pressure to build at this time. The £7,000 average build cost of the Kinnoull houses, let alone the £11,000 price tag, was almost double the actual sale price of new, albeit smaller, properties in Oakbank, a statistic which doubtless reflects the cost of prime building land and the quality of the new development. Prices which seem ludicrously cheap today had nevertheless been rising steeply, even as much as threefold in ten years in some areas. The local press of 1973 bemoaned 'the present rocketing price in private housing [which] has put even the cheapest of these out of the reach of many.' A further leap in the late 1970s pushed the price of the average detached Perth house to around £29,000 and yet another in 1983 to over £40,000. In 1988 the average Perth villa was changing hands for around £54,000, a figure which had almost trebled by the end of the century. The financial crisis which began in 2007 has successfully applied the brakes to runaway house prices which have since fallen in the Perth area by an average of about nine per cent.

By the mid-1970s the council had pinned their hopes of relieving the housing crisis on the westwards expansion of Letham but were held up for a number of years by the failure of the Scottish Development Department to make a firm decision on the line of the western bypass. The council had initially envisaged about 400 houses in that area but the Draft Tayside Structure Plan, which was published in 1979, increased that figure to a massive 1,200, of which over 400 were to be council-owned, though the council later decided against building there themselves. This was reckoned to be the last major housing development planned for Perth in the 20th century. When the last public enquiry into the line of the bypass had ended and permission to proceed was finally granted the big developers moved in, though they too held matters up by disputing with the council who should pay for the main distributor road and the creation of public amenity areas. Wimpey was the first to submit detailed plans and were followed by Barrett and A. & J. Stephen. There was further controversy when Norman Renfrew stepped down in 1996 as chairman of the Perthshire Housing Association citing as one reason the 'major tragedy' of there being no homes to rent at the western edge. And with no council housing either this large middle-class owner-occupied suburb is perhaps the ultimate local manifestation of Mrs Thatcher's 'property-owning democracy.' Its roots were well in evidence, though, in the work of David Beat and others, and it suddenly flourished in the early 1970s, well-watered by the advent of numerous building societies, the establishment of the Perth Property Agency (only the second of its kind in Scotland), and the

This plaque indicates the former premises in the Watergate of the Night Shelter for Females, one of the early institutions in the city devoted to the care of the homeless.
Courtesy of Iain McDonald, Glossop, Derbyshire.

phenomenon of rapidly rising house prices. And more is still to come. In 1991 plans were announced for a housing development in the Almond Valley, which by 1996 had become a huge and highly controversial project for a 1,000-home self-contained new village costing in the region of £100 million. This later grew to a proposed 1,800-home development which at the time of writing is the subject of an appeal to the Scottish government.

The homeless, like the poor, have always been with us and various institutions in Perth have cared for them over the years. One early example was the Night Shelter for Females which was opened in the Watergate in 1902, providing a bed for itinerant and destitute women. They were taken in at 7.00 pm each evening and given a simple meal of rolls and tea while spiritually uplifting literature was read to them. At 7.30 the following morning the doors were opened and they were sent on their way. Greyfriars, the council-run hostel in Princes Street, started life in the mid-1920s as urgently-needed temporary accommodation for those awaiting permanent homes. It was financed by Lord Forteviot who also provided money at the same time for the rebuilding of Skinnergate House, an institution for the homeless which originally dated from 1859. Perhaps he rather overdid the refurbishment as the press referred to it as 'an Hotel de Luxe for the toiling and too often homeless labourer.' By 1982, though, Skinnergate House, with a capacity of only 89 men, was unable to cope with the growing number of rough sleepers in Perth. This situation led to the founding of Perth Cyrenians, who took over the old abattoir in Shore Road and turned it into a comfortable home for eight men, and later provided another home in the Crieff Road area for recovering alcoholics. They are now based in St Paul's Square. The work of the Cyrenians has been complemented since the 1990s by day-care and hostel facilities provided by Churches Action for the Homeless, better known as CATH. Skinnergate House reopened in 2001 after a £1.7 million transformation and is now run by the Salvation Army. Some residents have the opportunity of graduating to one of the eight resettlement flats in the recently revamped Salvation Army building in South Street before returning to fully independent living.

The travelling community are by definition hard to pin down but the council made a big effort to provide a permanent site for them in the early 1980s. After swithering between former railway land at Tulloch and an area at Doubledykes, close to the Inveralmond Industrial Estate, they finally opted for the latter and incurred the anticipated bitter protestations from nearby residents and businessmen.

The housing of the elderly became the focus after World War Two, particularly in the wake of the opening of Bowerswell Home in 1950 as the city's memorial to the dead of that war. In the following decade the council opened Rosslyn House, the former poorhouse, as a second care home, and agreed to look for a suitable site for a purpose-built third. This only materialised in 1975 with the opening of North Inch House beside Balhousie Castle. Another council-run home, Beechgrove House, was opened on the site of the old Burghmuir Hospital in 1984. Kincarrathie House, the former home of A.K. Bell, was converted into another home for the elderly by the Gannochy Trust in 1961. Perth's first sheltered housing unit was established at North Muirton in 1973 and a second at Strathmore Street the following year. Others have opened in response to the gradual ageing of the population, including the Tayside Nursing Home (which has since closed and been demolished) and Viewlands House, both formerly owned by the General Accident. A children's home was established in 1950 at Cleeve, the former home of Sir Francis Norie-Miller, though it lasted only five years. Another, Colonsay House, was opened in North Muirton in 1974 and it too has closed. The big residential complex at Upper Springland for adults with physical or learning difficulties was completed by the mid-1980s. It was funded entirely by the Gannochy Trust and is owned and run by Capability Scotland.

CHAPTER ELEVEN

Transport: A Blessing and A Curse

TRANSPORT HAS BEEN both the making of Perth and its curse. The railway and the bus brought immense benefits to the city in terms of wealth and employment while the tram and the car conversely brought financial headaches and many tedious and ill-tempered years of serious traffic congestion.

The century began with the supremacy of the railway which linked Perth to almost all parts of Great Britain. The one thing, though, that a train could not do was provide in-town public transport and to fill the gap the first bus and tram services were developed. While Perth remained within its mediaeval bounds there was little need for public transport, but as it stretched south-westwards towards Cherrybank and as Scone, developing north-eastwards, gradually came within the orbit of central Perth for shopping and employment, the distance between these two points made some form of transport service desirable. A horse-drawn bus had been operating between Scone and Perth since the early 1860s but it was the decision to build a tramway, usually only found in the larger cities, that gave Perth both a status symbol and a transport system to be proud of.

The Perth and District Tramways Company was initially a private company operating horse-drawn cars. It was, however, coveted by the town council who after some preliminary posturing agreed to take over the company at a cost of £21,800 in 1903. The wisdom of such a move was debatable as within a relatively short time the tramway was losing money. In an attempt to staunch the outward flow of cash the council had decided by 1905 to do away with horses and power the trams by electricity instead, but to no avail – this in spite of the cheapest possible electricity being supplied by the council's own generating station. By 1910, and regarded at this time as one of the most important council services, the tramway was still losing money and the council were trying various measures to turn the finances around. These included the display of advertisements, both on the cars and along the routes, cheap return tickets and a limited Sunday service. The tramway limped along until 1925 when, facing stiff competition from cars and buses, the council seriously considered winding it up. The only problem, though, was that the tramway was by now around £30,000 in debt and there was still a faint hope that its fortunes could be revived and the debt paid off. The matter came to a sudden and dramatic conclusion on 7 November 1927 when with hardly any notice the newly formed Perth General Omnibus Company started up in direct competition with the tramway. At a meeting that very evening the council decided to phase out trams, buy nine buses at a cost of £14,000, hire others and start an immediate service.

The last tram ran in 1929 and by 1930 the rails were being lifted, leaving behind few physical reminders and plenty of memories. Some recalled thinking of tram drivers as sea captains with their ruddy cheeks exposed to the open air all year round, plying at a slow and stately speed the routes between the distant destinations of Scone and Cherrybank, the Cross and Craigie and the Cross and Dunkeld Road. In open country between Scone and Perth a top speed of 16 miles per hour was possible but in town, and in particular when negotiating a corner, the speed could

An electric-powered tram, photographed in 1910, trundles across Perth Bridge on its way to Cherrybank, the two passengers on the top enjoying the open views across the river. The advertisement on the side is for Robert Hay's drapery store in George Street which they will shortly be passing.
Courtesy of Perth Museum and Art Gallery, Perth and Kinross Council.

be as low as two. Others remembered the threepenny fare between Perth and Scone, the becushioned interiors and the less comfortable tops which were open to the elements.

Buses, however, were more popular with the Perth public, if only for their greater speed. By the middle of 1928 the Perth General Omnibus Company was finding the competition too fierce and agreed to sell its 12 buses to the council for the sum of around £9,000. Fares immediately went up: to pay for the bus war, for the recently purchased new buses and for a new corporation bus depot at Riggs Road which was completed in 1930. The council's victory over a rival bus company was, however, short-lived. In 1934 W. Alexander and Sons offered £22,000 for the corporation bus service, plus an annual payment of £1,500 for 21 years, and gave the council the right at the end of that period to resume bus operations if they so wished. Still servicing the huge debt incurred by the tramway the council found the offer too tempting to turn down. Many townspeople, though, had different ideas and not only organised a petition of several thousand signatures but protested so vociferously outside the council chambers that departing councillors required a police escort home. Alexander's ran the city bus service for much of the remainder of the century, operating latterly as Strathtay Scottish, until they ended up in a bus war with Stagecoach and went out of business.

A busy scene at Perth Harbour in c.1960.
Courtesy of Perth Museum and Art Gallery, Perth and Kinross Council.

Even though Perth has had direct trading links with Europe since mediaeval times, many visitors to this inland hill-surrounded city are surprised to find the presence of a harbour. A quay was situated at the foot of the High Street from the earliest days of the city's history until at least the 18th century, since when the servicing of ships has taken place at various points further downstream. The harbour in its present location dates from the earlier 19th century and was the home port for many ships, some locally built. Tall-masted sailing boats dominated the harbour in the early 20th century though they were gradually replaced by steam- and then diesel-powered vessels. Responsibility for the harbour was assumed by the town council in 1956 and is still vested in Perth and Kinross Council today. Much of the cargo either loaded or offloaded at Perth is connected with the Perthshire agricultural industry. Fertilisers arrive at high tide and potatoes and oats depart at the next; timber, cement and fuel for the neighbouring gas works were also regularly delivered. The harbour was still prospering by the end of the century though in the mid-1970s, when a controversial extension to the dock labour scheme was proposed, its survival seemed in doubt. At the present time, statistics over the past few years seem to indicate a slow

Bute Drive, North Muirton at 4.00 pm on 18 January 1993. The vehicle in the distance belongs to the water services department of Tayside Regional Council.
Courtesy of the A.K. Bell Library Local Studies Department, Perth and Kinross Council.
© Slim Shot Me Photography, Perth.

and steady decline in the number of ships using the harbour, a problem the authorities have grappled with – not always successfully – on many occasions over hundreds of years.

The Tay has contributed much to the wealth and stature of the city but on occasions there is a payback. The recorded history of Tay flooding goes back to 1209 when a flood swept away Perth's castle and drowned the king's son, and many serious floods have been regularly reported ever since. One of the first of the 20th century occurred in 1909 and plunged parts of the city into darkness when water seeped into the electricity generating station at the Shore. Further floods occurred in 1950 and 1974, the latter giving the new North Muirton estate, built on a flood plain, a four-feet deep reminder of its precariously low position beside the Tay, following which the council agreed to build a floodbank to protect its housing investment. While this proved effective against the flood of 1990, the worst since that of 1950, it could not withstand the devastating inundation of January 1993, which was caused by a period of heavy snow followed by a sudden thaw and which laid waste large areas of Perth and Perthshire. While awe-struck spectators in central Perth flocked to the river, wondering if the Queen's Bridge would survive the huge pressure of water and staring with mild amusement at the

Many Perth folk were saddened by the loss of the lime trees in Tay Street which were felled in October 1998 to allow work on the flood defences to proceed.
Courtesy of the A.K. Bell Library Local Studies Department, Perth and Kinross Council.

canoeists, the sand-bagged buildings and the submerged cars, the situation was becoming almost tragic in North Muirton and other parts of the city where hundreds of residents were being forced out of their homes, not to return for several months. This resulted in the massive multi-million pound flood prevention scheme which in the last years of the century was built between North Muirton and the harbour.

While the river has finally – perhaps – been tamed the weather has not. Flooding in recent years has resulted from monsoon-like downpours in the summer months which have inundated areas of the city, causing a substantial stone wall at Bowerswell to collapse and damaging retaining walls at the riverside beside Perth Bridge. Indeed the flooding of July 2010 which this author saw while on holiday, courtesy of YouTube, was described as the worst since that of 1993.

That Perth used to have a civil aerodrome with scheduled flights to other parts of the country is often as surprising to local residents as the presence of a harbour is to visitors. The building of an aerodrome was first proposed by the town council in 1934, in response to earlier encouragement from the government and the then Prince of Wales. This resulted in a flood of letters to the press, some from those who saw the financial benefits to industry and tourism, and others who saw it ultimately as part of the government's preparations for war. A 170-acre site at Newlands, just to the north-east of Scone, was purchased towards the end of that year and the new aerodrome was opened in June 1936 by Viscount Swinton, the Secretary of State for Air. Lord Provost Robert Nimmo stated at the ceremony that Perth had always been a transport centre and would not be left behind in air transport. Even so, from its earliest days, the aerodrome hosted an RAF Reserve flying training school run by Airwork Ltd on behalf of the Air Ministry and it was to Airwork that the council entrusted the management of the aerodrome. However, as far as the council was concerned, its main function was as a civil aerodrome and by the outbreak of war scheduled services had been established between Perth and Glasgow, Renfrew, Aberdeen, Inverness, Newcastle, Leeds, Doncaster, London and even Stavanger in Norway. Airlines such as North-Eastern Airways were keen to emphasise that onward flights from these destinations could be taken and stated in advertisements that 'passengers leaving Perth by air in the morning land at Amsterdam or Berlin the same day, or at Rome or Athens the next day.' A Perth-London airmail service was inaugurated in

Perth Aerodrome from the air, taken in 1948.
Courtesy of Ralph Tilston, Broughty Ferry.

1938, the first flight carrying greetings from Lord Provost Nimmo to the Lord Mayor of London and to the Member of Parliament for Perth, Thomas Hunter. Britain was close to war in that year and another training scheme, the Civil Air Guard, was launched whereby volunteer civilians were trained to fly on the understanding that they would join the RAF Reserves in time of emergency. Almost 250 applications were received for the training which was undertaken by the Strathtay Flying Club. Such preparations for war were seen as a boon by the council which received a much greater than anticipated income from the military use of the aerodrome.

The council's hope that the aerodrome would be as important to Perth as its railway station proved forlorn when after the war the government announced that Errol, not Scone, would be developed as the main civil airport for Perth and Dundee – a decision which, while ultimately abandoned, prompted the council to sell the aerodrome to Airwork in 1946. This, and the subsequent ending of its role as an RAF Reserve flying school, led to a change of direction in the mid-1950s from passenger services and military aviation to the training of commercial pilots and aeronautical engineers. Many overseas students were attracted to these courses (in 1965 there were 230 students from 47 countries) and

Pilots of the RAF Volunteer Reserve at Perth Aerodrome in 1948, with their Gipsy Moths behind them. Flying Officer (later Wing Commander) Eric Tilston is pictured fourth from the left. Courtesy of Ralph Tilston, Broughty Ferry.

what became known as Britain's air university, one of the largest flying schools in the world, gave Perth in the 1960s a 'United Nations flavour.' In 1993, and by now operating as Air Service Training (AST), the company announced plans to expand the aerodrome as the main passenger and freight airport for Tayside. Perth and Kinross District Council were in favour but Tayside Regional Council were not. In hindsight this was possibly a final attempt to ensure the survival of AST at the aerodrome as, in 1996 and just four months after the 60th anniversary of its opening, commercial pilot training ceased and the aerodrome was sold. This might have been the end of the story had Perth College not stepped in and taken over AST with a view to developing aeronautical engineering courses. In 2011 AST teamed up with ACS Aviation to provide, once again, commercial pilot training at the aerodrome.

The first major event in Perth's love-hate relationship with the car was a fatal road accident which took place on a Saturday evening in November 1901. Thomas Gourdie, a Glenfarg blacksmith, had been driving around the streets of Perth, visiting friends in various parts of the town and quite possibly, as young men do, showing off a little. Just prior to the accident he was seen driving at speed up the crowded High Street, in zig-zag fashion, forcing pedestrians to jump out of the way and causing one observer to comment that he, the driver, would kill someone if not careful. Tragically that was to prove true within minutes. Outside the General Post Office Gourdie took an unexpected swing into Scott Street and ploughed straight into a crowd of people in the road, coming to a halt with a wheel actually resting on a young boy. The boy died shortly afterwards and four others were injured. According to the press the furious crowd, quickly growing to an estimated 2,000 strong, first of all lifted the car off the boy's body and then turned on the driver and his car and vented their anger. The car was almost destroyed, with even the solid rubber tyres being slashed. Gourdie had most of his clothes ripped off and would possibly have been lynched had some of the crowd, and then the police, not intervened to protect him. The car was finally restarted and Gourdie was driven away to safety. He was allowed to return home that night but the following day was arrested and kept in custody while awaiting trial. The remorseful Gourdie was eventually found guilty of culpable homicide but recommended to leniency on account of a number of mitigating factors. These included his estimated speed of only four miles per hour which was deemed to be safe, the high

Frews Garage on the corner of Princes Street and Canal Street in 1922.
Courtesy of the A.K. Bell Library Local Studies Department, Perth and Kinross Council.

level of background noise in the street which prevented the car from being heard, the acknowledged tendency of some vehicles to get stuck in the tram lines (see the film *Genevieve* for evidence), and the fact that he was sober. He was sentenced to three months' imprisonment.

The post-World War One boom in car ownership was reflected in a flurry of newspaper advertisements such as one in 1922 by the Perth Garage, on the corner of York Place and Caledonian Road, who were sole agents for the Morris Oxford and the Austin 7 and who supplied petrol for all motorists. Frews were advertising themselves in 1923 as agents for Fiat, Talbot, Darracq and Ford and offered a battery service station and a parts and tyre service. Valentines, near the City Hall, were agents for Vauxhall, Alvis and Humber and by 1933 Strathmore Motors in Bridgend were offering new and used cars, a guarantee with every car over £35 and free driving tuition. And even though driving was described in 1922 as a slow and uncomfortable experience, because of potholed roads, car owners were liberated from the limitations of destination and departure time imposed by public transport and those of distance and incline imposed by bicycle. There really was a new and exhilarating sense of the freedom of the road.

Valentines Garage in King Edward Street on a snowy day.
Courtesy of Perth Museum and Art Gallery, Perth and Kinross Council.

To meet the demands of a new generation of motorists the council set about improving the city's roads. At the turn of the century those that were not already tarmacadamed were generally dusty in dry weather and muddy in wet. The surfacing work continued and was given a boost in 1912 when the council installed a 'bituminous macadam mixing plant' at Craigie Haugh, prompting the local press to look forward to a dust-free city. By the mid-1920s the council was spending large sums on extensive road improvements. In the later 1930s they undertook what was described as their 'most ambitious road improvement scheme of recent years' when, to ease the density of traffic at Muirton Park and the ice rink, they built a dual carriageway along that section of the Dunkeld Road. A number of bridges over railway lines were widened during this period, including the Glasgow Road bridge in 1930 and a little later the bridges at Dovecotland and Crieff road. The main bridge improvement, though, was the replacement of the unsightly Victoria Bridge. First announced in 1956 the initial proposals included a temporary bailey bridge to be built by the army between the foot of the High Street and Commercial Street, roughly following the line of the short-lived bridge which was washed away in the flood of 1621. This plan, designed to ease congestion during construction work, did not materialise. The new bridge, a graceful structure in stark contrast to its predecessor, was opened by the Queen in October 1960 and named the Queen's Bridge. Noticeable on the plaque at its western end is the absence of any reference to the second Queen Elizabeth. While letter boxes bearing the royal cipher ER II were blown up by the most extreme nationalists at the start of her reign, and were relatively cheap to replace, it was a different matter with a major £150,000 civil engineering project.

The romantic notion of the freedom of the open road, at least in the city, was somewhat short-lived as not long after the end of World War Two Perth began to suffer from a surfeit of traffic. The first attempt to relieve congestion was made in 1956 when the council introduced a one-way westward flow up the High Street from St John Street to St Paul's Church. The suburbs suffered too, as the following comment from a 1959 *Perthshire Advertiser* shows: 'Anybody who tries to drive through a housing scheme at night, with private cars parked on either side of the road, realises that it can sometimes be a hazardous journey.' In response the council began to incorporate garages and parking places in the Letham development. In the same year, 1959, a traffic census showed that 46 per

The Queen's Bridge being built underneath the old Victoria Bridge in 1959.
Courtesy of Perth Museum and Art Gallery, Perth and Kinross Council.

The opening of the Queen's Bridge in 1960. Queen Elizabeth is flanked by Lord Provost John T.
Young and Bert Crawford, Council Officer. The Louis Flood Collection.
Courtesy of Perth Museum and Art Gallery, Perth and Kinross Council.

cent of cars in Perth were through traffic which made the need for either a ring road or a bypass, both of which had been proposed in the 1940s, even more urgent. Traffic further increased in the following decade, thanks to ever-increasing levels of car ownership, cuts to the railway service, the growth of tourism and the opening of the Forth Road Bridge in 1964. At peak holiday times, particularly around the Glasgow Fair, there were traffic jams several miles long on the approaches to Perth and in the centre itself congestion was described as 'chaotic' and 'approaching gridlock.' Desperate drivers were even known to cut across the North Inch from Charlotte Street, pass under the dry arch of Perth Bridge and rejoin the queues in Tay Street. Congestion was in fact a national problem and one that was addressed in the Buchanan report of 1963 which proposed a number of solutions. These included the banning of cars from some parts of city centres, the demolition of buildings to create through roads, better public transport and controlled car parking, all of which the council considered and in part adopted.

The inner ring road, discussed since the 1940s and considerably modified since then, was finally agreed in principle by the council in

A policeman on point duty struggles to cope with the volume of traffic at the west end of Perth Bridge in 1959.
Courtesy of Perth Museum and Art Gallery, Perth and Kinross Council.

1971. Designed to keep through traffic out of the city centre, the plans were broadly similar to the existing inner ring today though initially they showed a new road proceeding west from Tay Street behind Marshall Place which had to be abandoned because of the cost. The only new section of the inner ring was therefore the swathe of road between Caledonian Road and Atholl Street which cut across land once occupied by the barracks. When it opened in 1976 the inner ring road was effectively complete.

The council had meanwhile been busy with other remedies, including increasing the number of one-way streets, widening streets such as the bottleneck at the foot of South Street near Speygate and Watergate and improving distributor roads such as Balhousie Street and Jeanfield Road. A new traffic and transport plan came into operation in 1973 and established the one-way two-loop traffic system which still, with minor alterations, applies today. It was initially unpopular and even the press described it as 'overkill' but its longevity is testimony to its success.

The biggest improvement to traffic congestion came with the construction of the bypass. First mooted in 1943 the bypass and other, somewhat outlandish, solutions to Perth's traffic problems were presented in a series of local and regional planning reports in the immediate post-war years. The bypass, running from Barnhill right round to Inveralmond, was the principal proposal and even then some thought that it should be continued over the river to the Blairgowrie road, as do supporters of the recently resurrected Cross Tay Link Road today. This was a bold plan and yet bolder still was the suggestion that strips be preserved at the side of the bypass for tree planting, parking and 'the landing and refuelling of light aeroplanes.' There was also a proposal to link the Edinburgh and Glasgow roads via a connecting road between Glenearn Road and Cherrybank, and indeed Glenearn Road was made wide enough to allow for at least some length of dual carriageway. Other plans included a new road to run parallel to a stretch of the Dundee Road to relieve pressure of traffic, and a new bridge adjacent to Perth Bridge which would convey traffic from Bridgend directly to the North Port. It was the Mears report of 1951, however, which was adopted by the council and which influenced the development of the city over the next 30 years or so. Not all the suggestions in this report were taken up: the diversion of Edinburgh Road traffic around the perimeter of the South Inch instead of through the middle was a laudable aim but never implemented.

After a frustrating quarter-century gestation period work finally began in 1973 on the first stage of the bypass, the Craigend interchange. This complex network of roads, a miniature Spaghetti Junction which required the excavation and reuse of 1.5 million tons of earth and rock, together with the first section of the bypass from Craigend to Broxden, was open by 1978. The completion of the bypass, however, was a controversial and tempestuous affair. The Friarton Bridge section was also opened in 1978 and immediately became the focus of a storm of complaints about the quality of the lighting, sign-posting and safety barriers. That winter many lorry drivers in Tayside, with the backing of their bosses, refused to cross the bridge in frosty weather until the barriers had been improved. The western side of the bypass proved to be even more of a problem. As a result of strong objections to the proposed route between Broxden and the Crieff Road a public enquiry was held in 1976 and the go-ahead given by the Secretary of State for Scotland. After further input from the regional council the public enquiry was reopened in 1978. In 1980, the year in which the M90 was finally completed between Edinburgh and Perth, another 'final' decision about the bypass route was reached which resulted in an appeal from a local farmer. This too was rejected whereupon the farmer threatened to take the case to the House of Lords. As soon as a compromise was reached another dispute blew up over the compulsory purchase order and yet another over the compensation due. The final 'final approval' was given in 1984 and the

The Friarton Bridge, formerly the M85 and as such the shortest motorway in Britain, spans the Tay beneath the cliffs of Kinnoull.

western bypass opened the following year. The various disputes not only held up the completion of the bypass for around ten years but, until agreement had been reached on its exact line, also progress on the housing development at the western edge.

Another way to keep city traffic moving was to keep roads clear of parked vehicles. 'No waiting' measures were introduced in the early 1960s, much to the annoyance of shopkeepers who felt the loss of trade, followed by the first yellow lines and the first traffic wardens. It was only in 1973, however, with the introduction of the traffic and transport plan, that miles of double yellow lines spread throughout the city centre. There were reports of tourists saying that they would not return to Perth because of the volume of traffic and parking restrictions, while High Street ironmongers Garvie and Syme said they were forced out of their shop by the omnipresence of yellow lines.

With these measures in place the provision of parking became urgent. When the old prison at Speygate was demolished in 1965 the council immediately turned the site into a car park and installed Perth's first parking ticket machine. More controversial that same year was the plan to use part of the North Inch behind Charlotte Street. This was strongly opposed by the townspeople whose Not an Inch off the Inch campaign forced the council to back down. Undeterred, the council tried the South Inch the following year and made another attempt on the North Inch in 1969, but had to admit defeat on both occasions after the same vigorous protests. Further demolition of old properties, including the old transport café on the South Inch in 1973, provided more parking, but such piecemeal provision and the genuine concerns of shopkeepers that customers had few places to park pushed the council towards a more radical solution – a multi-storey car park in Canal Street. While as many as six multi-storeys had initially been considered by the council in 1972 the first, after various bouts of indecision, was finally built as part of the shopping mall project and opened in 1986. The Kinnoull Street multi-storey, only the second, opened in 2000.

One of the most radical solutions to traffic congestion, first proposed in 1973, was to park cars on the edge of the city and ferry their occupants into a pedestrianised city centre by bus. This was later known as the park and ride scheme which was first tentatively launched at McDiarmid Park in the run-up to Christmas 1994 and has remained a fixture ever since, though now operating from Broxden. Thoughts of

Between the demolition of its old buildings in the 1950s and the subsequent construction of St John's Square, Meal Vennel was pressed into service as a temporary car park. The fire brigade tower and the gardens opposite the City Hall can be seen at the upper right of the photo.
Courtesy of Perth Museum and Art Gallery, Perth and Kinross Council.

pedestrianisation were first voiced in the 1960s and actively discussed by the council in the 1970s before getting the nod of approval in the 1980s. The last cars drove down the High Street in 1988 and the new-look High Street was formally opened in 1990. While the council could make some major decisions within a single day, as in the case of the tramway in 1927, others, such as pedestrianisation and park and ride, could literally take decades. The success of the High Street scheme encouraged the council to extend it into St John Street and also around St John's Kirk. Despite the initial opposition of most of that street's shopkeepers, the scheme was completed in 2003.

Pedestrians and cyclists were the intended beneficiaries of a new Tay crossing which was first mooted in 2006 by Sustrans as one of a number of lottery-supported Connect2 bridges across the country. The bridge would have linked the Isla Road with the North Inch, allowing cyclists from Scone and beyond to travel to Perth along a new cycleway, thus avoiding the heavy traffic on the main roads. Despite widespread public support – with the notable exception of North Inch golfers who objected to the bridge's proposed encroachment onto the golf course – the plans were abandoned when the costs soared and when a local organisation changed its mind about allowing access to the bridge across its land.

Looking back at the (almost) gridlocked Perth of the 1960s and the prediction made in 1970 that if car use continued to grow at the same rate as it had done the city would need a four-lane one-way system in the central area by the year 2000, then we have to be thankful for the decisions which restored the speed of through traffic to a reasonably acceptable level and that of travel in the city centre to a gentle walking pace.

CHAPTER TWELVE

Water, Sewage and the Story of Steamie Jeanie

TO IDENTIFY BY the frontage alone the one building in Perth which did so much to improve the daily lives of its inhabitants, and which today has a very different function, you would need some knowledge of Latin and a cryptic crossword mind. The Latin phrase *aquam igne et aqua haurio* (I draw water by fire and water), which is inscribed above the entrance to the Fergusson Gallery in Tay Street, is a clue to the original function of the building as the city's steam-powered waterworks. Even the engine house's chimney was, and remains, well disguised as a column topped with an urn. The largely unremembered Adam Anderson, who designed the building and who thus contributed greatly to the health of the city through the provision of a safe water supply, must rank as one of the heroes of 19th-century Perth.

The building which today functions as the award-winning Fergusson Gallery was originally built in the early 1830s as the city's waterworks.

Until 1832, when the waterworks were in operation if not yet complete, the city's drinking water was drawn from the heavily polluted lade, the waters of which were used for industrial purposes further upstream, and from the Tay at the North Inch which was chemically impure and considerably further away. Anderson's system drew water from the Tay opposite the waterworks, filtered it, stored it in the reservoir inside the cast iron dome, and from there pumped it to outlets around the city. In time, as the city grew, additional reservoirs were built at Wellshill, Burghmuir, Viewlands and Muirhall, the entire expanded system still being pumped by the engines in Tay Street. In the early days not all areas of Perth were within reach of the new supply. Bridgend, for example, received water from the Bridgend Water Company, though when it was analysed in 1875 it was found to contain considerable levels of organic animal matter.

Perth water, however, was not 100 per cent clean either and even before World War One there was a growing awareness that the purity of the water supply, designed in the 1820s, would no longer be adequate for the 1920s. Part of the problem was the fact that the original intake was from the tidal part of the Tay which washed sewage backwards and forwards over the collecting chamber with inevitable results. Lord Provost Archibald Ure Wotherspoon, responding to complaints about Perth water from the Scottish Board of Health, said in his Christmas message in 1919 that 'the question of a pure water supply must be dealt with without undue delay.' The council therefore decided in 1924 to approve a £290,000 scheme to bring three million gallons of water daily to the city from Loch Ordie near Dunkeld. Such massive expenditure would have increased the rate burden significantly and thus the proposed new supply was a highly controversial issue in local elections. A newly formed Ratepayers' Association argued their case so well that every candidate who supported the Loch Ordie scheme was defeated at the polls. By 1927 the council had given final approval to an alternative £125,000 scheme which involved taking water from the Tay at Woody Island, opposite Scone Palace, and pumping it to the waterworks at Tay Street before chlorinating it and pumping it to the city's old reservoirs at Burghmuir and Muirhall, and to a new one at Viewlands. The scheme was completed in 1930. The last major improvement to the water supply was the inauguration of the new waterworks at Gowans Terrace in 1965. As Princess Alexandra performed the opening ceremony the pumps in the Tay Street waterworks were switched off after more than 130 years of faithful service.

The safe removal of foul water was apparently not as high a priority as the bringing in of clean. Sewage had always been disposed of by pumping it straight into the Tay, though at the start of the 20th century this practice was causing concern among the city's water officials and also the fishing proprietors further downstream. A sewage treatment plant was discussed at the time but it was believed the expense would bankrupt the city. Perth philanthropist A.K. Bell, however, did not give up on the idea and at the time of the Loch Ordie debate was one of the few to champion the view that Perth's water problems would be better solved by removing sewage from the Tay locally rather than piping in an uncontaminated supply over a long distance. He therefore made over to the Gannochy Trust, in 1941, 120,000 shares in Arthur Bell & Sons for the purpose of funding new sewage treatment schemes for the city and for the towns and villages immediately upstream. The only proviso was that the trustees should make the funds available to the town and county authorities within 20 years of the gift, or in other words by 1961. This was duly done and the new sewage purification scheme at Sleepless Inch, beside the Tay and beneath the summit of Kinnoull Hill, was opened by Dr W.G. Farquharson, chairman of the Gannochy Trust, in 1971. At the ceremony he reminded the gathering that A.K. Bell had himself commissioned a full report into the feasibility of building a city sewage treatment plant as early as 1925 and this, finally, was the fulfilment of his wishes. Sewage from the east side of the Tay was now gathered beneath the grounds of Hillside Home before being pumped across the river in a pipe suspended from the railway bridge. Two other pumping stations, at the South Inch and Friarton, pumped the estimated daily Perth total of 21,000 tons of sewage (including industrial effluent) through three miles of piping to the purification plant at Sleepless Inch. Duly processed and rendered safe, the sludge was sold to farmers for manure and the liquid residue was returned to the Tay.

When considering the history of the utilities in Perth it is perhaps surprising to find that the city's gas works, also designed by Adam Anderson, were up and running several years before the waterworks. In production by 1824, the Perth Gas Light Company had filled the entire block between Charles Street, Canal Street, Scott Street and Victoria Street with a gas production plant, a gasometer for storage, and vast amounts of storage space for coal. A very obvious rival, the Perth New Gas Light Company, started up in 1844 at Blackfriars Wynd with a gasometer a third more capacious than at Charles Street. They amalgamated in 1868 and were taken over by the Gas Commissioners in 1871 who in turn passed their responsibilities to the town council in 1901. The need for a new gas works became apparent towards the end of the century when the old works struggled to meet the demand for fuel for

The city's gas works in 1909. A railway siding delivered the many tons of coal which were required each day to keep the city supplied with gas.
Courtesy of Perth Museum and Art Gallery, Perth and Kinross Council.

the increasing number of gas cookers and gas fires in the homes of both Perth and Scone. As gas production required a huge amount of coal (one day's record output of gas in 1940 required 120 tons of coal) it made sense to site the new gas works as near as possible to the harbour where coal was delivered. It was opened in 1901 and supplied the city right through the nationalisation of gas in 1949 until 1962 when Perth, newly connected to the developing national grid, began to receive its supply from Fife. Gas received a boost from the gradual introduction of central heating to Perth homes. Advertisements from 1959 offered systems from £250: 'And think of the labour you'll save! No fires to lay and light, no fuel to store and carry, no dust and ashes to clear up.' In 1975 homes in Perth were being converted to natural gas which was cheaper and, unlike town gas, not poisonous. Street lighting by gas was finally phased out in the 1960s but not before the following exchange in the letters column of the *Perthshire Advertiser*. Marjorie Dence, the owner of Perth Theatre, described the new electric lighting in Isla Road in 1957 as 'hideous', which prompted the response that 'the sodium light is nowhere near as hideous as the feeble, dismal, grossly inadequate light provided by its antiquated gas predecessors.'

The electricity generating station at the Shore was in operation by 1901 and within one year had over 200 customers and was powering electric street lighting in small areas of central Perth. By the early 1920s it was being adopted in more and more homes, particularly for lighting but also for cooking and other domestic purposes. Its use was encouraged in advertisements by the Perth Corporation Electricity Department such as this in 1921: 'For 5 hours out of 24 you live under artificial light, therefore use the best – electric.' By 1931 the generating station was 30 years old and with over 3,000 customers was approaching its maximum capacity. Even so, it was still regarded as one of the cheapest and best electricity supplies in the United Kingdom and the possibility then being discussed that in future the city might buy in a supply from the Grampian Electricity Supply Company was not widely welcomed.

These metal plaques, which relate to the first supply of electricity to the town, can be found in several places around Perth. Civic pride can again be seen in the prominence given to the coat of arms beneath which is the inscription Electric Lighting 1900.
Courtesy of Iain McDonald, Glossop, Derbyshire.

Grampian Electricity was based at Blackfriars in Perth and from its Rannoch hydro-electric power station (opened in 1930) was beginning to supply parts of rural Perthshire and Angus with electricity via its colossal and unpopular network of pylons. In 1933 the council reached an agreement with Grampian Electricity to take its main supply from them, though the council continued to administer the provision of electricity to the city. Power now came mainly from the hydro-electric schemes of highland Perthshire, though the generating station at the Shore, which had been transferred to Grampian Electricity, was still used to boost supplies during the winter and at other peak times. That same year, 1933, also saw the completion of not only the national grid, which stretched from central Scotland to the south coast of England, but also Grampian Electricity's Tummel Bridge hydro-electric power station which fed surplus power into the grid. Homes throughout Britain were now connecting to the electricity supply at a rate of 2,000 per day, and housewives were using the new source of power for vacuum cleaners, washing machines, kettles, irons as well as for cooking and lighting. The arrival of electricity in the home must have been a life-changing event, the only downside being the requirement of tenants to have a supply of coins for the meter.

Perth electricity continued to be among the cheapest in Scotland and was becoming the fuel of choice for more and more townspeople. The press in 1938 mentioned a doubling of usage in ten years and the building of substations to supply new housing at Muirton and Crieff Road. The war, of course, led to shortages of almost everything, including electricity, and it took some years for a degree of normality to return. The Perth Corporation Electricity Department urged its customers in 1946 to use as little power as possible in winter, and repeated the message in somewhat stronger terms the following year, which also happened to be the harshest winter in more than half a century. The message for 1947 read: 'It is absolutely essential to reduce electricity consumption at certain hours during the winter months. Electricity consumers are therefore urgently requested to refrain from switching on electric fires between the hours of eight and ten in the morning and four and six in the afternoon. Continuity of supply this winter can only be obtained with the help of consumers in reducing their demands at these times.' The North of Scotland Hydro-Electric Board took over responsibility for the city's supply in 1948 and as post-war restrictions eased so the love affair with all things electrical blossomed. Television was advertised in 1951 as 'coming your way' and sales received a huge boost when the BBC televised the coronation of the Queen in 1953.

When considering the advent of gas and electricity to Perth it should be remembered that both were entirely dependent on coal: coal to produce gas and coal to provide the heat source to make the steam to drive the electricity generators. Coal was also consumed in great quantities at the station and until the development of gas fires was the only heat source for most dwellings in the city. The *Perth Directory* for 1901–02 lists 26 coal dealers, including the Alloa Coal Company, the Co-operative Coal Society, and the Lochgelly Coal Company, whose livelihood helped make Perth the grimy, smoke-blanketed and sooty city it undoubtedly was. The evidence is no longer obvious, though it can still be seen on some older buildings and many will still remember the blackened walls of the General Post Office in the High Street.

The first telephones were installed in Perth in the 1880s and by the turn of the century the National Telephone Company had around 500 Perth subscribers. The exchange, for local calls only in those early days, was initially at 60 High Street before moving to first-floor premises in Scott Street. When the National Telephone Company was taken over by the Post Office in 1912, the exchange moved to the GPO's High Street building. The first installation, judging by the number, was that of Pullars who until the 1960s rejoiced in being Perth 1. When that number became untenable they opted for Perth 23456. Johnson Apparelmaster fell heir to the Pullars number and even though it nowadays has an extra six at the front the distant echo of Perth 1 can still be detected. The telephone system quickly developed and in 1885 a Perth-Dundee line was opened as the first stage in linking Dundee with Edinburgh and Glasgow. Engineers and dignitaries marked the occasion with conversation between the two cities and the whistling of *Auld Lang Syne* down

An early telephone exchange in Perth in the days of operators and party lines.
Courtesy of the A.K. Bell Library Local Studies Department, Perth and Kinross Council.

the wire. One of the biggest events in the history of the British telephone system was the introduction of subscriber trunk dialling which, following the opening of the new telephone exchange in Canal Street in 1963, allowed Perth residents to make trunk calls direct without having to go through an operator. The city's STD or area code, 01738, is still based on the original mnemonic system whereby 73 on the dial represented PE for Perth. By the later 1970s, when the chirrup of coloured trimphones was replacing the strident bell of 1950s black bakelite receivers, Perth subscribers could dial direct to 80 per cent of the world's telephones.

One of the most controversial of all public services in Perth, at least in its later years, was the wash-house. Colloquially known as the steamie, this institution, found in many a Scottish town, has been immortalised in a popular play of the same name by Tony Roper. The original public baths and wash-house building was erected in 1846 in Mill Street opposite where the Congregational Church now stands, evidence that cleanliness was indeed next to godliness. After almost 60 years of service Sir Robert and Lady Pullar donated £8,500 towards the cost of another wash-house which was opened in Canal Street in 1905. It quickly became one of the best-used institutions in the city, particularly among the poor,

The telephone exchange in Canal Crescent, photographed in 1988.
From the collection of the late Harry Chalmers, Perth.

prompting grateful comments to the donor such as, 'Oh Maister Pullar, it's just as guid as anither room... in the hoose.' However, in spite of its early opening time of 7.00 am its popularity led to complaints about it being too busy, which in turn led to calls for another wash-house to be built elsewhere in the city. By the 1930s the deterioration of the aged Mill Street wash-house only added to the pressure on the Canal Street building, which was now approaching crisis point. In 1938 the decision was taken to double its size whereupon Mill Street would be closed down, and this duly happened in 1952. Peace seems to have reigned in the wash-house in the 1950s where, though busy, housewives were able to do a week's worth of washing, drying and ironing cheaply and in only a few hours. By 1966 this wash-house too was feeling its age and when the council were advised that modernisation would cost £25,000 they swithered between building a new one or, as it ran at a loss, closing it altogether. This was the cue for Jean Hamilton to launch a campaign on behalf of the 1,200 housewives without washing facilities to keep the wash-house open. Steamie Jeanie, which became her nickname, began by saying that 'it would only be a mere male's idea to consider closing the baths' and pointed out that if the council felt able to subsidise the theatre then why not the wash-house? She then threatened to turn Perth into Chinatown by stringing her washing across George Street. A supporter chimed in with the comment that 'it seems incredible that this year [1969] a man can stand on the moon, yet next year I will have fewer facilities than my grannie had to do my washing.' The following year the council bowed to pressure and agreed to build a new wash-house, but the protests started again when the council were perceived to be dragging their feet. Finally in April 1973 the old wash-house closed as the adjacent new one opened, only to be condemned by the women's action committee as a 'glorified laundrette.' Mrs Hamilton may have won the battle but the council were ultimately proved correct when the new building immediately began to lose money. When it was argued that it would almost be cheaper to provide each wash-house user with her own washing machine then its days were numbered and it finally closed in 1976.

The original public baths and wash-house in Mill Street. The Sandeman Public Library and the North Church can be seen on the left.
Courtesy of Perth Museum and Art Gallery, Perth and Kinross Council.

The vacant space resulting from the demolition of the original wash-house in the early 1950s. The town's lade was briefly exposed until covered over. This photo was taken in 1954.
Courtesy of Perth Museum and Art Gallery, Perth and Kinross Council.

CHAPTER THIRTEEN

Art and Entertainment

IT WAS SAID by one Sir Arthur Somerville in the earlier years of the 20th century that England was 20 years behind Scotland in the musical training of teachers. Perhaps it was the enlightened fostering of music in schools that made Perth such a musical city in the 1920s for it seemed that almost every school, every church and every large business had its own choir. Together with local orchestras, operatic groups, band concerts and musical festivals, there were many opportunities to sing, play or just listen. Perth was also fortunate in having excellent music shops such as Methven, Simpson and Co., who were agents for the 'wonderful pianola', and Patersons, who sold both Bechstein and Steinway pianos. With other shops selling wireless radios there were as many opportunities for music-making and listening inside the home as outside.

That Perth developed into, above all, a singing city is quite remarkable when one considers that at the start of the Victorian era it had only one choir, that of the East Church whose conductor, David Peacock, was one of the great local historians of the 19th century. As the *Perthshire Advertiser* put it, in a musical retrospective of 1929, 'Mendelssohn was electrifying the musicians of Birmingham... with his *Elijah* when Fair City choralists were struggling to master elementary anthems... with an occasional attempt at a *Messiah* chorus.' While the blossoming of vocal music in the city was partly due to good teaching in the schools, it can also be attributed to the organists and choirmasters of local churches and in particular, perhaps, to those steeped in the Anglican choral tradition which flourished at St Ninian's Cathedral. Such highly talented and enthusiastic musicians as Frank Graves of Kinnoull Church, Fred Midgley of St John's, and Stephen Richardson of St Ninian's, who were all born south of the border, encouraged musical ventures well beyond church and cathedral confines. Graves did much to encourage the growth of music in Perth in the later 19th century. He had been the conductor of the Perth Musical Society which, according to his obituary, was the only musical organisation when he first came to the city. His amateur operatic society was the forerunner of several others. Stephen Richardson, who

The massed ranks of Mr Stephen Richardson's Choral Society, which later became Perth Choral Society, in the City Hall in c.1920. Richardson holds the baton at centre stage.
Courtesy of the A.K. Bell Library Local Studies Department, Perth and Kinross Council.

was a singing master at the Academy during the week, founded his eponymous choral society in 1890 which, after his death in 1937, developed into Perth Choral Society. It is now one of the city's best-loved musical organisations.

Stephen Richardson also played a major part in establishing the Perthshire Music Festival in 1921. It quickly developed into one of the biggest and best competition festivals in Scotland and by the time of the fourth festival in 1924 was offering 85 classes and attracting well over 500 competitors. Some classes, though, attracted only a single entrant and when this happened in 1932 the Inland Revenue were quick to point out that the performance could not be competitive and was therefore an entertainment and an entertainment tax should therefore be paid. Protestations were made and the Inland Revenue backed down. The organising committee has endeavoured to adapt to new musical developments over the years but were disappointed in the 1960s when, at a time when every schoolchild wanted a guitar, they did not receive a single entry in two years to their new guitar classes. 'We do try to keep abreast of new trends,' said the festival chairman, 'without being absolutely with-it.' The festival still flourishes, though now under the name Perform in Perth, and currently attracts around 3,000 performers each year, a figure which is sadly never remotely matched by audience numbers.

An offshoot from the earliest days of the festival was the Perth Madrigal Society which was founded by David Yacamini to take part in one of the festival classes. After a half-century of the highest-quality singing and following a series of declining audiences the society folded in 1978, prompting a wistful comment from Lady Jean Wemyss, the society's chairman, that 'no one seems to want to sing these days.' She was, however, a little premature with the obituary as the following year Henry Neil formed the popular singing group, Chansons, which inherited some of the Madrigal Society's funds and which therefore has a link, tenuous though it may be, with that decision in the mid-19th century to build an Anglican cathedral in Perth. Ten years later, in 1989, another highly successful singing group, a youth choir, was launched under the directorship of Marion Neilson who has only recently stepped down from this role. The high reputation of the Fair City Singers, forged by successes in national youth choir competitions, has led to international tours, several television appearances and a performance at the opening concert of the Millennium Dome at Greenwich. At least one member has since become an operatic soloist and another, Sam Stevenson (as she was then), was a star of the 2011 television series featuring Gareth Malone and the Military Wives Choir.

Perth has had an orchestral tradition going back to the 19th century though, as we saw in 1900, the amateur musicians of Perth Orchestral Society found some pieces rather challenging and probably should have left Schubert's *Unfinished* unbegun. The orchestra steadily improved in the post-war period under the baton of Richard McGlynn whose concert in 1930 was described as 'excellent', this in spite of the difficulty in getting local players to come forward and join the ranks. Later in the 1930s the orchestra found the expense of hiring professional wood and brass players prohibitive and resorted to using strings only. McGlynn's daughter, Flora, became one of the doyennes of Perth piano teachers after the war. The orchestra was revived in 1951 and gave its first concert in the theatre in 1953. It has had a series of excellent conductors in the past half-century but none as musically distinguished as the second, Dr

The first-known photo of Perth Symphony Orchestra, taken at their City Hall
concert in February 1955. Dr Béla de Csilléry conducts the orchestra and soloist
Shelagh Stamp in a performance of Beethoven's Piano Concerto No 1. The author's mother,
with the short dark hair, sits with the second violins.
Courtesy of the *Perthshire Advertiser* and Perth Symphony Orchestra.

Béla de Csilléry, who had studied with such greats of the 20th century
as Kodály, Hindemith and Ansermet and who took the orchestra to
perhaps undreamed of heights. It should perhaps be emphasised that the
City of Perth Sinfonia, the name recently adopted by the former Angus
Chamber Orchestra in honour of Perth's restored status, has no connection with Perth Orchestral Society.

Chasing hot on the heels of Perth Symphony Orchestra are those of
local schools and Perth Youth Orchestra. Founded in 1962 the youth
orchestra gave its first, well-received, performance in the City Hall in
1964, and in 1975 had the honour of being the only Scottish orchestra
asked to perform at the National Festival of Music for Youth (now
simply Music for Youth) in Croydon. It is today, at 50, a highly regarded
youth orchestra, a number of whose members have graduated to positions
with professional orchestras and some to successful careers as soloists.

Professional orchestras and musicians have also regularly visited the city. The London Philharmonic with Sir Thomas Beecham, the violinist Fritz Kreisler and singer Paul Robeson all came in the 1930s though attendances, at all but the Robeson concert which filled the City Hall, were described as 'deplorable.' Thus a pattern was established whereby every few years a top orchestra was enticed to Perth only to vow never to return due to the lack of support from the Perth public. The *Perthshire Advertiser* drew attention to the problem in 1972, saying that the city was in danger of becoming a cultural backwater, and in 1980 the manager of the Scottish Chamber Orchestra spoke out in strong terms when only 50 tickets were sold for a concert in the City Hall. He compared this with much smaller St Andrews where they would regularly sell 800. He complained that Perth was well-known for empty concert halls and added that 'no other orchestra could go on losing money the way we are doing in Perth.' Only at the end of the century was the cycle broken, when an annual series of concerts by Scotland's professional orchestras was, and continues to be, well patronised. A semi-professional orchestra, the Perth-based Sinfonia of Scotland, was founded in 1989 and officially launched two years later with backing from the district council and Scottish Enterprise Tayside. By 1995, however, it had been forced to close after running into financial difficulties.

Perth has had a long and generally happier relationship with opera.

Members of Perth Trades Silver Band, instruments at the ready, pose in front of the North Inch bandstand. This was taken in the 1920s and several proudly wear their war medals.
From the collection of the late Harry Chalmers, Perth.

Several amateur companies have come and gone leaving the field to Perth Amateur Operatic Society and Perth City Operatic Group (formerly the Cathedral Operatic Group). When in 1962 the fledgling Scottish Opera sent an appeal for funds to all Scottish local authorities, one of the first to respond positively was Perth Town Council. Scottish Opera subsequently chose to express their gratitude by making regular visits to Perth. In March 1971, for example, the Perth public were treated to six performances and four separate operas by Scottish Opera (complete with three conductors and two orchestras), a performance by the Choral Society and *White Horse Inn* by the Amateur Operatic Society. Such performances were not cheap to stage. Appearances by Scottish Opera were heavily subsidised and in 1980, despite a very successful run with *My Fair Lady*, the Amateur Operatic Society made a substantial loss thanks to demands for huge royalties and higher pay for the orchestra.

Other musical groups have flourished over the course of the century, such as the Perth and District Pipe Band which was founded in 1903 and Perth Silver Brass Band whose origins may be even older. The corporation band, one of several brass ensembles in the city, came in for criticism in 1927 when the local press complained about 'the same old threadbare tunes [being] trotted out Sunday after Sunday.' The catchy songs of Gilbert and Sullivan were a staple of their repertoire and, as the press said, this was the only contact with music for many Perth people. These bands would perform regularly in the North Inch bandstand, an elegant structure which had been bought from an exhibition in Edinburgh and presented to Perth by James F. Pullar in 1891. It was demolished in 1958.

For a relatively small city Perth has been successful in attracting some of the biggest names in pop, including Sandie Shaw, the Who, the Tremeloes, the Small Faces, the Yardbirds, the Kinks, the Bay City Rollers, John Mayall, Cream, Nazareth and Hawkwind. Genesis almost managed a performance in 1969 but arrived at the venue at 2.00 am, many hours after their audience had gone home, their van having broken down en route. In a curious juxtaposition of performer and audience, Alex Harvey, he of the sensational band, gave a concert in 1974 in aid of Craigclowan, Perth's only independent preparatory school. The Beatles never played Perth but did stay at the Salutation Hotel, affectionately known as the Sally, while performing in Dundee in 1963. Even the cocktail stick with which John Lennon stirred his drink was kept as a hallowed souvenir of an unpublicised and low-key visit to the city. One

The elaborately decorated late-Victorian bandstand, photographed in c.1914, which stood on the North Inch for almost 70 years before it was demolished in 1958.
Courtesy of the A.K. Bell Library Local Studies Department, Perth and Kinross Council.

of the biggest names to come to Perth in recent years was Elton John who played to a crowd of 16,000 at McDiarmid Park in 2008. The Radio One Club came to Perth on several occasions, not to the City Hall but to the more intimate atmosphere of the Sally where many a Perth pupil could be found lurking furtively during these live lunchtime broadcasts. As well as the big names, many local bands played in the pubs and clubs of 1960s Perth though by the end of the 1970s there was a noticeable decline in live music in the city.

Of local people and bands which made it to the big-time, one of the best known is Alan Gorrie of the Average White Band. He was described in the *Perthshire Advertiser* in 1971 as 'one Perth man who is sure to make a few headlines in the national music press.' Academy pupil Eve Beatson, professionally known as Eve Graham, enjoyed huge chart success in the late 1960s and 1970s as a member of the New Seekers and in 1984 Perth group Fiction Factory climbed high in the charts with (*Feels Like*) *Heaven*. Perth singer Elaine Simmons won ITV's *New Faces* in the 1970s

Young participants in Bill Wilkie's accordion festival in October 1956 entertain a small but
appreciative audience outside St John's Kirk. The Louis Flood Collection.
Courtesy of Perth Museum and Art Gallery, Perth and Kinross Council.

and subsequently carved out a singing career, even hosting her own
television show. There were doubtless many more: the author knows of
one studious and mild-mannered former Perth College lecturer who
casually mentioned that he had enjoyed a successful pop career in
Germany in the 1960s.

Traditional music has flourished in Perth, from folk music at the
Plough Inn where singers such as Sheila Douglas and Les Honeyman
often entertained, to the many Scottish dance bands in and around the
city. Ian Powrie and Jimmy Blue, from county rather than town, led two
of the most popular bands in the second half of the 20th century. Other
figures such as Mickie Ainsworth, Tom Wilkie, Pam Wilkie, Jimmy Cassidy,
Peter Bruce and many others contributed to a vibrant traditional music
scene in the Perth area. At the centre, though, was Perth-born Bill Wilkie
around whom it all revolved. A highly talented accordionist, he cut his
teeth playing alongside Peter Sellers in Ralph Reader's *Gang Show* during
the war. Back in Perth by 1950 he began one of the great Perth, and

indeed Scottish, musical events, the Perth All Scotland Accordion and Fiddle Festival in which the well-known names of Perth music, from Donald Maxwell to John Scrimger, and those of traditional music from the rest of the UK and abroad, regularly appear. Bill Wilkie opened a music shop in Canal Street in 1959 which, like the man himself, was for many years a local institution.

The low-key frontage and narrow entrance to Perth Theatre which was described at its opening as 'utilitarian'. In spite of such a disadvantage it nevertheless enjoyed a reputation as one of the most successful theatres in Scotland.

While there was much truth in the 1928 comment that Perth was an above-average musical city, the follow-on that the city was below average for drama might raise an eyebrow or two. This, after all, was a place with a long theatrical tradition: where famous names of the British stage performed at the Theatre Royal (more recently the home of Let's Eat) and at the Opera House (on the corner of Tay Street and Canal Street until destroyed by fire in 1984) and where the relatively new theatre had been opened with such a fanfare in 1900. John Savile was the original lessee of the theatre, later the owner, and was posthumously described in the *Perthshire Advertiser* in 1929 as having 'restored Perth to a recognised place on the dramatic circuit.' After his death in 1924, brought on, perhaps, by the fire at the theatre a few months earlier, his wife took over as owner and his daughter as manager and together they continued 'their predecessor's policy of raising the standard of the drama locally by engaging the best talent available, without regard to purely pecuniary considerations.' Mother and daughter took their final curtain call in 1934 whereupon the theatre was sold the following year to two young thespians, David Steuart and Marjorie Dence.

The new owners created a repertory theatre which, through passion, hard work and good business sense, gradually developed into one of the most successful and highly regarded in Scotland where, it was said, young actors regarded it as a privilege to get a job. Summer tours were started in 1941 and by 1960 Perth Theatre productions had been seen in around 50 towns and villages throughout Scotland, from Shetland to Wigtown. In 1945, aware that Perth could not sustain a two-week run of any play and that a two-week rehearsal period was better than one, Dence and Steuart took a bold decision to form a second theatre company in Kirkcaldy. This enabled each company to rehearse for two weeks and then present the play for one week at Perth and another week at Kirkcaldy. However, as Fife theatre-goers were thin on the ground they eventually had to abandon Kirkcaldy and the two companies instead presented different plays on alternate nights at Perth.

Finance has always been a problem for the theatre. In 1960, for example, its annual running costs totalled £45,000 to which the Arts Council made a donation of £7,000. Box office receipts made up some of the difference but there was still a significant funding gap which was filled by donations from both town and county councils and the local playgoers club. Dence and Steuart and all directors following them thus trod a fine line between the divergent demands of artistry and financial survival, a line made even finer after the popularisation of television. Dence encapsulated the situation in 1952 when she complained that even regular season ticket holders would cancel their seats if Shakespeare was put on. Success did come their way and, as the theatre's reputation grew, as it already had done to merit a command performance at Balmoral in 1938 and a visit from Princess Elizabeth in 1951, so local audiences grew too. Rewards came in the form of an MBE for Dence in 1952 and five years later an Arts Council Drama Award for both her and Steuart in recognition of 21 years of outstanding service to the theatre in Scotland.

The sudden death of Marjorie Dence in 1966 resulted in the brief appointment of Iain Cuthbertson as artistic director. He drew up ambitious and much-lauded plans for the theatre which were, alas, not supported by the theatre-going public, possibly, as has been suggested, owing to an over-emphasis on Scottish plays. His 'great experiment' ended with the theatre under threat of closure, his replacement by Joan Knight and the town council as the theatre's new owners. Knight quickly made her mark. The Oscar-winning film, *The Prime of Miss Jean Brodie*, was released in 1969 and was presented as a stage play at Perth the following year, breaking all box office records of the Dence and Steuart era. Further attendance records were set by *Cabaret* in 1973 (by which time Perth had the highest theatre-going audience per capita in Scotland) and *Piaf* in 1984 which starred Lesley Mackie. Knight retired in 1992, one of her last plays being the immensely moving *Shadowlands* which presaged her own death from cancer in 1996. Her legacy was a renovated, rejuvenated and award-winning theatre, one of the best attended in Scotland, thanks to a highly successful subscription scheme.

Many actors have trod the boards of Perth Theatre, some of whom like the late lamented Martyn James stayed and became well-known and well-loved locally, and others who moved on, sometimes to international fame and fortune. These include Canadian film star Donald Sutherland, Thelma Rogers who played Peggy Archer on the radio for many years, John Laurie (Private Frazer in *Dad's Army*), Gordon Jackson, Donald Pleasance, Edward Woodward, Lisa Goddard, Kevin Whately and many more. Stars of Perth Youth Theatre have also gone on to make names for themselves: Stuart Cosgrove for one, a broadcaster and leading Channel Four executive, and Joy Hendry who edits *Chapman*, one of Scotland's most influential literary magazines. Perth even has an Olivier award winner in the above-mentioned Lesley Mackie, who won in 1986 for her portrayal of Judy Garland in *Judy*, a musical play penned by her husband, Terry Wale.

A young Donald Sutherland on the left looks up at stern-faced David Steuart in the play John Knox at Perth Theatre in 1960.
Courtesy of Perth and Kinross Council Archive.

A night at the theatre can be expensive but not so the cinema which has been a popular form of entertainment ever since the

The former BB Cinerama in Victoria Street, one of the early cinemas in Perth,
showing the traces of a familiar history – cinema, bingo hall and then demolition.
From the collection of the late Harry Chalmers, Perth.

first films were shown in the City Hall and the theatre. Later, in the years immediately preceding World War One, came the purpose-built cinemas such as the Electric Theatre Company in Alexandra Street, La Scala in Scott Street and the King's Cinema in South Methven Street. The only surviving cinema in Perth today is the Playhouse which dates from 1933 and was the last to open. Others included the Alhambra (later the Gaumont and then the Odeon) in Kinnoull Street, which showed in 1929 the city's first 'talkie', *The King of the Khyber Rifles*, BB Cinerama in Victoria Street which in 1921 was advertising 'appropriate music by our own orchestra' and the Corona beneath the Guild Hall in the High Street. The advent of television dealt a major blow to local cinemas, though at least two found new roles as bingo halls. The Playhouse itself was threatened with closure in 1990 but a successful campaign saved the institution. It now has several screening rooms and by judicious juggling can show at least a dozen films each week, a distant echo of the heyday of the cinema in Perth.

While the art of reading had long been catered for by coffee houses and reading rooms around the city, not to mention numerous small society and church libraries, the first public lending and reference library in the modern sense was established in Kinnoull Street in 1898. The gift of Professor Archibald Sandeman and administered by the council, it developed into a much loved Perth institution. For the first 30 years of

Huge crowds in Kinnoull Street watch builders and civic dignitaries lay
the foundation stone of the Sandeman Public Library in c.1896.
Courtesy of the A.K. Bell Library Local Studies Department, Perth and Kinross Council.

its existence, however, the public were not permitted to browse the
shelves. Instead a catalogue was made available and borrowers made
their selection from this alone. In time, as new books were added and
others lost, the printed catalogue became increasingly out of date and,
as the cost of a new one was prohibitively expensive, librarians found
themselves struggling to find books from a catalogue several years old.
The solution, doubtless reluctantly arrived at by old-school librarians,
was to allow the public free access to the shelves where they were at
liberty to browse, to put books back in the wrong place and generally
annoy the staff. The new system, though, was popular and resulted in a
huge increase in borrowing levels which soared from around 63,000
issues in 1920 to around 250,000 in 1933. This led to the construction
of a library extension which was completed in 1934 and which in turn
led to a further doubling of issue figures by 1936. With the local press
publishing lists of new acquisitions, with newspapers and periodicals
available in the upstairs reading room, and with a children's corner, the
library was a valuable and appreciated resource in Perth.

The reference department and ladies' reading room on the first floor of the Sandeman Library.
In spite of the classical statuary, designed to elevate the thoughts, at least some
of the men seem more interested in the young ladies across the room.
Courtesy of the A.K. Bell Library Local Studies Department, Perth and Kinross Council.

After the war there was a gradual coming together of the Sandeman Library, almost exclusively for Perth residents, and the County Library in Rose Terrace, which was for residents of Perthshire outside the city. The town council agreed to relinquish its library powers to the county council and both services finally completed the merger in 1972, almost 50 years after co-operation between the two had first been discussed. The 1980s and 1990s were decades of considerable change as chief librarian Jim Guthrie updated services, increased staffing levels and fought long and hard, and ultimately successfully, for a new library which opened in York Place in 1994. The name of the A.K. Bell Library acknowledges the large donation of funds from the Gannochy Trust. The only other public library in Perth in recent years has been the Library for the Disabled in West Mill Street. This was supposed to have closed when the A.K. Bell Library opened, the latter having been well-equipped with a ramp for disabled access and an interior lift between floors, but so popular was the West Mill Street library as a meeting place for the disabled and so loud the public outcry when closure became imminent that funding was found and it has remained open to this day. The Sandeman Library,

A young Genevieve, the author's daughter, waits patiently for service in the
Sandeman children's library on the day of its final closure in 1994. Balloons,
a Thomas the Tank Engine train, colour and comfort indicate how far public libraries had
developed during the 96 years of the Sandeman's existence.
Courtesy of the A.K. Bell Library Local Studies Department, Perth and Kinross Council.

though, did close and remained firmly locked for a number of years until its resurrection as a pub.

The original collection of objects which developed into Perth Museum was housed behind the columned façade of the Marshall Monument, that splendidly classical edifice in George Street which was built by the Perth Literary and Antiquarian Society between 1822 and 1824. The Perthshire Society of Natural Science was founded in 1867 and created its own museum and library which were initially situated in Kirkside before moving, via St Ann's Lane, to Tay Street in 1881. It concentrated on the natural history of the area and was described by Patrick Geddes, one of the most distinguished sons of Perth, as the finest of its kind in Scotland. In time it became a victim of its own success as the volunteers who manned it could not cope with the increasingly large number of visitors nor could the society afford a professional curator. The society therefore offered the building and its contents, excluding the library, free of charge to the town council in 1896, a gift which was ultimately and

Not an everyday sight in Perth. A photograph of 1935 showing stuffed lions being moved from the former Perthshire Natural History Museum in Tay Street to their new home in the greatly enlarged museum in George Street.
Courtesy of Perth Museum and Art Gallery, Perth and Kinross Council.

slightly grudgingly accepted in 1902. The council in turn took over the Marshall Monument in 1914 and in 1934 both museums were amalgamated in the newly enlarged premises now known as Perth Museum and Art Gallery in George Street.

Perth's first art gallery was housed on the top floor of the Sandeman Library and at its opening in 1898 was bedecked with a loan exhibition of paintings by Velazquez, Rembrandt, Titian, Whistler, Constable, Gainsborough, Romney and Raeburn to name but a few. Other exhibitions, almost as impressive, followed. An Arts and Crafts display of over 800 exhibits was held in the gallery in 1904 and still ranks as the largest art event ever mounted in the city. Robert Hay Robertson, a local grocer and wine merchant, was the first convener of the council's Sandeman art committee and together with Robert Brough of McEwens department store, and others, was a founder member of the Perthshire Art Association in 1912. To this day amateur and professional artists display their work at the association's annual exhibitions which since 1952 have been held almost without exception at Perth Museum and Art Gallery.

Perth's first dedicated public art gallery was situated on the top floor of the
Sandeman Library. There was doubtless relief all round when the new
and more easily accessible art gallery was opened in 1935.
Courtesy of Perth Museum and Art Gallery, Perth and Kinross Council.

The Sandeman Gallery, while a powerful stimulant to the local arts
scene, was nevertheless an unsuitable place for a gallery on account of
its relatively small size and its location at the top of several flights of
stairs. The establishment of a new dedicated art gallery, larger and
accessible to all, was actively promoted by members of the Perthshire
Art Association and finally made possible by donations of money and
paintings from the estates of Robert Brough and Robert Hay Robertson
who both died in 1926. In 1929 the council approved the scheme to
replace slum dwellings with a new gallery adjoining the Marshall Monument and this was completed at a cost of around £40,000 in 1935. The
Duke and Duchess of York (later King George VI and Queen Elizabeth),
in the first official royal visit since 1914, performed the opening
ceremony and were given the freedom of Perth.

Jim Blair took over as museum curator in 1975 and with the support
of an excellent staff was largely responsible for the significant successes

of the service in the following years. One of the first major changes was the redisplay of the natural history section. Into the reserve collection went the stuffed lions and walruses, the butterflies and birds' eggs, most of which had been in Perth for at least half a century. Out went the old-fashioned display cases and dingy lighting, and in came a beautifully presented modern display of local flora and fauna. The museum service's crowning success was the bid to bring to Perth the works of J.D. Fergusson, one of the leading Scottish Colourists whose collection was valued at around £30 million. The council converted the Round House (the city waterworks in an earlier incarnation) and the new gallery opened in 1992, attracting over 10,000 visitors in only six months and

The royal opening of the newly enlarged Perth Museum and Art Gallery in George Street in 1935. Lord Provost Thomas Hunter leads the Duke and Duchess of York towards the large crowds which had gathered to watch. Courtesy of the A.K. Bell Library Local Studies Department, Perth and Kinross Council.

immediately winning the title of Scottish Museum of the Year. Also worthy of mention was the announcement in 2007 that the entire collection of Perth Museum and Art Gallery was a Recognised Collection of National Significance to Scotland.

Until the opening of the concert hall at Horsecross, and with the notable exception of the theatre, Perth lacked a dedicated arts venue. Church halls and public rooms filled the gap for amateur events and smaller shows but the bigger musical events were held in the City Halls, old and new. The old City Hall, built in 1845, was not a particularly attractive building, either inside or outside, and when, during the creation of King Edward Street, the demolition of neighbouring properties made it suddenly more prominent in the city centre as well as structurally weaker, there was considerable debate over whether to renovate and

The old City Hall, which dated from 1845, was not a particularly inspiring building though it played a significant part in the life of the city.
Courtesy of Perth Museum and Art Gallery, Perth and Kinross Council.

strengthen the old structure or build afresh. The building was part of Perth's history, where figures such as Garibaldi, Gladstone and Andrew Carnegie had been presented with the freedom of the city, and part of national history too as a speech given by Lord Rosebery, when in Perth to open the Sandeman Library, was reckoned to have averted an imminent war with France. In 1907, however, when a lump of plaster fell from the ceiling and caused a stampede for the door, the council decided to build a new hall on the same spot. Lord Provost James Cuthbert expressed the hope at the laying of the foundation stone in 1909 'that generations to come will praise the present community who had the foresight and courage to erect this beautiful building.' It was opened in 1911 and over the next 90 years or so played host to a huge range of events, from Saturday night dances to Sunday religious meetings, from society lectures to great prime ministerial speeches, from boxing to international badminton, from scout jumble sales to the library's book sales and from music festival competitions to the great orchestras of the world. Towards the end of the century the hall began to show its age: its facilities were too old-fashioned to compete with modern conference centres and it required increasing amounts of remedial work. It closed in 2005 and at the time of writing its future is still uncertain.

The new City Hall within a few years of its opening. Its closure after over 90 years of service has led to much thought – if not heated debate – about its future. Courtesy of the A.K. Bell Library Local Studies Department, Perth and Kinross Council.

While the City Hall was a generally satisfactory venue for music events, there was a growing feeling in the cultural community in the 1970s that Perth would benefit from an arts centre. The Junior Chamber of Commerce took up the idea in 1980 and after a feasibility study gave support to the proposed venture, only to back down when it became apparent that there was little public enthusiasm for it. The Scottish Arts Council had a similar experience in 1979, backing down when their suggestion that a Perth and Kinross District Arts Council be established failed to attract the anticipated levels of approval. There were further calls for an arts centre in the mid-1980s and various locations were considered, including the former Middle Church in Tay Street and, in a joint venture with a new library, the Pullars building. It was finally the radical proposal by the council in 1995 to mark the new millennium by replacing the City Hall with a 'golden tower' and a new conference and entertainment centre which subsequently led, much modified, to the new Perth Concert Hall.

Despite the lack of an arts centre the city has fostered the visual arts in various other ways. Regular exhibitions profiling the work of emerging artists and those whose reputation has long been secure can be enjoyed at Perth Museum and Art Gallery and at well-established galleries such

Part of David Annand's sculpture Nae Day Sae Dark which can be found in the middle of the pedestrianised High Street. It commemorates the life and work of the great Scottish poet, William Soutar, who lived, worked and died in the city.

as Frames, as indeed they once were at the Fair Maid's House until its closure as a gallery and craft shop in 1988. The Perthshire Public Art Trust has sponsored several works of public art around the city, ranging from David Annand's *Nae Day Sae Dark,* which commemorates the work of poet William Soutar, to the *Fair Maid of Perth* herself who sits on a bench in the pedestrianised High Street. Gillian Forbes' attractive sculptured panels on the walls of the flood defences in Tay Street are somewhat more comprehensible than the baffling *Vortex* (irreverently referred to by some as the cheesy wotsit) which, to save money, was made of concrete rather than stainless steel and which long stood outside the Playhouse cinema.

The Perth Festival of the Arts brings all the arts together in a ten-day cultural feast in May. Its origins go back to 1951 when, as a spin-off from the Festival of Britain, the city held an arts festival, the highlight of which was a day-long visit by Princess Elizabeth who attended a performance of *Twelfth Night* at the theatre – one Shakespeare play for which presumably no tickets were returned. Other events included the Scottish National Orchestra, Ballet Rambert, performances by theatre companies from Glasgow and Dundee, poetry recitals, exhibitions and even sporting events. The notion that the festival might be revived is attributed to Conrad Wilson, the music critic of *The Scotsman*, who described Perth as 'an ideal festival city – without a festival.' He further pointed out that 'ever since Scottish Opera first went there in the spring of 1966 Perth has had an annual festival in all but name.' Such comments set in motion a feasibility study, a commitment from the council to underwrite the event and the launch of the first festival in 1972 which featured the Scottish National Orchestra, Scottish Opera and brilliant pianist John

Ogdon. The festival quickly established itself as a fixture in the Scottish cultural scene and was even talked about as Scotland's second festival, after Edinburgh. With a professional administrator and a large budget, it continues to flourish and in the new era of inclusiveness has broadened its cultural base from the purely high-brow.

Of all the Perth people who have forged reputations as creators of art, no 20th-century person stands higher than the poet William Soutar. He is remembered primarily for his Scots verse but also for his diaries and the fact that he spent much of his adult life bedridden in his parents' home in Wilson Street. His reputation has steadily grown since his early death in 1943 to the extent that he is now regarded, by some at least, as one of the greatest of all Scottish poets.

Donald Paton celebrated 50 years as a local playwright in 1977, having had the satisfaction of seeing many plays published and some regularly performed including one for the Queen at Balmoral. His artistic output raised tens of thousands of pounds for charity, including over £30,000 for the Red Cross.

Your Festival Diary

Here is your complete guide to all the concerts, performances, events and exhibitions taking place in Perth during Festival Week. More detailed information can be obtained on application to Festival Headquarters, 13 High Street, or 'The Concorde', St. John's Square.

SUN 16
FESTIVAL SERVICE
GALA OPENING CONCERT
Perth Choral and Orchestral Societies
Conductor: John McLeod, Soloist: Patricia Hay

MON 17
YOUTH NIGHT   Perth Schools Brass Band
Perth Youth Orchestra
MUSICA A TRE
Perth Chamber Music Society

TUES 18
SCOTTISH OPERA
SCOTLAND ON THE SCREEN

WED 19
SCOTTISH OPERA
"SOUND FIESTA"

THUR 20
JOHN OGDON
A LATE NIGHT ENTERTAINMENT

FRI 21
SCOTTISH OPERA
BILL WILKIE CELEBRITY CONCERT

SAT 22
SCOTTISH OPERA
AN EVENING OF MILITARY MUSIC
(A special matinee will be presented in the afternoon at 3 pm for schoolchildren and pensioners)

SUN 23
THE PERNOD PROM
Perth's first Promenade Concert with the Scottish National Orchestra
Conducted by Alexander Gibson
Tickets for 600 promenaders at 25p each

An extract from the diary of events published for the first Perth Festival of the Arts in 1972. Courtesy of the A.K. Bell Library Local Studies Department, Perth and Kinross Council.

The best-known classically-trained Perth musicians of recent years are Donald Maxwell, son of the distinguished Perth Academy geography teacher, Kenneth MacAlpine, and George Donald, also formerly of Perth Academy. Donald Maxwell graduated through the ranks of amateur opera and, after a brief career following in his father's footsteps, started with Scottish Opera in 1976. By 1987 he was being described in the local press as Perth's first international opera star. Aberdeenshire-born George Donald came to Perth in the 1960s and after a successful career in teaching made a name for himself as the pianist with the highly popular *Scotland the What?* trio.

Several actors have passed through Perth Theatre on their way to fame and fortune but few have been home grown. Film star Ewan McGregor regards Crieff as his native town but he was born in Perth and made his first appearance in front of the cameras at the age of 16 while working as a stage hand at Perth Theatre in 1987. He played a Mozart horn concerto in a Grampian Television programme which focused on exceptionally talented young musicians. The *Perthshire Advertiser* noted that he had 'ambitions of becoming an actor.'

One Perth artist, D.P. Ramsay, had the distinction of painting what was probably the first oil portrait of the present Queen when she was about four years old. Showing the young princess in riding gear, the painting was latterly hung in Clarence House before being put into store at Windsor Castle. A more widely known artist, Sir David Young Cameron, died in the city in 1945, a mere hour after addressing the congregation of St John's Kirk on the subject *Beauty and the Church*, thus being summoned, as the press put it, 'from the Church Militant to the Church Triumphant.' Others include Scone-born William Miller Frazer who exhibited at the Royal Scottish Academy summer show every year between 1884 and 1961, a remarkable achievement unlikely ever to be surpassed, and Alexander Reid who won recognition as a theatre set and costume designer in Perth, London and New York in the later 20th century. Perth tailor and amateur artist Noel Hamilton first put paint to canvas in 1967 and quickly attained some considerable success when a still life was accepted for the Paris Salon in 1971 and a superb portrait of a dog, *Butch*, accepted for the Royal Academy summer exhibition the following year. *Butch* was subsequently displayed in the window of his George Street shop where he glowered at passers-by. Perth Museum and Art Gallery held a retrospective exhibition of Hamilton's work in 1977, attracting around 2,000 visitors and selling 17 paintings for a total of almost £6,000.

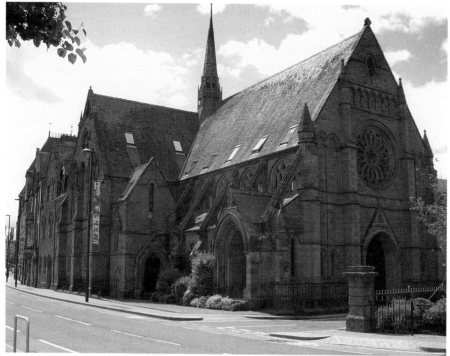

This attractive building, formerly the Free Middle Church, was targeted by Flicks of Brechin as a proposed £1 million nightclub for 1,000 people. In the early 1990s, after several years of objections, public enquiries and legal wrangles, they finally gave up the struggle. The building has since been converted into flats.

Entertainment has taken many other forms over the course of the century. There were the great annual gatherings for the Perth Show and for markets and fairs such as Little Dunning. Crowds large and small were attracted to fund-raising galas, bazaars, the South Inch shows, lectures, fireworks displays, flower shows, pierrots on the Inch, lantern slide shows, highland games and sporting events. Perth's history was celebrated in pageants such as that of 1932 to mark the centenary of the death of Sir Walter Scott, to whom Perth owes much, and another of 1949 when showbiz personalities Anna Neagle and Danny Kaye joined the crowds to watch tableaux of local historical events. National history was commemorated in 1921 in an Empire Day pageant entitled *Britannia and her Colonies*. The local gentry and aristocracy, and frequently royalty too, would attend Perth Hunt balls in County Buildings (better known as the Sheriff Court) which would be carefully decorated as a nightclub for the occasion. A young Princess Anne attended one of the balls in 1968, along with the Maharajah of Jodhpur and an eastern European princess, and was reported as being one of the last to leave. For those who stayed in, a wider choice of radio and television channels arrived in the 1980s with first Radio Tay and then Channel Four and cable television. More free channels became available following the digital switchover in 2010. Even patients in PRI could enjoy their own radio station – Hospital Radio Perth – which was launched in 1989 and has been named UK Hospital Radio of the Year four times, most recently in 2007. For those who enjoyed a night out there were numerous pubs to visit, such as the historic Glencoe and the Old Ship Inn, as well as several nightclubs to choose from. They were presumably highly profitable enterprises judging by the great efforts made by Flicks, the award-winning Brechin-based nightclub, to gain a foothold in the city, but in the popular imagination, if nowhere else, they were seen as noisy dens of drug and alcohol abuse, judging by the equally strenuous attempts to keep them out. The Ice Factory opened in 1994 and with its policy of bringing in top DJs became a popular venue before closing in 2009. Its location at the Shore was perhaps sufficiently distant from residential areas ever to have been a significant problem. The organisation behind Sportsters, however, in South Methven Street, had a tougher time. Despite the initial refusal of planning permission, following a plea by Councillor Joan McEwen on behalf of the elderly residents in that area, it finally opened in 2002 in the old Sharp's Institution building and was described at the time as the biggest-ever licensed trade investment in Perth. There was official recognition of the demand for entertainment in 1996 when the council proposed a huge leisure park for the sites at St Catherines recently vacated by Monax and the Wallace Works. They initially envisaged a multi-screen cinema, a bowling alley, a bingo hall, restaurants and a night club but when several companies pulled out they altered their plans accordingly. Despite the occasional failures there are still the hundreds of clubs and societies which provide leisure and entertainment on a small scale. If none of these should appeal there is always the simple pleasure of a walk round the Inch and a coffee in the café quarter.

CHAPTER FOURTEEN

The Sporting Life

THE NEWSPAPER TALKED of huge migrations of fans between Perth and Dundee to watch matches and of how 'confronting male supporters vied in drams and derisions that raised the on-field action to bonfire crackle.' While this may sound like a description of Tayside derbies between St Johnstone and a Dundee team, it actually refers to the fierce rivalry of cricket fans during the 'war of the roses' between Perthshire and Forfarshire. It always used to be said that Perth's game was cricket and while that may conjure up peaceful images of leather on willow, of polite applause rippling around the North Inch boundary and of flasks of tea and cucumber sandwiches, the reality was very different. The Perthshire-Forfarshire enmity, while in essence merely another facet of the age-old Perth-Dundee rivalry, was not helped by the collapse of the North Inch grandstand in 1903 which resulted in serious injuries to several spectators, including Forfarshire supporters, and claims for damages which took Perthshire several years to pay off. It was further reflected in an acrimonious dispute in 1911, conducted by letter and couched in the politest terms, about where and when the two teams should play. Little wonder, then, when local pride was at stake, that these matches could attract up to 10,000 jeering spectators, many brought in by special trains and many a little the worse for drink.

One of Scotland's earliest recorded cricket matches was played on the North Inch in around 1812. Perth Cricket Club was formed in 1827 and changed its name to the Perthshire Cricket Club in 1870. The 1890s were a successful period for Perthshire but better was still to come. No other club has come anywhere near, let alone match, their remarkable run of success in the Scottish Counties Championship which they won, in the 26 seasons between 1953 and 1978, no less than 20 times. Watching them, however,

In the author's opinion this hitherto unidentified photograph shows crowds gathered around the wreckage of the North Inch cricket pavilion which collapsed in 1903.
From the collection of the late Harry Chalmers, Perth.

were crowds generally numbering only a few hundred rather than the thousands of the pre-war era. In this their heyday, with a number of players such as Gordon Laing, Mike Kerrigan, Jimmy Brown and Len Dudman in the Scottish national side, and with Brown and Dudman reckoned to be of English county standard, they were a formidable team. Brown captained the national side for 12 years until stepping down in 1973, a lengthy record of service for which he was awarded the MBE. Statistics show that between roughly 1865 and 1950 Perthshire players had won 44 Scottish caps, a figure which, between 1951 and 1976, had rocketed to 210. These talented amateurs were aided in their efforts by club professionals who included Hugh Crosskill, Tom Lodge and even Wilfred Rhodes who, as a former Yorkshire and England player, was described as one of the greatest cricketers of the 20th century. He was, however, 60 years of age when he walked out to bat for Perthshire.

In 1978 Perthshire said farewell to its old pavilion, built to replace the one destroyed by suffragettes in 1913, and moved into the brand new Gannochy Sports Pavilion which they were to share with the Perthshire Rugby Club. That same year they beat Aberdeenshire to win the Scottish Championship one final time after which a gradual decline set in, which in turn resulted in an ignominious relegation from the National Cricket League and the club's virtual demise. The beginning of the fall from grace ironically coincided with the decision to admit women as full members of the club.

It was as an offshoot from the St Johnstone Cricket Club, one of the smaller local teams in Perth, that the city's (later) professional football team of the same name first took shape in 1884. Together with Fair City Athletic they were the leading teams in Perth during the later 19th and earlier 20th centuries. After some success in the Northern League Saints applied to join the Scottish Second Division and after an initial rejection were accepted in 1911. They were almost literally robbed of promotion in 1923 when they had to forfeit two points for fielding a player who had been signed after the permitted transfer date. Their rivals, Clydebank, whom Saints had just defeated, did not lose points despite having committed the same offence and were promoted instead. Saints turned the tables the following season when they were promoted in place of relegated Clydebank. Perth was described as having gone 'wild' that night with thousands lining the streets to welcome the team to a reception in the County Hotel. Promotion in 1924 coincided with the move from

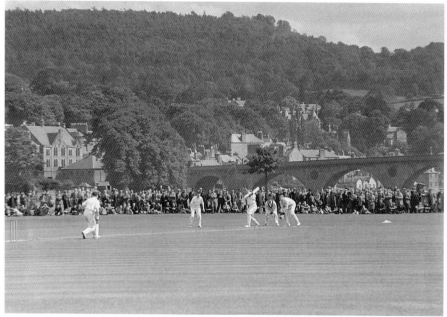

A good crowd of spectators watching a Perthshire versus Aberdeenshire cricket match on the North Inch in June 1951... The Louis Flood Collection.
Courtesy of Perth Museum and Art Gallery, Perth and Kinross Council.

their pitch at the Recreation Ground beside the South Inch to Muirton Park on the northern edge of the city. The first match was played there on Christmas Day 1924 and would have been watched not just by huge crowds of men and boys but also by a number of women who, as the press said, 'are now almost as enthusiastic supporters... as their male companions.'

With Saints now in the top rank of Scottish football and regularly attracting crowds of around 10,000 the management started buying new players. One popular acquisition was local boy Sandy McLaren who first signed for Saints in 1927 and went on to play in goal for Scotland. Relegation in 1930 ushered in new manager Tommy Muirhead who took the team back to the First Division in 1932 and to a Scottish Cup semi-final appearance in 1934. Football stopped at Muirton Park in 1940 and only resumed at the war's end, though the ensuing years were marked by dismal performance and depressing finances. By 1955 attendances had fallen to their lowest ever, and the club was so heavily in debt that they could not afford to pay close-season wages. Yet another manager was sacked in 1958 and in his place as part-time manager and coach came former Rangers and Scotland goalkeeper Bobby Brown who, with players such as the future Sir Alex Ferguson of Manchester United, took the team back to the First Division in two seasons. Brown and, from 1967, his successor Willie Ormond, both of whom went on to manage the national side, presided over one of the most successful periods in the club's history which included a Scottish League Cup final in 1969 and progression to the third round of the UEFA Cup in their first foray into Europe in 1971. Stars of this period were Henry Hall, John Connolly and Jim Pearson.

After Ormond's departure in 1973 the club sank into a long slow decline under a succession of managers, one of the few bright spots being the signing of a young Ally McCoist who went onto to much greater things with Rangers and Scotland. Perhaps the lowest period in the club's history occurred in 1984 and 1985 when Saints became the first club to plummet out of both the Premier League and the First Division in consecutive seasons, a distinction which somewhat dampened their centenary celebrations. Such poor team performances inevitably led to declining support, diminishing gate receipts and looming financial disaster.

... And an even better crowd at Muirton Park for a St Johnstone versus Forfar Athletic match in February 1950. The Louis Flood Collection. Courtesy of Perth Museum and Art Gallery, Perth and Kinross Council.

In a decision with far-reaching consequences the club's directors appointed local builder Geoff Brown as club chairman in 1986. Supporters
were initially sceptical, assuming he was eyeing up Muirton Park as a
development site, but were placated by his promise that Muirton would
'remain a sports stadium.' Hardly had he uttered those words when
supermarket giant Asda offered to buy the stadium for the site of a Perth
store and rehouse the club elsewhere in the city. Brown insisted he was
'in no way connected with the move' but, faced with a £200,000 debt
and weekly running costs of £3,500, eventually accepted the offer. The
brand new 10,000 all-seat stadium, McDiarmid Park, was opened on the
outskirts of Perth in 1989 and was named after farmer Bruce McDiarmid
who had made the land available at virtually no cost to the club. Saints
fanzine, *Wendy Who?*, thoughtfully provided readers with a free plastic
fork as an aid to removing the Muirton turf before the bulldozers moved
in. With a new chairman, a new manager in the shape of Alex Totten,
and a new stadium, a revitalised St Johnstone embarked on a new decade
which, while bringing not a little disappointment, also brought a season
of record profits, a Scottish League Cup final appearance and, in the last
full season of the 20th century, a welcome return to European football.

That end-of-century highpoint did not last. Sandy Clark, who had so
recently taken Saints into Europe, was sacked in 2001 for a string of poor
team performances and replaced by Billy Stark. Relegation and record
losses loomed in 2002, Stark too was replaced, and not even new manager John Connolly, star of the 1970s, could improve the club's fortunes.
However, following the appointment of Owen Coyle in 2005 things
began to look up: it's not often that Saints beat Rangers 2–0 at Ibrox but
that is what happened in a Scottish League Cup quarter-final fixture in
2006 – a game subsequently described as one of the greatest performances and results in the club's history. This would have delighted Saints
tea lady Aggie Moffat, who was long remembered for her public spat
with Rangers manager Graeme Souness and who retired the following year,
perhaps with this sweet memory in mind. With other successes following it was not long before Coyle was being eyed with interest by bigger
clubs south of the border, and a little over four years after he first came
to Perth he moved south to take over Burnley and steer them into the
English premiership. Saints themselves returned to top flight football in
2009 under the managership of Derek McInnes and when he too moved
south of the border in 2011 Steve Lomas stepped in to replace him. That

When McDiarmid Park was opened in 1989 it was regarded as one of the finest football stadiums in the country. Even the pitch looks immaculate with not just mere stripes in the grass but, as befits a Scottish team, tartan.

same year also saw the departure of club chairman Geoff Brown who had been at the helm for 25 years. A good 2011–12 season allowed Saints into the UEFA Europa League but they were knocked out early on by Turkish side Eskişehirspor.

Of the many amateur football teams in Perth, the two principal ones are Jeanfield Swifts and Kinnoull. And of football supporters none has been so keen in following the fortunes of the national side as 19-year-old Robbie Sterry who, mirroring the extravagant hopes and disastrous results of Scotland during the 1978 World Cup, set off to Argentina in April. Having been robbed of all his money en route he was nevertheless the first Scot to arrive at the team's venue and after a lifetime of experiences arrived home in October.

Local golfers like to claim that both James IV and his great-grandson James VI played in Perth in the 16th century. Another royal connection is remembered in the Perth Golfing Society which was founded in 1824 and first received royal patronage in 1833, a year earlier than the Royal and Ancient in St Andrews, since when it has been known as the Royal Perth Golfing Society. It functions today equally as a sporting and private dining club with clubrooms overlooking the southern end of the North Inch where the first of the ten tees was originally situated. The North Inch course was extended in 1924, following the gift of fields at South Muirton by the Hon. John Dewar, son of Lord Forteviot, and was taken into council ownership at the same time. By 1931 it was a busy course with well over 21,000 rounds played in that year. Today, as one of the oldest courses in Scotland, and with its attractive location beside the Tay, it provides an excellent golfing experience at a fraction of the cost of some courses south of the border. The King James VI Golf Club was founded in 1858 and moved in 1897 from the North Inch to Moncreiffe Island where Tom Morris designed the course. Craigie Hill is home to the most recent of the city's courses which opened in 1911. Local golfer and cricketer Joe Anderson assisted in the design of the course and while his father, Willie, basked in his local reputation as 'the grand old man of golf', it fell to Joe's daughter, Jessie, later Jessie Valentine, to launch her career from Craigie Hill as one of the most distinguished and successful of British woman golfers. She was already known to the Perth press by

Jessie Valentine sits proudly beside the Ladies Amateur Golf Championship Cup
(on the right) which she first won in 1937 as Jessie Anderson and twice more in the 1950s.
This photo was taken in 1955.
Courtesy of Perth Museum and Art Gallery, Perth and Kinross Council.

1931 as the 16-year-old Perth 'lady champion' and 'holder of all the available trophies at Craigie Hill.' In 1934 she was described as 'one of the foremost lady exponents of golf in the United Kingdom'. Fellow club member Willie Laidlaw was also becoming a national name at this time, though their paths were soon tragically to diverge. Pilot Officer William Laidlaw was killed in 1941 while Jessie went on to win the Scottish Ladies' Championship six times, the British Ladies' title three times, as well as French, Canadian and New Zealand titles. She died 65 years later in 2006.

Sharing the Inches with golfers, cattle and washing were the Perth races which were held on the North Inch as early as the mid-17th century. Seen by some as simply an excuse for the Perth Hunt balls, they were run for much of the 19th century on an oval track around the North Inch, and spectators were even provided with a grandstand beside the river, opposite the winning post and looking towards Rose Terrace. In 1908, flat racing on the Inch having been prohibited by the Jockey Club some years earlier, the Perth Hunt accepted the offer of Lord Mansfield to hold the races at Scone Palace, where they have been held ever since. As if to remind the public of their origins, the council first sponsored the City of Perth Gold Cup in 2000. And with sponsorship now provided by Aviva, and top jockeys competing for prize money in the tens of thousands, it has become a significant event in the British racing calendar.

The public swimming baths were built on the Dunkeld Road in 1887

Spectators gather round the finishing post at the Perth races on the North Inch.
A grandstand can be seen on the right of the photo, the bandstand in the background
and boats for hire in the foreground, all now long gone.
Courtesy of Perth Museum and Art Gallery, Perth and Kinross Council.

and despite their distance from the city centre were a popular Perth institution for about a century. By the mid-1930s they were recognised as falling 'considerably short of the required standard, both from a utilitarian and recreational point of view' and work began on the reconstruction of the entire building complete with a championship-standard pool. The extension required to house the new pool was built over the corporation bowling green which was given a new and more convenient home on the North Inch. The baths were reopened in 1937 and one of the first to benefit from the new facilities was Ronnie Burns, who was selected to swim for Britain at the Helsinki Olympics in 1952 and who won a Scottish title in 1953. His success at national level was followed by several others including Alec Galletly and the McClatchey brothers, John and Alan. Many, too, will remember the gold medals won by John's daughter, Caitlin, at the 2006 Commonwealth Games. The beginning of the end for the Dunkeld Road baths came in 1970 when Councillor Norman Renfrew first gave voice to what some in Perth had long been thinking: that it was shabby, out of date, cold and lacking in privacy. Serious consideration was given to a new pool in the late 1970s and, having considered building on the South Inch, and run into predictable fierce

The Dunkeld Road swimming baths were a popular Perth institution for almost a century. The Soldiers' Pool, as it was known, was the main one until the building of the championship-standard pool in the 1930s. Swimming clubs such as Pullars Penguins made good use of what became widely known as the Big Pool.
Courtesy of the A.K. Bell Library Local Studies Department, Perth and Kinross Council.

opposition, and at York Place, the council decided in 1982 to build on railway land at Glover Street instead. The new Perth Leisure Pool was opened in 1988 and welcomed around 60,000 people in the first 20 days. By the end of its first year it was in the top ten of chargeable-entrance attractions in Scotland.

Adjacent to Muirton Park on the Dunkeld Road, and even further out than the swimming baths, was the Central Scotland Ice Rink. Opened in 1936 and funded by the local authorities of Perthshire, Angus, Kinross-shire and Fife, the ice rink gave the sporting community of Perth a pre-eminence in both ice hockey and curling. Perth Panthers and Perth Black Hawks were the two main ice hockey teams in the city, the former having the edge thanks to the skills of several Canadian professionals. The Panthers won the Scottish National League on two occasions, though when this was replaced by the British National League in 1954 the additional costs of participation resulted in the demise of many Scottish clubs. Nevertheless six Scottish teams including Perth Panthers formed an amateur league, without the professional Canadian players, though this too folded in 1956 leaving the Panthers with virtually no opposition. The team was reformed in 2000 to play Dundee Tigers at the new Dundee Ice Arena, the first time the teams had played since the 1950s. A measure of just how strong the sport had been in Perth came in 2009 when former Perth Panther Ian Forbes, who had been a star player in the post-war period, was inducted posthumously into the British Ice Hockey Hall of Fame.

Curling in the post-war period grew in popularity among both men and women and successes were regularly achieved in the Scottish curling championships. The World Curling Championships have been held regularly in Perth since 1963, those of 1975 being described in the press as 'the biggest single money-spinning event ever to be staged in the city.' Scotland has won the men's competition several times and many Perth curlers of both sexes have figured prominently in the Scottish teams. The ice rink was caught up in the proposed redevelopment of Muirton Park by Asda and in 1988, with a view to moving to the site of the Dewars bonded warehouse in Glover Street, applied for permission to demolish that landmark building. It was a highly controversial application but one that eventually won the day: the Dewars building was demolished by 1989 and the new Dewars Centre opened the following year. The first event in the building, already condemned as a 'giant shed', was not an international curling match or something similarly suitable, but a bird show.

The red-brick exterior of the Dewars Centre, described as 'respectable and stodgy' by architectural historian, John Gifford, is nevertheless an echo of the Dewars bonded warehouse which formerly occupied the site.

Other sports have flourished in Perth, with several clubs having a distinguished history and many players performing at national level. Perthshire Rugby Club, one of the oldest in Scotland, was formed in around 1869 and has since merged with local rivals, Perth Academicals. Saturday afternoon matches on the North Inch still attract a good crowd of touchline spectators. Women's hockey has been particularly successful at producing international standard players such as Betty Gavigan, Eileen Nicoll, Marietta Craigie and Alison Ramsay. Marietta retired from playing in 1983 as the most-capped player in Scottish women's hockey, with 73 to her name, while Alison was selected for the 1988 and 1992 British Olympic teams, returning from Barcelona with a bronze medal. Tennis is also a popular Perth sport and the city boasts a number of clubs. Elena Baltacha, daughter of former St Johnstone player Sergei, honed her skills sufficiently well as a teenager on local courts to make her 11th appearance in the Wimbledon ladies' singles in 2012 and on more than one occasion has held the British number one spot. Other notable sporting personalities, to name just a few, include Hilda Millar, one of the finest post-war shots in Britain of either sex; motorcyclist Jimmy Buchan who enjoyed success in the Isle of Man TT races in the 1950s; David Campbell, a British canoe champion in the 1950s; Tommy and Norman Dickson, father and son, who both competed at a high level in motor-racing; David Banks who skied for Scotland; Maureen McLeish and Don Halliday who ran for Scotland; Alistair McCann who won a bronze medal for trampolining at the 1976 Olympics; Doug Holden and Dougie Reid who boxed for Scotland; and top Scottish badminton players Charlie Gallagher, Anthony Gallagher and Aileen Nairn. An avenue of trees was planted on the North Inch in 1973 to commemorate at least some of these sporting achievements, though sadly they did not survive the attention of local vandals.

In his Christmas message of 1919 the lord provost said that 'sport and recreation should be encouraged and fostered,' and the council quickly set about providing new sporting facilities. Bowling greens were opened on the South Inch and Dunkeld Road, as were quoiting and putting greens, which in the case of the last mentioned became extremely popular: around 81,000 rounds of putting were played on the North Inch course in 1925 which equates to about 260 rounds every day of every six-day week. Corporation tennis courts were established at Darnhall Drive and, as we have seen, the council took over the North Inch golf course, all within five years of that Christmas message. Later developments include the South Inch boating pond in 1931, the pitch and putt course in 1960, the acquisition of Rodney Pavilion as a small sports centre in 1987, the new skatepark on the South Inch in 2002, and the George Duncan Athletics Arena in the grounds of Perth Grammar School in 2005.

One of the biggest boosts to sport in the history of the city was the building of Bell's Sports Centre which came at a time when shorter working hours, earlier retirement and longer holidays meant more time for recreation. In 1959 the council first proposed incorporating some of the grounds of Balhousie Castle into the North Inch and building a changing room and shower block for the convenience of those who used the Inch for sport. Firm plans for the centre, to be funded by the Gannochy Trust, were announced in 1964 and work began two years later. Its construction was beset with difficulties, from the earliest planning days when the radical design incurred objections from influential bodies, to the awkward manoeuvring of the 36-metre-long arch ribs through the streets of Perth and to the major fire in the dome which delayed the opening by several months. It was opened in 1968 and a number of famous

A peaceful view of the South Inch bowling green, possibly in the 1950s.
Courtesy of the A.K. Bell Library Local Studies Department, Perth and Kinross Council.

A photo taken in c.1967 showing the construction of Bell's Sports Centre.
Courtesy of Perth and Kinross Council Archive.

sporting names were quickly attracted to it, not least of them the former leader of the Liberal Democrats, Sir Menzies Campbell, who in an earlier role as a distinguished British athlete, was invited to test the material to be used as the running track. Others included past and future Wimbledon champions Lew Hoad, Ann Jones and Virginia Wade, who competed in the Dewar Cup in 1969. The centre has been extended over the years and together with its link to the adjacent rugby and cricket pavilion is now one of the biggest sports complexes in Scotland.

Exercise for many people, though, can consist of a gentle stroll and the council over the years has provided many pleasant walks. In 1910 Lord Elibank gifted the Buckie Braes at Cherrybank to the council whereupon they created a 'pleasure ground' with swings and picnic tables. The acquisition of Kinnoull Hill was first discussed by the council in 1919 but it was only in 1923, when the hill was on the open market, that Lord Dewar, fearing that a new owner might refuse access to the townspeople, stepped in and bought it for the city. Paths were created, new planting carried out, and in what was described as a very feudal ceremony Lord Dewar handed the hill over in 1924. It has since been

Boys and girls making use of the newly laid out 'pleasure ground' at Buckie Braes in 1911.
Courtesy of Perth Museum and Art Gallery, Perth and Kinross Council.

gently improved with nature trails, car parking, picnic tables, and in 1968 by the acquisition of the Kinnoull Hill tower. The hill, though, is carefully watched by the Perth Civic Trust and others for any sign of over-development. Another hilly beauty spot, St Magdalene's Hill, was given to Perth in 1954 by the Duncan Trust, whose chairman was Sir Stanley Norie-Miller. A.K. Bell purchased Quarrymill (and subsequently transferred it to the Gannochy Trust) 'for the public benefit', but a dumping ground for Scone residents was probably not the benefit he had envisaged. In 1933 the Annaty Burn, which flows through Quarrymill, was described as being full of domestic rubbish, iron bedsteads, old bicycles, tyres, bedding and frying pans, and again in 1975 as being choked with 'an amazing accumulation of litter.' Indeed, when members of the Perth Junior Chamber of Commerce and local scouts and guides mounted a clean-up operation they removed 16 tons of rubbish. Thus began a transformation which ultimately led to its opening in 1987 as a beautiful and peaceful woodland park, extending over 30 acres between Perth and Scone. The city's riverside walk, which now stretches between Perth Bridge and the railway bridge, originated in 1933 when General

The duck pond at the Quarrymill Woodland Park on a summer's morning.

Accident purchased the grounds of Rodney, demolished the southernmost of the surviving gable ends which had disfigured the Victoria Bridge for so long, and opened the grounds the following year as a recreation area for its staff, complete with bowling green and tennis courts. In 1971, having been extended as far as the new Commercial Street development, it was handed over to the council as a public park for all Perth residents to enjoy. The opening of Bellwood Park in 1993 completed the walk. One of the most recent of public open spaces is the Millennium Park which opened in 2007 on the lower slopes of Kinnoull. The land was purchased by the Jonathan Gloag Trust and leased at a minimal rent to the Bridgend, Gannochy and Kinnoull Community Council for the benefit of the community.

Perth is indeed fortunate in its open spaces and in the range of spectator and participatory sports available. However, of all the tales of sporting prowess featured in a century's worth of local newspapers, none has surpassed that of the Perth Railway Club's ladies' darts team who in 1981 took on a team of men from Houston, Texas, by telephone. After an hour of play during which the Texans had accumulated a considerable lead and British Telecom a hefty profit of £250, the phone call suddenly ended due to 'technical difficulties' – or so they said…

CHAPTER FIFTEEN

Perth at War

PERTH HAS ALWAYS been strategically important in Scotland, both geographically as a gateway town to the highlands, and, until the close of the mediaeval period, if not Jacobite times, one of the politically eminent cities in the kingdom. As such, it has been viewed as a prime military target by invading armies. The Romans were active all around the area, long before Perth came into being; Robert the Bruce recaptured the town from the English by scaling the walls, in legend at least; Oliver Cromwell built a huge citadel, roughly where the South Inch car park now is, and in doing so destroyed many of the city's old buildings; Jacobite armies made a beeline for it; and in the wake of the '45 it was heavily garrisoned for many years. Perth is a city well acquainted with the tribulations of war.

A later 19th-century view of the Queen's Barracks' parade ground showing the
presentation of colours to the militia.
Courtesy of Perth Museum and Art Gallery, Perth and Kinross Council.

After many years of troops in their thousands camping on both Inches, a barracks was built on the lands of Drumhar in around 1794. It is believed to have derived the name Queen's Barracks from the Queen's Own Regiment of Dragoons who were the first regiment to occupy it. The regiment long associated with the barracks, however, was The Black Watch which was first raised in 1739 as Crawford's Highlanders. Its nickname, The Black Watch, is thought to have come from the dark colours of its tartan and its function as a watchful presence over potentially rebellious highland clans. It was moulded into its 20th-century format in the Cardwell and Childers reforms of the 1870s and 1880s whereby it merged with the 73rd (Perthshire) Regiment of Foot under the name of The Black Watch (The Royal Highlanders). The reforms further established the recruiting ground as Perthshire, Angus and Fife, in theory if not in practice, and made the Queen's Barracks their permanent home or depot.

The regiment served in all the major British conflicts of the 20th century, from South Africa and two world wars to Korea, Kenya, Cyprus, Northern Ireland and, in 2003-04, Iraq. Most recently, as a battalion of the

The entrance to the Queen's Barracks on the corner of Barrack Street and Atholl Street. Following the departure of The Black Watch the barracks were taken over by the town council and eventually demolished in c.1968. Courtesy of Perth Museum and Art Gallery, Perth and Kinross Council.

Royal Regiment of Scotland, the men of The Black Watch have served in Afghanistan. It was also the last British military unit to leave Pakistan in 1948 and Hong Kong in 1997. Volunteers have long played an important role in supplementing the regular army and many of those from Perth and Perthshire ended up in the 6th Battalion The Black Watch. This had the distinction of being the only battalion of the regiment to be awarded the Croix de Guerre in World War One. After serving in the British Expeditionary Force in World War Two the 6th Battalion was evacuated from Dunkirk in 1940 and went on to serve in North Africa, Italy and Greece.

The 1st Battalion The Black Watch, together with many Perth territorials in the Royal Army Service Corps, all serving in the 51st (Highland) Division, was caught up in the battle and surrender at St Valery in Normandy in June 1940, an event which was described by Eric Linklater as having as big an impact on Scotland as Flodden had in 1513. With their backs to the sea and making an heroic last stand against a rampant German army which had just expelled the bulk of the British Expeditionary Force from mainland Europe at Dunkirk, they had little alternative to surrendering. Some escaped but many more young Perthshire lads spent the next five years as prisoners of war. In the confusion of retreat the story goes that Captain Peter Norwell, of the High Street shoe shop, met Major David K. Thomson, later lord provost, of the whisky firm, on the cliffs of St Valery and tossed a coin to decide which way to go. Norwell went one way and with his men managed to descend the cliffs with the aid of a makeshift rope and, having made contact with a British boat, escaped back to the UK. Thomson, together with Captain Rodger Stewart, son of Perth's late medical officer of health, Charles Parker Stewart, tried to make his way through the chaos of St Valery to make contact with Lt Colonel T. Harris Hunter of the *Perthshire Constitutional* whose father was the MP for Perth. However, before they were in a position to attempt an escape the news came of the surrender which left them 'completely shocked and stunned.' There was indeed a sense that the only men standing between Hitler and his complete domination of mainland Europe were the businessmen of the Fair City. There was a sad end to the story for Captain Stewart who, near the end of the war, suffered fatal wounds during an air attack on a column of prisoners. He lived long enough to be returned to the UK where he was reunited with his wife and introduced to his son for the first time, before dying a mere six days after VE Day. (After the first edition of this book was published in 2008, the author was delighted to receive a letter from Captain Stewart's son who, like his grandfather before him, had followed a medical career.)

A interesting consequence of the surrender at St Valery was the creation of a new dance, *The Reel of the 51st Division*. The story goes that Lt Jimmy Atkinson, while on the long march into captivity in Austria, spent his time mentally devising a new reel. It was based on the diagonal cross of St Andrew, which at that time was the shoulder badge of the division, and timed to the rhythm of marching feet. He and fellow enthusiasts, including Lt Colonel T. Harris Hunter, developed it at their POW camp and then tried to send details back to Scotland by letter. German censors, however, were suspicious of the diagrams and only approved the letter once a demonstration of the dance had been given. Mrs Harris Hunter duly received it, practised the reel with her Scottish country dance group in Perth and later sold copies of it to raise money

The little-known Korean War memorial which can be found in a close off the Old High Street. The roof and spire of St Paul's Church can be seen at the top of the photo.

for the Red Cross and their work for prisoners of war. Traditionalists still insist it should be danced by men only.

Well over 1,000 Perth men gave their lives in the wars of the 20th century, the great majority during World War One. Most towns, villages, churches and large businesses honoured their fallen sons by establishing memorials, ranging from stone monuments dominating village centres to modest plaques on factory walls. The Pullars memorial, for example, can still be seen on the wall of Pullar House in Kinnoull Street, and that of the City of Perth Co-operative Society, which until recently was attached to a wall in the Skinnergate, is now on the North Inch. The city commemorated its war dead in particularly practical ways: the restoration of St John's Kirk (in memory of the dead of the whole county) after the first war and the conversion of Bowerswell House into the Bowerswell Memorial Homes (recently transferred to the Caledonia Housing Association) after the second. Several fund-raising events were held for the latter, including in 1948 a trio of singing bus conductresses who paraded through the town with a banner on the bus inviting the public to 'Help to keep the old well at Bowerswell.' Rather more flamboyant was Buchanan Dunsmore, owner of a local drapery store, who flew eight models from London to give a fashion show in Perth in aid of funds. Princess Margaret opened both the home and the 20 small cottages in the grounds in 1950. St John's Kirk also has two stained glass memorial windows, one to members of the East Church congregation who fell in the first war and the other to those who died while serving with the 6th Battalion The Black Watch in the second. The only Black Watch casualties from Perth since 1945 have been William Shaw and Barry Stephen who were killed in action in Korea in 1952 and in Iraq in 2003, respectively. The latter's name appears on the memorial to the Black Watch dead of Iraq which stands in the grounds of Balhousie Castle.

Those who returned alive at the end of World War One, either from active service or from prisoner of war camps, were suitably fêted, usually with a parade through the city streets, a civic welcome and, in 1919, a banquet in the City Hall. The 51st (Highland) Division, accompanied by the massed pipes and drums, received a civic welcome in Perth in 1946, but an even bigger event was to come the following year with the presentation of the freedom of the city to The Black Watch. Thousands came to the ceremony on the North Inch to see the future Queen Mother, as Colonel-in-Chief, accept the honour on behalf of the regiment. With the honour came the right to march through the streets of Perth with fixed bayonets and bands playing, a right which they exercised in 1958 to mark the 50th anniversary of the 6th Battalion and again in 1978 when they bore their old colours to Balhousie Castle. Field Marshal Earl Wavell, whose long career in The Black Watch, latterly as Colonel of the Regiment, was drawing to a close, also received the freedom of Perth at the same ceremony. His life was commemorated in 1966 with the opening of a memorial garden and gate at Balhousie Castle, and almost 40 years later, in 2004, Prince Charles declared open the Queen Mother memorial gates nearby.

Later, as war and post-war austerity receded into the memory, came the reminiscing. As early as 1922 Perth people were making trips to the battlefields of Flanders under the auspices of the Church Army and in 1960 Lord Provost John Young visited St Valery to mark the 20th anniversary of the battle. A happier though still moving occasion was the great reunion of the 51st (Highland) Division in 1963, the first since the war, which was held on the North Inch and which attracted crowds estimated at around 20,000. Former soldiers and their families from all over the UK and overseas attended and were put in touch with old comrades in arms thanks to a stream of messages being broadcast over a loudspeaker throughout the day. One of the highlights was the appearance of Mrs Perla Siedle Gibson, the Lady in White, who had stood on the quayside at Durban in South Africa, welcoming the troopship convoys from the UK. The author's father remembered the emotion of pulling into that safe haven after the dangerous Atlantic journey and hearing the patriotic songs she sang. Then in the 1990s came the 50th anniversaries: a small party returned to St Valery in 1990, trees were planted outside Bell's Sports Centre in 1992 in remembrance of El Alamein and three years later there was a huge parade of veterans, one of the largest in the country, through the streets of Perth to mark Victory in Europe Day. A memorial to the officers and men of the 51st (Highland) Division was also unveiled on the North Inch. A parade of D-Day veterans was held in 2004 to mark the 60th anniversary and at the same time the Royal British Legion was granted the freedom of Perth.

In the 1960s, almost a decade after The Black Watch's brief but bloody confrontation in Korea, the military began their withdrawal from Perth. The first to go were the regular soldiers of The Black Watch who, when plans to build a new depot at Spoutwells near Scone came

The Queen (later the Queen Mother) at the ceremony on the North Inch in 1947
to present the Freedom of Perth to The Black Watch. Lord Provost John Ure Primrose
is on the right of the photo. The Louis Flood Collection.
Courtesy of Perth Museum and Art Gallery, Perth and Kinross Council.

The great parade through Perth in 1995 to mark the 50th anniversary of Victory in Europe Day.
Courtesy of the A.K. Bell Library Local Studies Department, Perth and Kinross Council.

The winds of war blow through this poignant memorial to the officers and men of the
51st (Highland) Division which was unveiled on the North Inch in c.1995.

to naught, marched out of the Queen's Barracks for the last time in
1961. The departure for their new depot at Stirling Castle was watched
by thousands of spectators lining the streets. Work on the demolition of
the barracks began in 1966 and on completion the site was used initially
as a car park until the new police headquarters was built there. The
regimental headquarters, meanwhile, together with the regimental museum,
was established at Balhousie Castle beside the North Inch, and at the
time of writing the museum is about to undergo a major redevelopment.
After a number of years in Perth the Infantry Records Office, complete
with 24 tons of records and equipment, was transferred to York in 1964.
The 51st (Highland) Division was disbanded in 1967 while The Black
Watch, after several threats to its existence, finally merged with other
Scottish regiments in 2006 to become The Black Watch, 3rd Battalion,
The Royal Regiment of Scotland. Even ex-servicemen's clubs have
folded owing to a general lack of support, including the Royal Army
Service Corps Club in 2001, the Black Watch Club in Stormont Street in
2008 and the former Royal British Legion Club in 2011. Bucking the
trend, though, are the territorials or, to give them their proper name, the

A view of Balhousie Castle, the regimental headquarters of The Black Watch, with the memorial gate to Field Marshall Earl Wavell in the foreground.
By kind permission of the Trustees of The Black Watch (Royal Highland Regiment).

51st Highland, 7th Battalion, The Royal Regiment of Scotland, who have maintained their presence in Perth, latterly at a new Queen's Barracks on the Dunkeld Road which was opened by the Queen Mother in 1975.

No one could have been in any doubt in 1914 that Perth was a military town. The streets were full of soldiers who were either based in Perth or, in the great mobilisation of regulars and territorials in the Highland area (which was being organised by the military authorities in Perth), merely passing through. Many buildings were adapted for war purposes, such as the school board's premises in Rose Terrace which became an administrative base and home for Belgian refugees, schools which became recruiting centres, the Conservative Club in George Street which became a club for soldiers and the former infirmary at York Place and the poorhouse which both became war hospitals. The Wauchope and Black Watch Memorial Home in Scott Street, which had been opened in 1903, was particularly busy providing beds and meals for soldiers in transit, either on their way to the front or returning battle-weary from it. On one night in 1918 three soldiers arrived at the home at 1.30 am, just back from France via a late train. According to the home's annual report, 'they were shown into a clean little room with three beds. It was long since they had slept on sheets. One sat down, gazed round him, and with a voice broken with emotion exclaimed, "Man, Jock, this is heaven."'

The station was a focal point during both world wars, when thousands of servicemen passed through it, heading to and from the military and naval bases further north and south. During World War One the Perthshire Women's Patriotic Committee ran the Perthshire Patriotic Barrow which was a somewhat grand name for a glorified tea trolley. It was manned almost 24 hours a day by a band of volunteers who dispensed tea, cocoa, sandwiches, fruit, cigarettes and even the occasional posy of flowers to the hundreds of servicemen who briefly stopped at the station each day. School teachers, for example, did their bit by manning the barrow in the early morning before doing a full day's work at school. A list of donations to the barrow was published in the local press in 1916 and many ordinary housewives in the area were recorded as having made cakes and sandwiches; one of the few males listed, however, was no less a figure than the Marquis of Breadalbane who supplied the Bovril. In the first year of war alone the volunteers who manned the barrow reckoned they served around 50,000 grateful young men.

This building, adjacent to the entrance to the Scott Street car park, was formerly the Wauchope and Black Watch Memorial Home where thousands of World War One soldiers found a temporary refuge from the discomforts of war. Despite the fading lettering the name can still be made out on the side wall.

While many local men volunteered for the services in the early days of war, there were many too who had no wish to go, either because of family and business commitments or later because the reality of life in the trenches was becoming all too apparent. Conscription was introduced and tribunals set up to determine whether or not men had acceptable reasons for not joining up. Employers, increasingly short of manpower, spoke in support of their employees at such tribunals, arguing in some cases that the work was of national importance, but unless it was not suitable for a woman or an older man, the employee was usually told to report for military service. As the late Bill Harding said in *On Flows the Tay*, by the end of 1916 there were hardly any men left in the city between the ages of 18 and 41.

The lack of manpower had a significant effect on the workplace. By the end of 1914, less than five months after the declaration of war, Pullars had lost 20 per cent of their male staff, Campbells 25 per cent, and other factories were probably hit in a similar way. By the end of 1916 40 per cent of male workers at Pullars had joined up and almost 70 per cent at Campbells. On the other hand both Pullars and Campbells had less work coming in, as with fewer social events being held there was a corresponding drop in items of evening dress being sent in for cleaning. The Wallace Works was affected by a shortage of flax, and orders began to dry up at the Balhousie Works as carpets were seen as a luxury and therefore not being bought.

While men were in the services it fell to women not just to support the war effort – by voluntary work, knitting comforts for the troops, donating money and filling the gaps in the workplace with a 50-hour

The Army Pay Office in Atholl Street during World War One where, it is believed, film star Ronald Colman worked. The women clearly outnumber the men who are either elderly or possibly, having been wounded, no longer fit for active service.
Courtesy of the A.K. Bell Library Local Studies Department, Perth and Kinross Council.

week – but in a time of shortages to provide food (including growing vegetables), clothing and shelter for their families. Long years without a husband and coping with rising prices and shortages of almost everything meant that the home front, while less dangerous, was every bit as gruelling as life in the field.

Life, in fact, was difficult for everyone. While soldiers at the front were regarded as heroes and universally admired, those who were based in Perth, either heading for Flanders or home on furlough, made the most of local pubs – and local girls – and were regarded by the authorities as an irritant. The police were kept busy with a variety of petty offences, including bigamy, prostitution and drunkenness which tended to follow in the military's wake. The council was snowed under with an avalanche of new regulations, but had fewer and fewer staff to carry them out. Food shortages from the earliest days of the war resulted in dramatically increased prices and demands from unions for higher pay for workers. The city's undoubted patriotism did not always extend to altruism.

And of course there was the endless toll of human life. While the war may have begun with a bang of the big guns it ended with a whimper of relief. Quietness and calm were the first reactions to the armistice, followed by the hoisting of flags on public buildings and the ringing of the St John's bells. Work stopped and a 'joyous and animated crowd' filled the High Street which, as the afternoon wore on, 'burst into flame' with the city's youth parading through the newly relit streets singing patriotic songs. Only the old were restrained, remembering. The public packed into the City Hall that evening to roar their approval of the speeches and The Black Watch band and to sing the national anthem and *Rule Britannia*. There were loud cheers for Field Marshal Haig and also for Lloyd George, 'the greatest of all British statesmen since William Pitt.' By midnight the streets were peaceful again.

The Treaty of Versailles, which officially ended the war to end all wars, was signed in 1919, but was described by those prescient enough to see it as the peace to end all peace, for within 20 years Europe was once again at war. Despite the government's policy of appeasement in the run-up to war and the hopes of many that war could be avoided, most people feared that Hitler's aggression would lead to another conflict. One of the main worries was the power of the Luftwaffe which was graphically demonstrated to the world during the Spanish Civil War. The bombing of the little Basque town of Guernica in 1937, the subsequent depiction of the event in Picasso's painting and, perhaps most poignantly, the arrival in Perth of Basque refugee children in 1938 brought home the fact that every village, town and city in Britain was within reach of German bombers. To counter the threat many young volunteers were trained to fly at the aerodrome at Scone under the auspices of the RAF Volunteer Reserve. Battle of Britain ace 'Ginger' Lacey and Perth-born Neil Cameron, Marshal of the Royal Air Force, Chief of the Defence Staff and later Lord Cameron of Balhousie, both started their distinguished careers at Scone during this period, as did two well-known local residents, Squadron Leader Alfie Smith and Wing Commander Eric Tilston.

In Perth, the first significant preparations for war were made in 1938 when Air Raid Precautions (ARP) wardens were recruited and plans made for the distribution of gas masks. By 1939 the ARP service was well-manned with 1,500 volunteers under training, all managed from a control centre in the basement of the museum and art gallery. Air raid sirens were installed at four points in the city: at the fire station in King Edward

Princess Mary, the then Princess Royal (who bears a distinct resemblance to her great-niece, the present Princess Royal) and honorary Controller-Commandant of the ATS, visits the interior of an air raid shelter at Balhousie Castle in 1946. The Louis Flood Collection.
Courtesy of Perth Museum and Art Gallery, Perth and Kinross Council.

Street, at the electricity station at the Shore, at the Dewars building on the Glasgow Road and at the swimming baths on the Dunkeld Road. These were supplemented by the Pullars 'bummer', the siren that in peacetime announced to its workers, and indeed to much of the city, the beginning and end of the working day. Air raid shelters were established at various positions around the city, including at all city schools, and Pullars provided shelters along Kinnoull Street, mainly for the use of their own employees but open to anyone outside working hours. By the autumn of 1940 over 400 shelters had been built in Perth, providing accommodation for over 14,000 people. In the event the only bombs which landed on the city were those aimed at the Moncreiffe railway tunnel which dropped close to what is now Craigclowan Preparatory School, and those which landed in the harbour and which were found in 1968. In the absence of any serious bombing raid, exercises were held which were based on the premise, for example, that Perth had been subjected to a four-hour bombing blitz with buildings destroyed and many killed, or that a heavy air attack was to be followed by invasion.

In 1941 all men between the ages of 18 and 60 had to register for civil defence duties (the new term for ARP work) and over 5,000 duly did so, though there were almost 3,000 claims for exemption. The following year all women between the ages of 20 and 45 had to register for fire-watching duties, unless they had very young children to look after. Civil defence was administered by the council with a remit widened to include fire fighting, rescue, decontamination, first aid and emergency relief. In 1944, with the war swinging the allies' way, civil defence duties were lightened. The blackout, described as 'the worst of all our many wartime burdens', was relaxed in September 1944 and crowds filled the High Street to welcome back the lights.

The Perth battalion of the Home Guard, officially the 6th Perthshire Battalion Home Guard and originally known as the Local Defence Volunteers, was raised in May 1940 and within days of its formation had around 500 registered members. The majority were aged between 40 and 65, and as they climbed the steps to the recruiting office in the premises of solicitors McCash and Hunter in Kinnoull Street (the commanding officer for much of the war was Lt Colonel Alan Hunter), they must have known that they were signing up for a physically tough life of training, exercises, possible combat, and, at the end of a lengthy working day, more long hours spent guarding buildings such as the gas works and

Children of Robert Douglas Memorial School in the neighbouring village of Scone
clutch their gas masks, a scene repeated on many a day in Perth
and throughout the country during World War Two.
Courtesy of Perth Museum and Art Gallery, Perth and Kinross Council.

the station, away from family and fireside. One recruit was James Grassie, the physical education master at the Academy, who had risen through the ranks from private to captain in World War One and who in doing so had earned the DSO. He served as one of the senior officers in the Perth Home Guard. After more than four years of service the Home Guard was stood down, the occasion being marked by a pipe band parade through the streets of Perth in December 1944. There was no happy end to Grassie's war as his daughter, Helen, was killed in the Bourne End rail disaster in September 1945 and subsequently commemorated on the Perth Academy war memorial. His son, Duncan, though, followed in his father's footsteps and as an officer of The Black Watch earned a commendation for bravery in the Mau Mau uprising in Kenya in 1954.

Senior cabinet minister Sir John Anderson said in 1940 that 'in the main, we have to look to the women to see us through.' Thousands of Perth women had already responded to the call by joining the services, by working in munitions factories, in the Women's Land Army, in hospitals or other forms of national work, while others replaced the menfolk in shops, offices and factories. Some of the jobs were physically tough and included police work, driving trains and cleaning engines. To free younger

Women cleaning railway engines at the Perth engine sheds in c.1943.
Courtesy of the A.K. Bell Library Local Studies Department, Perth and Kinross Council.

mothers for such war work the council opened day nurseries at Muirton, Friarton and elsewhere in the city. The Women's Voluntary Service (wvs) was another channel for their energies and operated from the museum and art gallery under council supervision. Their main responsibility was primarily civil defence and included the organisation and care of evacuees, ambulance driving and assisting as nursing auxiliaries. They also undertook more mundane duties such as distributing food and clothing parcels sent from overseas, meeting convalescent troops at the station, manning the Citizens Advice Bureau in South St John's Place, and even making Christmas puddings.

Many women also helped the Red Cross with their various activities. With so many Perth and Perthshire men having been captured at St Valery in 1940, one of the most important roles of the Red Cross locally was to send food parcels to prisoner of war camps overseas. Working from their base in Tay Street's County Buildings, and with the help and advice of dieticians, they put together 6,000 food parcels every week which were shipped to Lisbon, forwarded by train to Geneva and then distributed

Queen Elizabeth (later the Queen Mother) visiting the Red Cross parcels depot in 1944.
Courtesy of the A.K. Bell Library Local Studies Department, Perth and Kinross Council.

to the camps by the International Red Cross. When the then Queen visited Perth in September 1944 she placed the final item in the millionth parcel packed.

Youth organisations also played their part, though several scout troops and Boys' Brigade companies had to amalgamate when their halls were taken over by the military or when leaders joined up. They were taught how to deal with incendiary bombs and how to act as stretcher bearers. They leafleted every house in Perth for Warship Week in 1942, collected waste paper and did forestry work on summer camps. Guides were equally busy washing dishes at the station canteen, making temperature charts for hospitals, digging for victory, collecting sphagnum moss for dressings and even empty cotton reels for use in field telephones. The Girls' Guildry made comforts for the troops and knitted bedspreads for hospitals. The elderly too gave up the hard-won rest of old age to help younger family members, busy on war work, with household duties. It seemed that almost everyone was involved to some degree with the war effort, though Lord Provost Nimmo was at pains to point out in 1941 that some were still not doing their bit. Such chiding seems to have worked as in 1943 he admitted that 'there can be few who are not pulling their weight.'

Fund-raising was a vitally important part of the war effort and Perth people were particularly generous in giving to various causes, often giving more per capita than other towns and cities in Scotland. Children in several areas of the city held street concerts in aid of the Spitfire Fund, Gannochy folk held a concert to support the Perth Prisoner of War Fund, local farmers held an auction to raise funds for the Red Cross, while firms such as the GA and Dewars made six-figure donations to War Weapons Week, all in 1940. In 1942 the city and county together raised over £1.6 million for Warship Week, more than double the original target, and were thus able to 'buy' two warships outright, *Highlander* bought by the city and *Hamilton* by the county. That same year Perth and the surrounding area raised £160,000 in a ten-week campaign to buy five tanks and the RAF was similarly supported with the Wings for Victory campaign.

A group of boys in Scone in c.1940 collect saucepans from housewives seemingly eager to give. Signs on the cart proclaim 'Collecting Aluminium for Aeroplanes' and 'Give to Defend Your Liberty.'
Courtesy of Perth Museum and Art Gallery, Perth and Kinross Council.

Perth played host to two groups of incomers in the early years of the war, and indeed it was on the night of 1 September 1939, before war was even declared, that the first trainloads of evacuees from Glasgow arrived at the station to be met by the wvs. They were not universally welcomed as the local press reported that many householders seemed more upset at having evacuees thrust upon them than they were at the outbreak of war. According to a pre-war survey less than one per cent of Perth house-holders were prepared to take them if required. In the end the majority of that first wave of evacuees drifted back to Glasgow within a few weeks of arrival, following which the council successfully persuaded the government that the city should no longer be an evacuee reception centre. Their brief stay, though, necessitated a two-shift system at two city schools whereby pupils from four Glasgow schools shared the facilities at Southern District and St John's Roman Catholic primary. Polish troops also arri-ved in Perth after the outbreak of war and have left their mark on the city ever since. One notable event during their stay was an open-air Mass on the North Inch in 1941 to celebrate the Feast of Corpus Christi, which was attended by a number of distinguished exiled Poles. They left in 1942 after an 18-month stay and presented the city with a bronze plaque which is now on the wall of the old City Chambers at the foot of the High Street. Around 400 Polish servicemen are buried in war graves at Wellshill Cemetery where there was once also a plaque to those

During the 1940s a temporary wooden bridge, built by the military, spanned the Tay between the North Inch and the grounds of what is now Upper Springland.
Courtesy of Perth Museum and Art Gallery, Perth and Kinross Council.

who died in the Katyn massacre of 1940. There was a bristle of indignation when this plaque was removed by a district councillor in 1976, prior to the visit of a Polish consul, 'in the interests of good relations.'

Those first evacuees arrived at a dark and sand-bagged station already well-prepared for whatever German bombers might throw at them. As in World War One hundreds of thousands of troops passed through the station during the war and Perth people did their best to make that stay, however brief, as pleasant as possible. A YMCA canteen and a St Andrews Ambulance Association casualty rest room were opened at the station in the first year of war and were staffed by women from the WVS. The canteen was open from at least 4.30 am to 1.30 am and provided gallons of tea each day, while servicemen in the rest room could make use of a 'books for the troops' service provided by the Sandeman Library. To maximise the military use of the railway the general public were actively discouraged from travelling by train. Posters asking 'Is your journey really necessary?' were generally unnecessary themselves as few people willingly resorted to overcrowded, dimly-lit and partly-vandalised trains with the bare minimum of dining facilities and ill-furnished lavatories. The war-wounded also arrived by train as did, from 1944, the sick and injured from London hospitals which had been damaged by V1 and V2 flying bomb attacks. They were met by a long line of ambulances and other vehicles which ran from the station platform right down to York Place, ready to take them to hospitals in Perth, Bridge of Earn and Fife.

For those running businesses and shops in Perth the war years were mixed. Within two months of war starting the GA had lost 27 per cent of its male employees to the services. Big increases in excise duty hit the whisky firms and the closure of hotels affected both the laundry and soft drinks businesses. Petrol rationing and the absence of men took many cars off the road and thus had an adverse effect on motor insurance, the GA's main source of home income. But they generally survived and some even prospered: Thomsons, for example, who started winning major government contracts for laundry work for hospitals and the services, and the GA who described business in 1943 as 'amazingly good.' Small businesses such as the one-man branch of the Caledonian Insurance Company at the foot of the High Street were at the mercy of a powerful moral pressure on young single men to join up. That one man, the author's father, was persuaded by a friend to visit the local recruiting office with a view to finding out more. Almost inevitably they emerged, in a certain degree of shock, as the latest raw recruits to the RAF, instructed to report for duty the following day. The bosses in the Dundee head office were appalled at such irresponsibility and were left with the job of closing down the Perth office for the duration of the war. Ironically the one who made the initial suggestion failed his medical and was sent home.

The shopping experience was as frustrating for the shopkeeper, who had to deal with the unreliable and irregular delivery of goods, as it was for the shopper who had to cope with queues, ration cards and empty shelves. There were probably many advertisements similar in tone to that by ironmongers Garvie and Syme, apologising for the lack of sauce-pans on sale: 'It is our regret that we cannot supply you with all you want – the need for munitions must come first.' If food was missing from the shops then many families at least had the opportunity to grow their own. Gardens were given over to vegetables rather than flowers and the council made available a number of new allotments – at Muirton and Cherrybank and elsewhere – to help the townsfolk 'Dig for Victory.' Part of the Academy playing fields were under cultivation though the council rejected a government suggestion to plough the Inches. If all else failed there was always the British Restaurant at 97 South Street where a three-course lunch could be had for under a shilling (around £0.04).

Despite the shortages, disrupted family life, the threat of bombing and invasion, gas masks, the taped-up windows, the disappearing railings, the blackout and a host of other inconveniences, many people who went through the war years still look back on them with nostalgia. For the one thing that lingers is that often-mentioned wartime spirit of mucking in, of make-do-and-mend, of comradeship in the face of shared adversity. And those who were single young women at the time still remember the joy of dancing at York House and the wide choice of partners.

The end of the war in Europe was celebrated on 8 May 1945. Shops, brightly decorated with red, white and blue, were busy in the morning with customers anticipating a holiday. Flags were hoisted and people sported victory posies but there was little cheering or laughter on this damp day, just 'a general murmur of excitement and gladness.' The streets were virtually empty as Churchill broadcast to the nation at 3.00 pm after which the bells of St John's rang out and church services were held. A pipe band processed along the High Street and small celebrations were held in streets around the city. In the evening the City Chambers were floodlit and the fairy lights were burning once again along Tay Street. VJ

Day and the end of Word War Two was celebrated on 15 August and announced by a radio broadcast by Attlee at midnight. Thoughts of rolling over and going back to sleep were dispelled by four pipers who played beneath the City Chambers' floodlighting and led the nocturnal celebrations. The following day there were again services of thanksgiving, a parade by the pipes and drums of The Black Watch on the North Inch, and performances by both the Perth Silver Band on the South Inch and the regimental dance band in the evening.

There was no speedy return to normality after the war and for some there were completely new lives to begin. Forty newly-weds, some of them perhaps those girls who had so much enjoyed the dancing in York House, set sail for Canada in 1946 to join their new husbands. Sport and entertainment picked up again fairly quickly though the more pressing issue of the availability of food, clothing and household goods lingered for several years more. Food shortages, however, were marginally eased by donations from the Empire and the USA: the Bertha Home received almost 50 kilograms of sultanas from South Africa in 1946, gas works staff received several consignments of food from their counterparts in Perth, Australia and in 1948 a vanload of boxes labelled 'Yankee Friendship' was delivered to the city. Sweets were returning to the shops in 1946 and bread was becoming whiter again, but good clothing was scarce and queuing was still an irritating part of everyday life. The de-rationing of sugar in 1953 was described as the second-biggest event of the year, the coronation presumably taking first place, and meat and butter, the final items to be de-rationed, were once again freely available in 1954. While 15 long years of rationing had not been a pleasurable experience for the British people they were probably physically healthier and literally in better shape than their descendants half a century later.

In 1974 the *Perthshire Advertiser* gave the public a brief reminder of those dark days of 1940 when the threat of invasion was very real and when church bells were to remain silent unless invasion was imminent. They recounted the story of the recently-deceased John Henderson, the deaf bell-ringer of St John's Kirk, who had been given a code word in a sealed envelope at the beginning of the war. If a soldier from the barracks ever came with a similar sealed envelope he was required to open both and then, should the code words be the same, ring the bells to warn the townspeople that danger was nigh. He finally opened the envelope a year or two before he died to find the word was 'fairmaid.'

CHAPTER SIXTEEN

The People of Perth

GENETICALLY, THE PEOPLE of Perth are a pretty mixed bunch. Those who first built their huts beside the Tay, on the wet and wooded flatlands beneath the hills of Kinnoull and Moncreiffe, were probably Pictish who, in the mid-ninth century, as their authority waned, relinquished power to the Scots from the west. It is quite possible, too, that the Vikings and maybe even the Romans, left a small genetic inheritance, as did perhaps the early traders from mainland Europe. It is difficult to assess the genetic make-up of the citizens since those earliest days as records of immigration and emigration were not kept. However, war and disease, pilgrimages and peripatetic parliaments, clearances and the railway and a variety of other social and economic factors would have ensured the constant ebb and flow of peoples and consequently a well-mixed population.

The first modern census to require details of birthplace was that of 1851. In that year the population of Perth was almost 24,000, of which only 14,000 – a little over half – had actually been born in the city. Of the remaining 10,000 or so, 5,000 had been born in the county, 3,500 were born elsewhere in Scotland and 1,500 were born outside Scotland altogether. Of this last-mentioned figure the majority came from Ireland and a sizeable minority from south of the border. This great influx of people is explained, in part at least, by the agricultural reforms of the later 18th and early 19th centuries which resulted in a considerable flow of redundant agricultural labourers into the towns, and by the coming of the railway to Perth which brought the English and the Irish. Their spiritual needs were met by new Anglican and Roman Catholic churches and by the Gaelic Chapel. The 800 speakers of Gaelic listed in the 1901 census of Perth and a flourishing Perth Gaelic Society at that same time, in a town where the language is believed to have died out in later mediaeval times, illustrate very well the drift of Highland folk into the towns of the lowlands. By the time of the 1931 census, when the city's population was up to almost 35,000, only 23,000, or roughly two-thirds of the population, had been born in either the city or the county,

This uninspiring building, now a nightclub, was once the spiritual home for the several hundred Gaelic speakers in the city. Built in Canal Street in 1787 it could hold 800 worshippers. The spire of St John's Episcopal Church can be seen in the background.

the remainder hailing from elsewhere in Scotland or England. That sense that many of us will have, of belonging to Perth and being 100 per cent Scottish, may in fact be only skin-deep: a little digging around the base of the family tree may well reveal roots going back to the Highlands, England or Ireland.

No matter their ethnic origin, the people of Perth are as proud of the city's history as they are conscious of its status. It is a source of pride that at least two royal James's are associated with the city, one whose fondness for golf is remembered in the King James VI Golf Club and the other, James I, whose penchant for tennis led indirectly to a grisly end in the sewers of Blackfriars and subsequently a memorial plaque opposite the North Inch. They will also let it be known that the city was once the capital of Scotland, and while it was certainly one of the chief towns in the mediaeval kingdom it is perhaps anachronistic to use the word 'capital.' However, the Battle of the Clans, the Gowrie Conspiracy and the start of Reformation violence are known by many to be significant events in the history of both the city and the nation.

The murder of James I at Blackfriars in 1437 gave his successors reason to believe that Edinburgh wasn't such a bad place after all and thus hastened the development of that city as Scotland's capital in the modern sense. Despite abandoning Perth for Edinburgh royalty has maintained loose links with the city over the centuries. Both James I and Margaret Tudor (the widow of James IV and sister of Henry VIII of England) are buried somewhere in the vicinity of the King James VI Hospital. Perth was perhaps a little wary of royal houses after the political turbulence of the 17th and 18th centuries, and the gift of the Gowrie House to the Duke of Cumberland after Culloden should be regarded as more of a political gesture than one of affection. It fell to Victoria to rehabilitate the Hanoverians in the eyes of the people of Perth who gave her a warm welcome on her visit to the city in 1842. The warmth felt for Victoria was probably compounded in her later years by the presence in the city of The Black Watch who fought

A view of Parliament Close in 1966. Although in poor condition and although no firm evidence exists to indicate that a parliament ever sat in this precise spot, the very name added to Perth's sense of its own history and importance.
From the collection of the late
Harry Chalmers, Perth.

loyally for Queen and country in the wars of that century. Since Victoria, other members of the royal family have visited Perth. There have been the official visits to The Black Watch, particularly by the late Queen Mother, and other visits to open, for example, the hospital in 1914, the art gallery in 1935, Bowerswell in 1950, the Queen's Bridge in 1960, the leisure pool in 1988 and the new library in 1995. There have also been many unofficial visits for reasons as mundane as shopping, weddings and social events. Any royal visit, official or otherwise, always attracted spectators, and even the knowledge in 1950 that the soon-to-be Queen Mother would be passing through the city – without stopping – was enough to bring crowds onto the pavements to line the royal route.

The four coronations of the 20th century were great occasions for Perth people to celebrate royalty. Apart from the bunting and decorations, the

Great crowds attend the celebrations on the North Inch to mark
the coronation of King George V in 1911.
Courtesy of the A.K. Bell Library Local Studies Department, Perth and Kinross Council.

church services and the music, that of Edward VII in 1902 featured a sports meeting on the North Inch which was attended by 20,000 spectators, and a cake and wine banquet in the old City Hall. George V's in 1911 was similar with a colourful pageant on the North Inch, watched by almost 30,000 people, and a sit-down lunch in the new City Hall for 650 older residents who were treated to two bridies, a tart, three cakes and either a bottle of lemonade or a cup of tea. In the evening there was dancing on the North Inch to the music of The Black Watch Band and the Perth Pipe Band before people headed off to Craigie Knowes for a celebratory bonfire. The 1937 celebrations were more subdued because of the international political situation, but Perth was still gaily decorated and there were formal entertainments as well as spontaneous street parties. 'The carnival spirit' was particularly noticeable 'in working-class quarters,' said the local press. On the death of George VI in 1952 Princess Elizabeth was proclaimed Queen by Lord Provost Primrose at the Mercat Cross in the presence of a Black Watch guard of honour and the Perth High Constables. The council, meanwhile, sent a loyal address to the new Queen on behalf of the people of the city. The coronation in 1953 was a more joyous affair with military and fancy dress parades, bonfires, fireworks and street parties. Sixty years after her accession the people of Perth held some of the biggest celebrations in Scotland to mark the Diamond Jubilee and not a few were surprised at the depth of genuine joy which manifested itself both locally and across the country in the summer of 2012.

The aristocracy and gentry, in contrast, remained aloof from Perth. Some indeed had town houses within the city and others served as provost, but in general there seems to have been a recognition on their part that the city's ancient rights and privileges had been stoically defended by burgesses over the centuries and that this was their domain. While Lord Scone briefly represented Perth in Parliament and the major county families were regular attendees at Perth Hunt balls, the true aristocracy of 20th-century Perth were the leaders of business and industry who were intimately connected with its governance, who funded civic improvements and who were held in the highest regard by the townspeople. Some, of course, like the Pullars, the Dewars and the Norie-Millers, were in time honoured with titles, and others, like the Bells, for whatever reason, were not.

If royal connections and its place in Scottish history gave Perth a good conceit of itself, then so did the fine Georgian buildings which developed alongside both the North and South Inches in the later 18th and early 19th centuries. These were much admired by early tourists and visitors to the town and gave Perth an architectural eminence within Scotland. In addition, a beautiful setting beside the river and its position as the county town of Perthshire – with all the connotations that has – have combined to give the city an air of genteel respectability. But that, of course, is only part of the story because Perth was also an industrialised factory city, an agricultural centre, a railway hub and a home to the military, and it is this tension between occupations, classes and social groups, between Tories and Nationalists, between fine architecture and slum housing, between town and country that has made Perth the interesting city of contrasts it is today.

It is a said with some truth that nothing unites a people more than a common enemy. Hence another distinguishing feature of Perth people is a certain distrust of that upstart city down the river, Dundee. As local historian R.S. Fittis said, '"Bonny Dundee" and the "Fair City", the sister-burghs of the Tay, have been more famed in history for their mutual jealousies and bickerings than for mutual friendship and good-neighbourhood.' He cites two main reasons for this, both dating from mediaeval times when Perth, if not the larger centre of population, was more influential in the affairs of the nation. The first of these was Perth's preferential rights of navigation on the river and the other, Perth's legally enshrined precedence over Dundee. A letter to the *Perthshire Constitutional* in May 1919 shows this attitude superbly. Concerning Dundee's early move to honour Earl Haig after the war, the writer, who signed himself Enterprise, stated: 'I am the last man in the world who would

The Scottish Urban Archaeological Trust investigated the site of Cromwell's citadel
on the South Inch in 1999. This shows some of the stonework uncovered.
Courtesy of the A.K. Bell Library Local Studies Department, Perth and Kinross Council.

suggest that Perth should follow the example of Dundee. Of all the towns in Scotland, and of all the peoples in Scotland, Dundee and Dundonians are the last I should copy... As usurpers they have few equals. That which does not belong to them they claim without hesitation or a blush.' Today there is still a degree of competition between the two though any surviving rivalry is generally good-natured.

A further example of the city uniting against an external threat occurred in May 1951 when a BBC radio programme, entitled *The Fair City*, gently chided Perth for allowing the destruction of its old buildings. Over the ensuing weeks the sense of outrage in the press against such slander was huge. 'One of the worst things that has happened to Perth within this century', said one listener, which was not bad going for a 60-minute broadcast on the Scottish Home Service.

As many will now admit, though, the sentiments expressed in that radio broadcast were accurate. Far too few of Perth's old buildings have survived. Cromwell visited the city in the 1650s and, having destroyed much of the old town in order to build his citadel on the South Inch, can be blamed for at least some of the loss. The council has frequently been blamed in more recent years but such criticism is unfair when one

Though the Cross in the High Street was removed in 1765 the empty space continued to be known by that name, and ceremonies such as the proclamation of a new monarch were held there until 1910. Perth's ancient and central meeting place was not easily forgotten.
Courtesy of Perth Museum and Art Gallery, Perth and Kinross Council.

considers the intense pressure they were under to get rid of slums and build anew. Following the death of Queen Victoria there was an appreciation that the old order was changing, 'yielding place to new', and one can perhaps detect a resurgent sense of local history in the bid to have part of the old Mercat Cross returned to the city in 1906. Originally situated in the High Street, between Kirkgate and Skinnergate, the whole structure was removed in 1765 to allow the easier movement of carts and carriages. The shaft ended up in the grounds of Fingask whose owner at the time, William Murray Thriepland, declined to give it back, and is still at Fingask to this day. The design of the new Mercat Cross, which was unveiled in King Edward Street in 1913, was closely based on the old one. Several organisations, including Perth and Kinross Heritage Trust and the council's archive, local studies and museum services now actively promote the preservation of all aspects of old Perth, whether it be architecture, artefact or the written word. Early on the scene, though, was Perth Civic Trust which was founded in 1967 in response to the proposed redevelopment of Commercial Street and the demolition of other historic buildings at that time. One of the trust's earliest successes, under the leadership of eminent archaeologist, the late Dr Margaret Stewart, was

The unveiling of the new Mercat Cross in King Edward Street in 1913. The head of
Edward VII was sculpted by a local man, James Ness. The first proclamation of a
new monarch from the platform at the top was that of King Edward VIII in 1936.
Courtesy of Perth Museum and Art Gallery, Perth and Kinross Council.

the preservation of the waterworks and they have since fought long and
hard to preserve Perth's built environment as well as encourage good
contemporary architecture. Shortly after Perth Civic Trust was formed,
the redevelopment of prime commercial plots in the High Street, and
elsewhere in the city, gave archaeologists (prime amongst them those of
the now defunct Perth-based Scottish Urban Archaeological Trust) the
opportunity to carry out extensive investigations into Perth's mediaeval
past. The Marks and Spencer site on the north side of the High Street
was the first major excavation, the company initially allowing archaeologists three months to complete their dig. But then came the superlatives
– 'the largest ever urban excavation in Scotland' and 'potentially the most
significant archaeological site in Europe' – followed by more money and
many more months of work. The dig finished more than two years later
in 1977 having yielded a huge amount of information about life in the
mediaeval burgh and further stimulated an interest in the city's history
among the inhabitants.

Most people who do more than just pass through will have their own opinions on the city. These can range from a single person's view that it is 'a very married place' to those of a disaffected youth whose comment could be rephrased as 'not much goes on here.' On the other hand the elderly might say that it is an excellent place to retire to, central and neither too big nor too small, and parents might say that with its good schools and sporting and cultural facilities it is a fine place to bring up a family. As for the inhabitants, though, opinions are not so good. Even Onlooker, the *Perthshire Advertiser* columnist with a Biblical turn of phrase, stated in 1922 that 'Perthites are a strange people who taketh not well to strangers, and who looketh upon them, yea even with the eyes of suspicion from the toe to the crown of

Excavations at 75 High Street, before the present Marks and Spencer store was built, showing a mediaeval wattle trackway and building timbers.
Crown Copyright Historic Scotland.

the head.' Perhaps he was thinking of the time in 1906 when German gipsies, in an act of mediaeval vindictiveness, were driven out of the city by a group of townspeople. He added that 'Perthites are a jealous people who do watch their neighbours carefully and are much learned in their affairs.' Things were no better 30 years later when that same newspaper described Perth folk as 'suspicious', 'stand-offish', 'snobbish', 'smug' and 'frostily indifferent', before modifying those less than flattering terms into a people 'minding their own business', 'living and letting live' and being 'courteous and incurious.' They took a decided turn for the worse in 1971 when the *Courier* published the following comments from a young man who had been in the city for over two years: 'Perth people take great pride in their Fair City but they couldn't care less about newcomers. Married couples who have settled in the city take ages before they are accepted and this clannishness affects even their young families. The one good thing about Perth is that it is a fine place for passing through. And I am leaving it for good, I hope, next week.' Much, though, depends on one's personal outlook and there are doubt-less many incomers who regard Perth as a welcoming and friendly city.

IN MEMORIAM
OF REMAINS UNCOVERED
IN PERTH CITY CENTRE
JUNE 1991

Archaeological excavations in Perth city centre
uncovered a number of mediaeval human remains
which were subsequently reburied in Wellshill
cemetery in 1991. While Perth may now have a well-
mixed population there is at least the possibility that
some Perth residents today will descend from
someone buried in this particular spot.

Perth people were also inclined to take the law into their own hands. Earlier chapters have drawn attention to the angry mob which necessitated police protection for the Rev. David Manuel during the dispute with his assistant, for the driver of the car involved in Perth's first fatal road accident, for town council members taking difficult decisions and for those taking part in industrial disputes. Prone to violence though they may have been, Perth people have also been surprisingly prudish. In 1972 the performance at the Sally of Cuddly Kim, described as an exotic dancer, was cancelled after protests from the public, and the following year topless dancer Angie suffered the same experience when the licensee at The Plough gave in to police pressure. As recently as 1989 a Perth news-agent was on trial for selling top-shelf soft porn and the *Sunday Sport* was reported to the Advertising Standards Authority for putting up what some Perth folk considered to be offensive posters. Even the window displays in the Ann Summers shop were a bit too racy for some.

However, Perth folk are good at enjoying themselves and the millennium eve party on 31 December 1999 was every bit as good as the coronation and end-of-war celebrations of the past. 'What a party!' exclaimed the *Perthshire Advertiser* and proceeded to recount how 15,000 revellers on the North Inch enjoyed a 'spectacular and dazzling display of fireworks and searchlights' and how people young and old danced, sang and toasted their way into the year 2000, 'ensuring a mega-millennium hang-over for many.' Hogmanay had been a day of numerous family events, such as the Imagination Market in the City Hall. Five thousand people took part in a torch-lit procession through the streets of Perth and were entertained on the way by street artists and a pipe band.

Provost Mike O'Malley welcomed the crowds to the North Inch where four stages had been erected for the night's events. Quite a party indeed, and yet there were only four arrests for anti-social behaviour.

For all the perceived imperfections of Perth people we are a resilient bunch. We have sent our men off to all the major wars of the 20th century, leaving the women to man the home front. We have seen the decline and demise of our great home-grown industries and struggled hard to establish new ones. We have built a greater Perth, beautified the city and knocked down the slums, though in doing so we have also lost some of the city's vennels, closes and quaint corners. We have released the city, to a certain extent at least, from the stranglehold of traffic. We have restored some of our great public buildings and built new ones. We have fostered the arts and encouraged sport and leisure. Decent sanitation and public services have improved the health and eased the lives of our citizens. If that were not enough then we have also coped with changing moralities, global warming, decimalisation, emigration, immigration, pollution, drug abuse, teenagers, Europe, divorce, the Internet and, for better or worse, increasing wealth. The 20th century was indeed a century of change and we survived it.

CHAPTER SEVENTEEN

Into the New Century

THE FIRST CHAPTER of the first edition began with the brave death of soldier James Ames, and by way of underlining Perth's enduring – though diminishing – connection with the military, the final chapter of the second begins with the tragic death of soldier James Collinson. This former pupil of Perth Grammar School would have had little idea, as he signed up for the army, that his name would come to feature regularly in the local and national press in subsequent years. He had the great misfortune to be sent to Deepcut Barracks in Surrey, a name already tragically tainted by the controversial deaths of three young army trainees. On 23 March 2002 James Collinson became the fourth. Police and army investigations were carried out and even the investigations themselves were investigated, such was the dissatisfaction amongst the families when the results were made public. In James's case, as with that of two others, neither suicide nor murder could be proven and the coroner had to record an open verdict. The families, the press and Members of Parliament have called in vain for a public enquiry, a demand repeated ten years after his death by James's mother, Yvonne, who believes her son probably died as a result of a prank that went terribly wrong. James's parents have fought long and hard for the truth and all in Perth will surely hope they find some comfort from the naming of a new street – Collinson View – in their son's memory.

A story with a much happier ending was also frequently in the news at that time. The project which ended up as Perth Concert Hall was first publicly discussed in the mid-1990s as a way of marking the new millennium by redeveloping the Horsecross area. Supported from the outset by the Gannochy Trust it nevertheless quickly ran into problems when the Millennium Commission declined to follow suit. Revised plans for a concert hall were still strongly backed by the Gannochy Trust but once again the whole project was jeopardised by a lukewarm response to the request for lottery funding. Nothing daunted, the Gannochy Trust upped their contribution to almost £5 million – their largest donation to date – and with funding from other donors as well, including the council and Norwich Union, the project finally moved to the planning stage. Following an architectural competition, a distinguished panel of judges selected

An 18th-century tenement (left), a 19th-century factory (in the distance) and a 20th-century public building (right) flank the 21st-century concert hall. The Gannochy Trust, which celebrated its 75th anniversary in 2012, made a very substantial donation towards the cost of construction

the winning design and construction work began in 2003. The £19.5 million Perth Concert Hall – a name chosen by the Gannochy trustees to emphasise its artistic and therefore charitable status – was opened in 2005 and although designed principally as a concert auditorium is nevertheless equally suitable for conferences or even sporting events. It has been an undoubted success, catering to all tastes, attracting large audiences from a wide area and winning major awards for business tourism. Even party conferences have been regularly enticed back to Perth because of it.

The siting of any major building away from the immediate centre of the city almost always impacts on its surroundings and the concert hall has been no exception. While still at the planning stage, the 1980s scheme to create a shopping mall, or a new street, between High Street and Mill Street (close to the proposed new hall), was once again being considered, and later, long before Woolworths had even closed, there was talk of the building being demolished to make way for a shopping development. By late 2007 talk had progressed into a planning application which had the backing of the council (if not that of the Architectural Heritage Society of Scotland), but when the financial crisis started to bite the private developers had a change of heart and, instead of demolishing the old Woolworth building, converted it into modern retail units.

The Gannochy Trust celebrated its 75th anniversary in 2012 by coming out of the shadows in which it had long dwelt and receiving the congratulations of the many organisations it has supported over the years. Until relatively recently it had a policy of keeping quiet about its affairs and this author, in an earlier incarnation as reference librarian in the Sandeman Library, well remembers the difficulties of eliciting any information from its staff at all. Even the large projects supported by the trust in Perth – Bell's Sports Centre, Perth Leisure Pool, Dewars Centre and the A.K. Bell Library to name a few – played down the Gannochy name, though there is an exception in the Gannochy Sports Complex as the enlarged facilities at Bell's Sports Centre are now known. The new spirit of openness – the Gannochy *glasnost* – was marked by the publication of a short history of the trust in the summer of 2012.

As previously mentioned, the Gannochy Trust was established by Arthur Kinmond Bell in 1937 when he transferred to it the Gannochy housing estate, together with other lands and properties which he or Arthur Bell & Sons had owned. The income deriving from these properties was to be used principally to maintain and enlarge the estate, with any surplus going to clubs and organisations in the local area. For the first 20 years the surplus income was enough to make a number of small annual charitable donations. And then it came to light that, thanks to a legal oversight which had gone unnoticed for 15 years, the trust was actually far wealthier than the trustees could ever have dreamed. Bell's Sports Centre, funded from a now healthily glowing bank account, was the trust's first major project and many others since then have been financially supported, either wholly or in part, including the above-mentioned public buildings, the Upper Springland complex, the Cornhill Macmillan Centre, Perth Theatre, Perth Festival of the Arts and many more worthy causes in the city and surrounding area. A change in the terms of the 1937 Trust Deed, made in 1967, allowed the trustees to spread their new-found wealth over the whole of Scotland rather than just Perthshire to which they had originally been restricted. Beneficiaries since 1967 have included organisations such as the National Galleries of Scotland, Scottish Opera, the Scottish universities (particularly those of Dundee and Stirling) and the Royal Society of Edinburgh, as well as a host of societies, charities and youth organisations the length of the country. Perth remains the focus, though, and it is worth remembering that the city would be a very different place had it not been for the generosity of the Gannochy Trust.

Another major project which had Gannochy Trust backing fell at the last hurdle when it failed to secure additional lottery funding. Plans for a national garden for Scotland were announced in 2000 and enthusiastically backed by the council which saw its potential to become Perthshire's biggest tourist attraction. The multi-million pound development was planned for Broxden, on the outskirts of Perth, and was to include a museum devoted to tartan as well as a park and ride facility for the city. Despite the Scottish Tartans Authority quickly pulling out, plans went ahead for the national garden, to be known as The Calyx, and in 2007 a request was submitted for lottery funding totalling £25 million. By now the hugely ambitious scheme encompassed a 60-acre garden and a staff of around 200 which, it was reckoned, would generate an estimated income of £20–30 million per year. However, within months of the news that no lottery funding would be forthcoming the project was dropped.

As work began on the construction of one large building – the concert hall – the demolition of another was beginning to be openly discussed and argued around the city. Perth's City Hall had been opened in 1911 and had served the city well for almost a century. But when major conferences started avoiding Perth, or using the Dewars Centre instead, and when repair and maintenance costs began to reach unacceptable levels, the council took the decision in 2005 to close its doors for the last time. One of the first proponents of demolition was former council planning director, Denis Munro, who suggested in his book, *A Vision of Perth*, published in 2000, that the creation of a civic square in front of St John's Kirk would be beneficial in a number of ways. He has since completely changed his mind on the issue and is now strongly opposed to demolition but the idea has taken root and has a number of powerful advocates, not least of them the Perthshire Chamber of Commerce and Perth Civic Trust. Despite Munro's book, the council were initially in favour of converting the hall into a shopping centre and gave a London firm, Wharfside Regeneration, the go-ahead to start work. The firm succeeded in obtaining detailed planning permission for their proposals as well as consent from Historic Scotland but eventually fell victim to the recession when they could not attract enough retailers to fill the commercial units available. The original plans foresaw completion in late 2007 but with 2009 coming into view and no actual work on the City Hall having been carried out at all, the council were accused of dithering and the clamour for demolition began to grow. In September 2009 the council finally gave up on Wharfside and the future of the old hall was suddenly very much in doubt. After much public debate and wars of words in the local press the council, in June 2010, voted in favour of demolition and the creation of a civic square, a project that was estimated would take four years and cost £3 million. However, advocates of retaining the hall, either in full or in part, kept submitting alternative proposals, and there was further bad news for the council when it became known that the decision to demolish had been taken not by the full council but by the ten members of the development control committee who had decided the matter by seven votes to three. The retention lobby were infuriated that such a momentous decision had effectively been made by only seven out of 41 councillors. But even this was not the end of the story as Historic Scotland in May 2012 over-turned the council's decision on the grounds that they had failed to demonstrate sufficient efforts had been made to retain the building and that alternatives to demolition had not been fully explored. 'For lease' signs are once again on display outside the City Hall whose future is no clearer than it was ten years ago.

Running concurrently with the later stages of the City Hall saga has been that of the Shore Road incinerator, an issue which, far from divid-ing the city, has brought almost everyone together in condemnation. The story began innocently enough when Holden Environmental submitted a planning application in December 2005 requesting outline planning permission for a waste to energy facility at their existing waste recycling centre at Shore Road. The arguments looked persuasive: it would reduce traffic on Shore Road and provide jobs, while the creation of energy from waste would reduce the need for wind farms and thus protect the rural Perthshire environment. And when it was further pointed out that by cut-ting down on landfill it would be a meaningful contribution to the obli-gations and targets set out in the National Waste Strategy for Scotland then, as they say in modern parlance, the application seemed to tick all the boxes. The planning officer asked for more detailed and specific informa-tion about the proposed waste to energy plant but was told by Holden Environmental that no such information could be provided until other investors joined the scheme, whereupon more detailed proposals would be drawn up. Potential investors, they pointed out, would not look at the scheme unless outline planning permission were already in place. It seemed

Price 85p   Tuesday, March 10, 2009   www.perthshireadvertiser.co.uk

SPOT THE CHIMNEY?

£100 MILLION INVESTMENT: The 260-feet chimney stack (pictured above in this artist's drawing) would change Perth's iconic skyline.

The *Perthshire Advertiser* first broke the waste-to-energy incinerator story in 2008. Articles and images such as this have helped to mobilise the campaign against Grundon's proposals. Courtesy of the *Perthshire Advertiser*.

a reasonable argument and, despite the misgivings of one or two council colleagues and SEPA officials about the lack of detailed information, the planning officer decided to recommend approval in outline, providing full details regarding noise, emissions and dust, as well as the layout of the site and its appearance, were made available at the reserved matters stage. Formal outline permission was granted on 9 March 2006.

By that summer Grundon Waste Management, a company based in Oxfordshire, had emerged as the investor Holden Environmental were looking for and were quick to explain their plans to the council. Officials were seemingly taken aback by what they were proposing and in October raised concerns about the sheer scale of the whole undertaking including the chimney stack, its proximity to the city centre and the impact it would have on the city's appearance. Correspondence in the spring of 2008 shows that relations between the council and Grundon were already becoming difficult, with the the former insisting that the proposed plant should be close in scale to the application for which outline consent had been originally granted, and the latter replying that the council should have realised from hints such as 'a multi-million pound investment' that it would be a sizeable undertaking.

Then in September 2008 the *Perthshire Advertiser* got hold of the story and when it was made clear just how high the chimney stack would be (80 metres), and what might be belching out of it, the townspeople started fighting back in earnest. MPs and MSPs took notice and Councillor Peter Barrett and former council chief executive Jim Cormie emerged as leaders of the opposition along with members of the Bridgend, Gannochy and Kinnoull Community Council. Public meetings were held, attended by hundreds of outraged local residents who demanded that the council revoke the outline planning consent in its entirety rather than merely refusing permission for the detailed plans presented. Compensating Grundon would have been an expensive option but one that would have brought the whole matter to a swift conclusion. Instead the council took a risk and in November 2009 would only go so far as refusing detailed planning permission, thus allowing Grundon to keep a foot in the door. They appealed unsuccessfully to the Scottish government and then came back in 2011 with revised plans, this time with two chimney stacks (albeit significantly lower in height), and these plans too were rejected by the council in February 2012. Grundon have said they will appeal again, arguing that the council, by granting outline permission in 2006, have agreed in principle to the idea of a waste incinerator at Shore Road. Whether or not that initial permission was granted in error, as campaigners have argued, or out of naivety or even just good faith, the ramifications have been enormous and have cast a long shadow over what should have been a joyous run-up to the Perth 800 celebrations.

The fact that Perth has been a royal burgh since the mid-1120s, in the time of David I, might lead one to wonder why Perth 800 was celebrated in 2010 and not in the 1920s. What was being celebrated was not, in fact, the 800th anniversary of the royal burgh but that of the first charter, or possibly first surviving charter, which was granted by William the Lion and which confirmed the status and privileges granted some 80 years earlier. And even then, historians are not absolutely sure of the date of that charter, which could have been drawn up at any time between 1205 and 1210. However, the decision to mark the anniversary in 2010 accorded with the commemorative plaque on the Queen's Bridge which was opened in 1960 on what was believed at that time to be the 750th anniversary of the charter.

The highlight of the celebrations was Perth Day on 3 July which featured a host of sparkling events, including a huge military parade, a visit from Prince Edward and exhibitions and displays. With crowds

The Olympic torch was paraded through Perth on 12 June 2012.

pouring into the city for this event and even more descending on Scone Palace for the Scottish Game Fair, traffic congestion was expected to be a serious problem. No sensible father would even consider arranging his daughter's wedding on such a day, but that, in fact, is exactly what this author did... Later in the summer a well-attended two-day conference devoted to aspects of the history of Perth – *Perth: a Place in History* – was held in the concert hall and was graced by an array of excellent speakers and historians. One of the final events was Perth Lightnight at the end of November, a stunning open-air evening of music and fireworks which used the river and bridges as a backdrop. Adding to the spectacle were the trees of the Norie-Miller Riverside Walk which had been illuminated for the occasion. It proved to be a fitting conclusion to the 800th anniversary celebrations as, with the eyes of the vast crowd turned skywards, the first snows of a long and particularly hard winter began to float down. A permanent memorial to Perth 800 was the large sculpture of a grouse which was gifted to the people of the city by the Edrington Group, owners of the *Famous Grouse* whisky, and which now stands in the middle of the Broxden roundabout at the south-western entrance to Perth. Nocturnal illumination by solar power has since been installed. Perth may not have a £40 million National Garden for Scotland at Broxden but at least it has a gigantic metal grouse.

Provost Liz Grant presents the keys of the city of Perth to the Queen.
The ceremony took place on 6 July 2012 in Tay Street and was watched by the
Duke of Edinburgh and the Lord Lieutenant of Perth and Kinross, Brigadier Melville Jameson.
Courtesy of the Perthshire Picture Agency.

While Perth 800 had been a year of celebration it had had a serious purpose too, for local residents had emerged from it more aware of just how historic their city was. It also proved to be a springboard for the final push towards city status, a campaign which had been gathering momentum for several years, and indeed almost from the time when the council had originally decided against participating in the millennium and Golden Jubilee competitions for that very award. The campaign was, of course, successful and the result, when announced on 14 March 2012, was the start of what proved to be a memorable summer. Weather-wise, summer itself began shortly after the announcement, and with temperatures nudging 21 degrees some residents could be seen sitting in their gardens in the warm March air, sipping wine by candlelight. The sunshine did not last but spirits were lifted again by the arrival in Perth of the Olympic torch in June, which featured a relay of runners taking it in turns to hold the flame aloft while passing through the crowd-filled streets of the city centre. The Queen and Duke of Edinburgh made a formal visit on 6 July, she to receive the keys of the new city and he to be given

its freedom. And at the end of July and throughout August spirits were
further raised by the astonishing success of British athletes at the London
Olympics and Paralympics. The whole country shared in the joy of these
games and of the success of Andy Murray at both the Olympics and the
US tennis open championship: he who but for a reorganisation of local
government in the 1970s might still be regarded as a Perthshire lad. It had
been a summer never to forget, and, for the people of Perth in particular,
one that had been heralded by the news in March that Perth, finally, was
a city again.

Index

Luath Press Limited

committed to publishing well written books worth reading

LUATH PRESS takes its name from Robert Burns, whose little collie Luath (*Gael.,* swift or nimble) tripped up Jean Armour at a wedding and gave him the chance to speak to the woman who was to be his wife and the abiding love of his life. Burns called one of 'The Twa Dogs' Luath after Cuchullin's hunting dog in Ossian's *Fingal*. Luath Press was established in 1981 in the heart of Burns country, and is now based a few steps up the road from Burns' first lodgings on Edinburgh's Royal Mile.

Luath offers you distinctive writing with a hint of unexpected pleasures.

Most bookshops in the UK, the US, Canada, Australia, New Zealand and parts of Europe either carry our books in stock or can order them for you. To order direct from us, please send a £sterling cheque, postal order, international money order or your credit card details (number, address of cardholder and expiry date) to us at the address below. Please add post and packing as follows: UK – £1.00 per delivery address; overseas surface mail – £2.50 per delivery address; overseas air-mail – £3.50 for the first book to each delivery address, plus £1.00 for each additional book by airmail to the same address. If your order is a gift, we will happily enclose your card or message at no extra charge.

Luath Press Limited
543/2 Castlehill
The Royal Mile
Edinburgh EH1 2ND
Scotland
Telephone: 0131 225 4326 (24 hours)
Fax: 0131 225 4324
email: sales@luath.co.uk
Website: www.luath.co.uk